Stuck in Place

Stuck in Place

Urban Neighborhoods
and the End of Progress
toward Racial Equality

PATRICK SHARKEY

THE UNIVERSITY OF CHICAGO PRESS

Chicago and London

Patrick Sharkey is
associate professor
of sociology at New
York University and
an affiliated member
of the faculty at the
Robert F. Wagner
School for Public
Service.

The University of Chicago Press, Chicago 60637
The University of Chicago Press, Ltd., London
© 2013 by The University of Chicago
All rights reserved. Published 2013.
Printed in the United States of America.

20 19 18 17 16 15 14 13   1 2 3 4 5

ISBN-13: 978-0-226-92424-3 (cloth)
ISBN-13: 978-0-226-92425-0 (paper)
ISBN-13: 978-0-226-92426-7 (e-book)
ISBN-10: 0-226-92424-6 (cloth)
ISBN-10: 0-226-92425-4 (paper)
ISBN-10: 0-226-92426-2 (e-book)

Library of Congress-in-Publication Data

Sharkey, Patrick
    Stuck in place : urban neighborhoods and the end of progress
toward racial equality / by Patrick Sharkey.
        pages ; cm
    Includes bibliographical references and index.
    ISBN-13: 978-0-226-92424-3 (cloth : alkaline paper)
    ISBN-10: 0-226-92424-6 (cloth : alkaline paper)
    ISBN-13: 978-0-226-92425-0 (paperback : alkaline paper)
    ISBN-10: 0-226-92425-4 (paperback : alkaline paper)
    [etc.]
    1. African American neighborhoods—Social aspects.
2. African American neighborhoods—Economic aspects.
3. Urban African Americans—Social conditions.   4. Urban
African Americans—Civil rights.   5. Discrimination in housing—
United States.   6. Equality—United States.   I. Title.
    E185.86.S514 2012
    323.1196'073—dc23
                                                        2012017909

⊗ This paper meets the requirements of ANSI/NISO Z39.48-1992
(Permanence of Paper).

Contents

Acknowledgments

This project evolved in several stages, and I received a tremendous amount of feedback and support at each stage. The idea for the project emerged when I was in graduate school. While reading the literature on intergenerational economic mobility, I wondered why there was no equivalent research on mobility into and out of poor and affluent neighborhoods across generations. I brought the question to the three faculty members who had given me the most guidance while I was at Harvard—Robert Sampson, William Julius Wilson, and Chris Winship—and they all agreed that it was an important gap in the literature. That was the beginning of my dissertation.

Since those initial meetings, these three advisers and mentors have spent much more time responding to my questions, thoughts, and ideas than I deserve. Bill Wilson, whose research on urban poverty inspired me to become a sociologist, provided extensive feedback and pushed me to think more broadly about the implications of my findings for understanding racial inequality in America. Chris Winship spent hours with me discussing tricky methodological issues, conceptual problems, and strategies for refining and improving the analyses I was proposing. I thank them both for their insight, for their advice and suggestions, and for their support throughout graduate school and beyond.

Rob Sampson was the chair of my dissertation committee. When I heard Rob was coming to Harvard, a year after I had arrived to begin grad school, I was thrilled—but I had no idea what an impact he would have on my development as a sociologist. This book, along with all of my work, bears the unmistakable imprint of the countless conversations I have had with Rob discussing ideas, planning courses, puzzling over methods, and interpreting results. Many of the ideas that I put forth in the book are influenced by his research, by the collaborative research we have conducted together, and by the feedback that Rob has given me throughout the development of the manuscript. I am enormously grateful for his mentorship.

Beyond my three advisers, I was lucky enough to be able to interact with a group of thoughtful and incisive people while completing my graduate work. Christopher Jencks and Jim Quane were particularly helpful in guiding my thinking throughout the early stages of the project, and I benefited tremendously from the feedback of other faculty, researchers, and peers during (and after) graduate school, including Corina Graif, David Harding, Joel Horwich, Elisabeth Jacobs, Pam Joshi, Therese Leung, Jal Mehta, Pam Metz, Bikila Ochoa, Jennifer Sykes-McLaughlin, Laura Tach, Chris Wimer, and Scott Winship.

When I finished my doctoral work the strongest parts of the project were the descriptive analyses demonstrating the degree to which neighborhood inequality is passed on across generations. My committee members urged me to make it something more, and it was only after I left grad school that I began to focus primary attention on the *consequences* of persistent neighborhood inequality. I spent two years in the Robert Wood Johnson Health & Society Scholars Program at Columbia University, pushing this project forward and beginning new lines of research as well. During this period I received excellent advice and feedback on the project from Peter Bearman and Bruce Link, and I was able to draw on the knowledge and the ideas of a wonderful and diverse group of fellow scholars in the program and faculty at Columbia, including jimi adams, Lisa Bates, Maria Glymour, Gina Lovasi, Kathy Neckerman, Ezra Susser, and Julien Teitler. I thank them all.

I began an extended collaboration with my friend Felix Elwert during this time as well. Felix and I spent several years coming up with a strategy that would allow us to identify the effect of living in poor neighborhoods over multiple generations. This collaboration resulted in the analyses that are presented in chapter 5 of the book and also in a stand-alone journal article published in the *American Journal of Sociology* in 2011. It has been a tremendous experience to work with Felix, and our conversations have been crucial in refining my thinking about the cumulative effects of neighborhood poverty. We benefited also from the thoughts and comments of David Harding, Robert Mare, Steve Raudenbush, and Geoff Wodtke, all of whom provided important feedback on this part of the project.

When I finished my fellowship and began teaching at New York University, the book project was much more expansive than when I left graduate school, but it was not complete. One of the central questions that remained underdeveloped was "What next?" That is, how can public policies disrupt or confront the problem of multigenerational neighborhood disadvantage? In considering this question, I was heavily influenced by the thoughts of Larry Aber, a colleague and mentor at NYU. Hoping to take advantage of Larry's expertise on issues surrounding neighborhood inequality, child development, and public policy, I asked him if he would be willing to read the concluding chapter of the manuscript. When we met a few weeks later, Larry had read the entire manuscript and had an array of ideas and questions about the overarching argument of the book and about specific sections, paragraphs, and sentences throughout the book. I am extremely grateful to Larry for his willingness to read the book and share his thoughts with me, which were highly influential in the revision process and in the writing of the concluding chapter.

My colleagues in the Sociology Department at NYU also have been remarkably generous in offering their feedback on different pieces of the manuscript. In particular, Richard Arum, Dalton Conley, Steven Lukes, Gerald Marwell, Harvey Molotch, Caroline Persell, Florencia Torche, and Larry Wu have, at various points, provided specific ideas or comments that have stuck in my mind and made their way into the book, in one form or another. Others have provided similarly important comments in informal conversations or during presentations of the research; these others include Xavier de Souza Briggs, Tom Cook, Kathy Edin, Herbert Gans, Michael Hout, and Loic Wacquant. I thank all of these individuals for contributing to the final product.

With a draft of the complete manuscript in hand, in the spring of 2011 I had the rare opportunity to sit in a room with some of the leading scholars in the field and hear what they thought about the book. Jeff Manza, the chair of NYU's Sociology Department at the time, expended a great deal of effort organizing this informal book workshop designed to generate feedback on the manuscript before its publication. This is only one example of Jeff taking extraordinary steps to support junior faculty in the department, and all of his efforts are greatly appreciated. It was something of a shock to hear that the people we asked to take part in the workshop actually agreed to travel to New York City to spend several hours discussing an unpublished book manuscript, but they did and it was an invaluable experience that improved the manuscript dramatically. A few weeks later I sat down with Lance Freeman, who also had read the manuscript but was unable to attend the workshop, and discussed his perspective on the book. To Lance, Jeff, and all of the participants in the workshop—John Goering, Eric Klinenberg, John Logan, John Mollenkopf, and Deirdre Royster—I cannot thank you enough for your generosity, your time, and your insight.

Now that the book is finally complete, it is sobering to think about all of the people and institutions that have provided the resources and support necessary to carry out the research. During graduate school I received dissertation support from Harvard's Project on Justice, Welfare, and Economics and research grants from the Institute for Quantitative Social Science and the Horowitz Foundation for Social Policy. My affiliations with Harvard's Multidisciplinary Program in Inequality and Social Policy and, later, with the Robert Wood Johnson Health & Society Scholars Program provided the resources that allowed me to focus on the research and also offered stimulating intellectual communities. The Pew Charitable Trusts' Economic Mobility Project provided support to study the role of neighborhoods in explaining racial gaps in economic mobility, and I thank Erin Currier, Ianna Kachoris, and Scott Winship in particular for their excellent comments on analyses of economic mobility that were conducted for a report submitted to Pew—some of this analysis also appears in chapter 4 of the book. Felix Elwert and I received support from the Panel Study of Income Dynamics' Small Grants Competition, which allowed us to refine the analysis of multigenerational neighborhood effects presented in chapter 5. At a more general level, researchers and staff from the PSID have been supportive of this research from the outset, and their assistance to me and to the research community as a whole has helped to make the PSID an extremely valuable resource. Donna Nordquist in particular does a tremendous job in coordinating the application process for the PSID restricted-use geocode data, and I thank her for the help she has provided me over the last several years.

Doug Mitchell at the University of Chicago Press has been instrumental in encouraging me and in pushing the book forward at every step, and I owe him an enormous debt of gratitude for his work on the project. I thank Tim McGovern as well, along with the anonymous reviewers solicited by the press, who provided me with thoughtful, constructive comments early in the development of the project and again on the complete manuscript.

This book took much longer than I thought it would to complete. When I began this project I was an unmarried graduate student living in Cambridge, MA. As the book moves to publication, my wife Alyssa and I have two kids and have now spent several years living in the middle of Manhattan. Alyssa has put up with the ebb and flow of my moods as we have gone through grad school, marriage, and parenthood together—she remains an inspiration in my life, and I thank her for all of her support. Thomas and Kate allow me to forget about my research for hours at a time and focus on how much fun it is to have two little kids. My brothers Kevin and Brendan are two of my closest friends, biggest advocates, and most vocal critics, and I thank them for all of these roles. While I have settled on the cushy academic life, they have been teaching the children and organizing the workers that I study, and their perspectives have been invaluable for my own research. And, finally, I thank my parents Eileen and Tom Sharkey for their remarkable support, for their thoughtful feedback on my ideas and interest in my research, and for demonstrating how to live a dedicated, inspired professional life while being extraordinary parents. This book is dedicated to them.

| Chapter 1 | **Introduction** |

"A remarkable development has taken place in America over the last dozen years: for the first time in the history of the republic, truly large and growing numbers of American blacks have been moving into the middle class, so that by now these numbers can reasonably be said to add up to a *majority* of black Americans—a slender majority, but a majority nonetheless. . . . It is real progress, a massive achievement; and to all appearances it is here to stay."
— Ben J. Wattenberg and Richard M. Scammon, 1973[1]

One common viewpoint during the civil rights era, held among many policy makers, activists, and academics alike, was that advances in civil rights would mark the beginning of a movement toward racial equality. From this perspective, the end of legal discrimination meant the removal of barriers blocking African Americans from accessing the resources and opportunities necessary for economic and social mobility— open and fair housing, equal employment opportunity, political power, access to integrated schools and higher education. The alternative viewpoint, expressed in documents like the Moynihan Report and the Kerner Commission Report, was that racial equality, in economic terms, would be a goal much more difficult to attain than racial equality in legal terms.

The passage with which I begin the book, written at the tail end of the civil rights era and at the cusp of a national economic downturn, reflects a consistent set of empirical findings providing at least partial support for the former, optimistic view.[2] The authors' conclusion that "truly large and growing numbers of American blacks have been moving into the middle class" was based on an analysis of data gathered in 1970, a time when much of the evidence available suggested that black/white inequality was on the decline. The claims made by Wattenberg and Scammon were somewhat exaggerated, as they were based on a definition of middle-class status that included essentially any family living outside of deep poverty. But the progress they described was real, even if it was more nuanced than these authors let on. Specific segments of the black population had, in fact, been able to take advantage of expanded civil rights and affirmative action programs, which resulted in a rapid expansion of the black professional class in both the private and public sectors.[3]

Wattenberg and Scammon were correct in describing the economic advancement among African Americans as "real progress, a massive achievement"—but for the purposes of this book, the key phrase is the one that follows: "and to all appearances it is here to stay." If these authors were correct in describing the tremendous economic advancement made by black Americans in the civil rights era, were they also correct in forecasting the continued decline of racial inequality?

The data reveal a complex answer. By some measures, African Americans have continued to make marginal progress toward economic equality since the beginning of the 1970s. It is common to hear about the continuing expansion of the black middle class, for instance—and while there is a slightly greater presence of African Americans in the middle and the high ends of the income distribution, a close look at the data shows that the overall level of economic advancement among African Americans has been remarkably limited.[4]

Consider the graph shown in figure 1.1, which shows the proportion of African Americans in each fifth of the U.S. income distribution over time.[5] If the distribution of income among African Americans was the same as that for the nation as a whole, we would expect to find about 20 percent of African Americans in the poorest fifth of the income distribution, 20 percent in the richest fifth, and so forth. It is no surprise that this has never been true over the past forty years. What is surprising is how stable the distribution of African Americans has been over time. At the start of the 1970s, roughly 39 percent of African Americans were in the poorest quintile—that is, the bottom 20 percent—of the U.S. income distribution. Now, at the end of the 2000s, about 33 percent of African Americans are among the poorest fifth of the U.S. population. Back at the start of the 1970s, about 65 percent of African Americans were in the bottom 40 percent of the income distribution; now, it's about 58 percent. Over this entire period, the portion of African Americans in the richest part of the income distribution has barely changed— about 8 percent of blacks were in the richest fifth of the income distribution in 1971, and just 9 percent were in the top fifth of the distribution in 2010. All of these figures suggest some positive change, but it is trivial change when compared to the severe racial inequality that was present at the start of the 1970s and that continues to exist today. Further, newly available evidence indicates that the gains in economic status made by African Americans are eroding during the current economic downturn.[6]

The narrative of the expansion of the black middle class gets even more complicated when one considers how the U.S. population has changed over time and who is counted as "black" in America. The nation has seen an explosion of immigration since the passage of the Hart-Cellar Act in 1965,

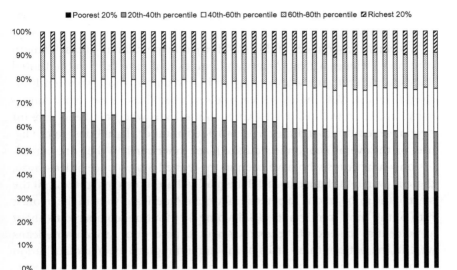

Figure 1.1. The proportion of black Americans in each fifth of the overall U.S. income distribution, from 1971 to 2010. Source: Author's tabulations based on figures from the March supplement to the Current Population Survey.

which overrode the previous national origins quota system and rapidly changed the flow of immigrants coming to the United States.[7] Whereas in the early part of the century most immigrants came from Europe, a majority of immigrants now arrive from Latin America, the Caribbean, Africa, Asia, and the Middle East.[8] There are two consequences of these changes that affect how we interpret trends in racial inequality. First, it is important to recognize that most of the growth in the immigrant population has occurred in the lower segments of the income distribution. This means that one of the reasons why blacks appear to be moving slightly upward in the income distribution is that an influx of immigrants has moved into the lower portion of the distribution, providing an artificial "bump" upward. If we consider African Americans' absolute income, rather than their relative position within the income distribution, new research shows virtually no improvement over time.[9] African American men have experienced no growth in income whatsoever, and the gains in income made by African American women, due to steadily increasing labor force participation, have been smaller than those of white women.

A second consequence of this shift is that the population of black Americans now includes African American families that have been in the United States for several generations along with newcomers who have recently arrived from the West Indies, Africa, or elsewhere. These "new" black Americans have fared well relative to African Americans who have been here for several generations, and they have provided another slight boost to the figures on the overall economic status of black Americans.[10] When one considers only Americans who have been in the United States since at least 1970, there is even less change in racial inequality than shown in figure 1.1. At the start of the 1970s, about 40 percent of African Americans were in the poorest fifth of the "non-immigrant" U.S. income distribution, compared to about 35 percent at the end of the 2000s. About 82 percent of African Americans were in the bottom three-fifths of the non-immigrant income distribution at the start of the 1970s, compared to 78 percent at the end of the 2000s. What these figures tell us is that when we consider only families that have been in the country for the last several decades, we see virtually no progress toward racial equality.

An alternative way to track patterns of change among the population of African Americans who have been in the United States since the 1960s (and much earlier) is to track families over multiple generations and examine how the current generation of African American adults is doing, in economic terms, relative to how their parents did. The good news that emerges from this comparison is that the average African American has moved upward in the income distribution to a position that is very slightly higher than her parents occupied a generation ago. But a closer look reveals a less optimistic picture. The proportion of African Americans who have made substantial advancement—defined as those who move into a higher quintile of the income distribution than their parents—is extremely low, particularly when compared with whites. By contrast, there has been an extraordinary amount of *downward* economic mobility among African American families that were doing fairly well a generation ago. A majority of African Americans whose parents were in the middle class have fallen downward into a lower segment of today's income distribution.[11] Whereas white children raised in middle- and upper-income families have much higher income than their parents when they reach adulthood, black children raised in similar families have substantially lower income than their parents. For instance, if we focus only on the middle of the income distribution, a recent study shows that white children raised in families in the middle of the income distribution earned, on average, about $74,000 annual income as adults, almost $20,000 per year more than their parents (in adjusted dollars). Black children raised in families in the same segment of the income distribution earned about $45,000 income per year, $9,000 less than their parents.[12] Much of the progress that was the source of such optimism a generation ago has been lost in the current generation.

These figures reveal a portrait of severe, and persistent, racial inequality. It is a picture that is particularly troubling when one considers that this is the generation of African American children raised in the civil rights era, the first cohort of children able to take advantage of expanded civil rights as they completed their schooling and entered the labor market. If one had assumed in 1968 that freedom from legalized discrimination was the crucial step in the path toward racial equality, then one might have also assumed that the children who were raised in this period should have benefited most from the expansion of civil rights in the 1960s. Yet this is a generation of African American children who have made virtually no economic progress relative to their parents. How is it that the first generation of children able to take advantage of expanded civil rights has made so little progress toward economic equality?

When researchers analyze economic inequality or economic mobility across racial or ethnic groups, they often focus on characteristics of individuals and families within these groups, things like human capital, family structure, or culture. In other words, they focus on factors that lie within the home or within the individual as explanations for the divergent economic outcomes of different racial and ethnic groups in America. This research offers valuable insights into the sources of inequality—but it often overlooks or minimizes the role of forces that lie outside the individual, or outside the home environment, that influence the fortunes of different racial and ethnic groups.

This book looks beyond the individual and the family to understand inequality and mobility. I focus on the importance of places—communities and cities—as crucial sites for the transmission of racial inequality in the post civil rights era. I argue that to understand why the children of the civil rights era have made such minimal progress toward racial equality, we need to consider what has happened to the communities and cities in which they have lived over the past four decades. African Americans have been attached to places where discrimination has remained prevalent despite the advances in civil rights made in the 1960s; where political decisions and social policies have led to severe disinvestment and persistent, rigid segregation;

where the employment base that supported a middle-class urban population has migrated away, contracted, or collapsed; and where the impact of punitive criminal justice policies has been concentrated.

But understanding the forces that have affected urban communities, and the consequences of these forces, is not sufficient for understanding the transmission of racial inequality to the current generation. In addition, it is essential to consider how places are passed on from parents to children, how changes in urban communities have been experienced by families, and how these changes have affected the trajectories of families, over time and across generations. To understand racial inequality today, it is crucial to approach racial inequality from a multigenerational perspective.

This is the core idea that distinguishes this book from the set of recent studies that have examined the relationship between places and inequality.[13] In this book I analyze the trajectories of individual families in combination with the trajectories of the places they occupy. The logic underlying this approach is intuitive—if we want to understand how neighborhoods and cities alter the trajectories of families, it is essential to consider the types of environments in which families live over long periods of time and over an extended period of a family's history. If growing up in a poor or violent neighborhood alters the schooling opportunities of a child, affects who serves as his role models, exposes him to pollutants in the air and soil, leads to consistently high levels of stress, and limits his economic opportunities, then it is logical to assume that the impact of the environment would be more pronounced for a child who spends the duration of his childhood years in the disadvantaged setting, relative to a child who spends only a few years in this setting before moving out. If a child is raised by a parent who grew up in a similarly disadvantaged neighborhood—a parent who was taught in similarly deficient learning environments, who witnessed the same violence, who also had few employment opportunities—it is reasonable to think that the effects of the environment would be amplified, reinforced by the consistency of disadvantage as experienced over generations of a family.[14]

These assumptions lie at the heart of the analysis presented throughout the book, which examines the trajectories of a national sample of children who were raised during the civil rights era—the generation of children who inherited racial inequality from a previous era and reproduced this inequality in their own lifetimes. What I find is that it is impossible to understand racial inequality in the current generation without looking back to the neighborhoods and cities occupied by the previous generation. There are three reasons why this is so. First, neighborhood disadvantage and advantage are remarkably stable—families that currently live in an impoverished neighborhood are overwhelmingly likely to have lived in a similarly poor neighborhood for multiple generations. Second, the effects of neighborhood disadvantage experienced during childhood continue to have strong impacts as individuals move into adulthood—as a consequence, racial inequality that is present today is, in large part, a product of the extreme disadvantage in the neighborhoods of African Americans a generation ago. Third, the effect of living within severely disadvantaged communities accumulates over generations. The consequences of living within deprived residential environments over multiple generations are much more severe than the consequences of living in a poor neighborhood at a single point in time, or even in a single generation. In short, the story of racial inequality in the current generation must be thought of as a continuation of a story that extends well back in time.

Urban Neighborhoods and Racial Inequality from 1968 Forward

There is no clear marker indicating how far back one must go in order to understand current patterns of racial inequality in America's neighborhoods—but I begin in the late 1960s, for two reasons. The first is that the end of the 1960s can be seen as the dawn of a new era for African Americans in the United States. This period marked the tail end of the civil rights era and the beginning of a new period in American history, one in which racial inequality was no longer imposed and maintained by law. It was a time of social unrest, but also a period when the formal barriers upholding racial inequality in our legal system were slowly being torn down. The second reason is practical—one of the most remarkable surveys of American families ever conducted began in 1968, providing data that allow one to track the fortunes of black and white families over time in close detail and thus to generate evidence on the destinations, both geographic and economic, of black and white children who were raised in the civil rights era.

One downside of using a national dataset that began in 1968 is that it is impossible to analyze the trajectories of groups other than African Americans and whites, because there simply were not enough families from other racial and ethnic groups present in the original sample.[15] For this reason, I focus primarily on blacks and whites—this focus is not due to lack of interest in the fortunes of other groups, nor is it due to a belief that these other groups have been unimportant to understanding racial and ethnic inequality. Immigration and the growing ethnic diversity in the nation have been enormously important for urban areas, a fact that emerges clearly in the analysis of neighborhood change in chapter 6. However, in an analysis that considers the trajectories of families over multiple generations, it is simply not possible to make reliable statements about the fortunes of other groups in America.[16]

With a main focus on the fortunes of African Americans and whites, data from the Panel Study of Income Dynamics (PSID) provide evidence on questions that have taken decades to answer: Did African American children of the civil rights era advance out of America's poorest neighborhoods? Did mobility out of the ghetto lead to economic and social mobility? Or, has the racial inequality that led to the civil rights legislation simply been passed on to the current generation of black and white adults?

To answer these questions, I begin by turning back to the 1968 Fair Housing Act, a piece of legislation that was passed in one of the most tumultuous periods in the last half century. The legislation was passed years after the other major civil rights bills, at a time when schools and workplaces were already on the slow path toward integration. Segregationists had fought against integration in the workplace and in the schools—but the neighborhood was their last stand, and they had dug in their heels to resist residential integration. The turning point came with the assassination of Martin Luther King, Jr. When the nation's cities erupted in response to King's death, including the neighborhoods surrounding the Capitol building, there was a brief moment of opportunity for fair housing advocates. The injustice of racial inequality and the danger of inaction could not have been clearer. It was in this explosive environment that the Fair Housing Act was passed by a reluctant Congress.[17]

The legislation made discrimination in the public and private housing markets illegal, and carried with it the hope that America's neighborhoods would no longer be divided by race. But in reality, the act was largely symbolic. The compromises that led to its passage gutted the enforcement mechanisms that were part of the original legislation and made it extremely difficult to prosecute cases of discrimination. Considering the impotence of the law and the fierce resistance to the very idea of residential integration, it would have been irrational to have expected that whites would suddenly accept black neighbors with open arms, or that black families would eagerly move into neighborhoods where they knew they would be treated with hostility. It would have been irrational to have expected that America's neighborhoods would integrate overnight—and those that may have had such optimistic expectations would have been severely disappointed by the persistence of segregation in the decades following the legislation.[18]

We are now four decades removed from the tension surrounding the period. A generation of black and white children has entered adulthood during a time in which housing discrimination is no longer officially sanctioned by law, a time in which social norms have gradually changed, and the memory of de jure segregation has faded. One could argue that the true test of the civil rights era did not lie with the generation of adults who lived through the civil rights period; the true test arrived with the next generation, who offer the best indication of whether the Fair Housing Act and other civil rights legislation succeeded in opening up pathways of upward mobility out of the ghetto for African Americans. And it is only now that we have the data available to assess whether the children of the civil rights era have achieved the promises of the period.

Based on the optimism that surrounded the Fair Housing Act, one might have guessed that the data would serve as confirmation that the children who were raised during the era of civil rights have made progress relative to their parents, even if equality has not yet been reached. Given the freedom of residential mobility, one might have guessed that a large segment of African American children has advanced out of the segregated, poor communities occupied by their parents and into neighborhoods that are similar to those occupied by whites with similar financial circumstances.

Instead, the data that I will present tell us that the story of neighborhoods and race in America is one of enduring, *inherited* inequality. Despite the high hopes of the civil rights era, the finding that emerges very clearly is that the stark racial inequality in America's neighborhoods that existed in the 1970s has been passed on, with little change, to the current generation. Relative to their parents, the current generation of African American adults has made virtually no advancement in residential America—the children who were raised in the most disadvantaged areas during the civil rights period are overwhelmingly likely to now raise their own children in remarkably similar environments. For the families living in today's ghettos, the challenges and risks associated with life in America's poorest neighborhoods represent a continuation of a family history of disadvantage. As I will document later in the book, over 70 percent of African Americans who live in today's poorest, most racially segregated neighborhoods are from the same families that lived in the ghettos of the 1970s.

To put it differently, the American ghetto appears to be inherited. In the same way that genetic background and financial wealth are passed down from parents to children, the neighborhood environments in which black and white Americans live have been passed down across generations, a process that has continued even in the post civil rights era. In order to avoid confusion, it is important to clarify what I mean when I refer to the "inheritance of the ghetto." I do not mean that children grow up and remain in the same physical space, but rather that children grow up and remain in the same type of environment. The level of poverty and the racial composition of families' neighborhood environments remain incredibly similar across generations of family members.

This empirical observation raises several questions about racial inequality and America's urban neighborhoods that form the focus of this book. First, four decades after the passage of the Fair Housing Act, why is it that African Americans have made virtually no advancement out of the nation's poorest, most disadvantaged neighborhoods? Secondly, does the transmission of neighborhood disadvantage to the current generation of African Americans help to explain the lack of progress toward racial equality in the economic sphere? At a more general level, what have been the consequences of persistent exposure to the nation's poorest neighborhoods, over multiple generations, for African Americans? And lastly, what can be done to end the cycle of multigenerational neighborhood disadvantage—that is, the problem of the inherited ghetto?

Coming to terms with the consequences of the urban ghetto becomes considerably more complex when we consider racial inequality from a multigenerational perspective, as this perspective forces one to move beyond the experiences of a single individual in a single lifetime and to consider the legacy of disadvantage as experienced over generations of a family. In later chapters I demonstrate that neighborhood inequalities experienced during childhood are an important reason why the current generation of black adults has experienced so much more downward economic mobility than whites. Moreover, the impact of disadvantages experienced during childhood is not felt in only a single lifetime, but lingers on to affect children in the next generation.

These empirical findings suggest that to understand American inequality—and particularly racial inequality—a shift of thinking is necessary. We must think about inequality as something that occurs over long periods of time and structures the opportunities available to families over multiple generations. Thinking in terms of generations, not snapshots in an individual's life, presents imposing challenges when we begin to consider how to confront the problem of concentrated poverty in urban neighborhoods and the related problem of persistent racial inequality. It means that to understand the full impact of urban ghettos we must consider the disadvantages faced by children in poor or violent neighborhoods in relation to a history of disadvantage experienced by family members. It means, further, that we must think about policies that do more than provide a short-lived excursion out of the ghetto, and instead consider investments and interventions with the potential to alter the trajectories of families, and alter the trajectories of the neighborhoods they occupy, in ways that will persist over long periods of time.

These are challenging goals, but evidence presented later in the book provides a hopeful vision for the segment of families that continue to live in the most disadvantaged neighborhoods. In chapter 6 I review research demonstrating that when families are provided the chance to escape the nation's most disadvantaged, most violent ghetto neighborhoods, there is encouraging evidence suggesting that children benefit substantially. Even more encouraging, I present new evidence showing that African American children living in the most disadvantaged neighborhoods experience considerable economic mobility when their neighborhoods undergo a transformation that brings about new economic opportunities and chips away at racial segregation.

This evidence, in combination with what we have learned from a series of experimental and quasi-experimental residential mobility programs, suggests a revised and expanded approach to confronting the problem of concentrated poverty in America's cities. While taking steps to enhance families' ability to live wherever they choose is essential, attempting to engineer the movement of large numbers of families from specified high-poverty neighborhoods to specified destination neighborhoods should not be a primary policy approach to ending the cycle of multigenerational disadvantage. The evidence available suggests that mobility out of ghetto neighborhoods is likely to be effective only if the programs are targeted toward families living in the nation's most violent, poorest, most racially segregated neighborhoods that volunteer to move, and if intensive services are provided to families as they settle in new communities. Attempting to disperse families from a broader range of poor urban neighborhoods, as has been suggested by several prominent academics and politicians, is unlikely to improve the life chances of children in families that move and could have severe unanticipated consequences, such as political backlash and the creation of new high-poverty communities. In addition to targeted mobility programs, I argue for a policy agenda designed to generate intensive and sustained investments in the nation's most disadvantaged neighborhoods with the dual goals of avoiding areas characterized by high levels of concentrated joblessness and creating areas that feature safe, enriching environments for youth. The strategies that I review are designed to make the urban ghetto less pernicious, and to alter the pattern of multigenerational disadvantage that I uncover in my analyses. The concluding chapter describes several programs that provide a template for what types of interventions might be effective in attaining these goals.

More important than any specific ideas or programs are two key principles that underlie all of the policies I discuss. The first principle is that to confront the problem of multigenerational disadvantage requires policies that have the potential to reach multiple generations of family members, to generate a lasting impact on families, and to be sustained over time. Point-in-time investments, even if they are based on promising ideas and strong theory, are unlikely to have transformative impacts on families that have lived in disadvantaged communities over decades and generations. I argue, in other words, for a "durable" urban policy agenda. Second, the place-based investments that I propose can only be effective as complementary measures initiated in support of a broad-based policy agenda designed to promote urban prosperity through investments in human capital, affordable and quality housing, health, economic competitiveness, and social integration. Policy experiments from the past several decades have made clear that place-based programs, by themselves, are likely to be overwhelmed by broader forces affecting the fortunes of entire segments of the urban populace, entire cities, and entire metropolitan areas. At the same time, broad-based policies designed to promote metropolitan-wide prosperity are not sufficient for ending the problem of the inherited ghetto. Even in times of urban growth, disadvantaged communities and specific segments of urban populations have been left behind, and these same communities are hit hardest in times of downturn. Place- or area-based programs that support broader metropolitan policies have the potential to ensure that no communities are left behind as a city experiences growth, and that no communities are abandoned and left to deteriorate during times of downturn.

These ideas are described in detail in the concluding chapter, but before getting to the analyses I have described or to the details of the strategies that I will propose, a more basic set of questions needs to be addressed: First, what do I mean when I use the term "ghetto"? Second, why focus on the ghetto, or on neighborhood environments more generally, as a key to racial inequality? Third, why focus on continuity and change over generations, as opposed to the experiences of an individual child or family?

Neighborhood Inequality and the American Ghetto

The term "ghetto" has a long history and has come to be thought of, defined, and measured in very different ways by social scientists, journalists, and the public at large.[19] Beginning with W. E. B. DuBois's research in Philadelphia and St. Clair Drake and Horace Cayton's work in Chicago,[20] in the American context the term has come to be used almost exclusively to characterize the residential environments of African Americans.[21]

To define the concept I borrow and expand upon an elegant definition supplied by Talja Blokland, a Dutch sociologist who defines the ghetto as the "spatial expression of social processes"—including processes of social and economic exclusion, exploitation, abandonment, disinvestment, and racial stigmatization and domination.[22] The ghetto is the result of these processes, an area characterized by racial and economic segregation and lacking the basic institutional, economic, and political resources that foster healthy and successful development in childhood and economic and social mobility in adulthood. While this theoretical definition is broad, its breadth is necessary in order to encompass the variation in the processes leading to urban ghettos in various times and places.

The theoretical definition of the "ghetto" is useful for providing a general idea about the concept under study, but it is less useful for providing concrete examples of what is and what is not an urban ghetto. Ideally one would operationalize ghetto neighborhoods by gathering historical data and interpreting the different forces at work in creating areas of concentrated disadvantage. There are many excellent examples of this work in urban sociology.[23] For studies designed to analyze the prevalence of exposure to urban ghettos among a large, national sample, and the consequences of life in the ghetto over multiple generations, this approach is not feasible. Instead, it is necessary to operationalize the concept of ghetto neighborhoods with identifiable markers that are commonly linked with the social processes described in the theoretical definition. In this effort I follow the lead of arguably the most prominent scholar of the urban ghetto of the last several decades, William Julius Wilson, and characterize urban ghettos on the basis of the concentration of poverty and the interaction between race and concentrated poverty, using data from decennial censuses aggregated to the level of the census tract. This is an imperfect approach, but it is an approach that captures the most salient feature of the post-industrial urban ghetto: the concentration of poverty and its differential impact on racial and ethnic groups, most notably African Americans.

With this definition in hand, let us consider why the study of urban ghettos is important for understanding American inequality more broadly. The vast majority of research describing inequality focuses on indicators of social or economic status that exist at the level of the individual or the family, such as income or wealth, occupational status, or educational attainment. One could make the case that these dimensions of stratification are the major fault lines by which American society is organized. One might also claim that the inequality that is so visible across America's neighborhoods is simply derivative from inequality in these other domains—for instance, African Americans may live in poor neighborhoods simply because they can't afford to live in more affluent areas, and thus the presence of black ghettos may be entirely attributable to racial inequality in income or wealth.

This book rests on the claim that research on individual income, education, and occupations, while essential, is insufficient for developing a complete picture of inequality in America. The primary reason why this is so is that inequality does not exist exclusively at the level of the individual or the family; rather, various forms of inequality are organized or clustered in social settings like neighborhoods, schools, and political districts, and these social settings represent crucial sites at which American inequality is generated, maintained, and reinforced.[24]

Perhaps the most powerful evidence of this fact of social life comes from a basic yet profound finding in ecological research, which is that a wide range of social phenomena such as violence, joblessness, and physical and mental health outcomes tend to be clustered together in space.[25] Why might this be so? To begin to answer this question, consider the way in which various aspects of social life are organized by geography, including schools, government and electoral districts, and other local institutions. The fact that schools are typically organized and partially funded by residential districts means that the quality of one's educational opportunities depends directly on where one lives. Regardless of a family's own income, living in areas with minimal resources for public education means that a child's learning opportunities may suffer based solely on the income of her neighbors. Add in the fact that violence, drug markets, and gang activities are often organized by territory (that is, by spatial boundaries located within disadvantaged areas), and it becomes clear why there is such tremendous variation in the schooling experiences of American youth. It is not surprising that quality teachers are unwilling to devote their energies to teaching in schools where safety and discipline become more important than learning, where violence can be as great a concern as educational advancement. It is also unsurprising that children in extremely disadvantaged neighborhoods are much more likely to drop out than similar children in economically diverse neighborhoods, or that neighborhood disadvantage has been found to be closely linked with children's performance on cognitive tests, even after accounting for a wide range of individual and family characteristics.[26]

Our nation's educational system is just one of many institutions that link individuals' residential locations with their life chances. For example, researchers have demonstrated that residents of poor and segregated neighborhoods have less political influence than residents of neighborhoods with more racial and economic diversity.[27] A great deal of evidence suggests that the spatial locations of jobs and industry, and the relationship between the types of jobs available in an area and the types of people living in the area, have important influences on the likelihood that individuals will be able to find and maintain steady employment.[28] The quality of public amenities such as parks, libraries, and recreation centers, the effectiveness of public servants such as the police, and the degree of exposure to violence, gangs, toxic soil, and clean air all depend directly on where one lives.[29] In these and other ways, the spatial clustering of social phenomena, economic opportunities, environmental resources and hazards, and public institutions has important implications for the life chances of individuals.

To truly understand inequality in America, then, it is necessary to move beyond a focus on income, occupation, and education, the traditional markers of socioeconomic status, and to consider the ways in which inequality is organized in space. In doing so, we find that the neighborhood is an *independent* dimension of stratification, meaning the residential patterning of American neighborhoods is not explained by these other dimensions of stratification—income, occupation, or education. An extensive research literature shows that after accounting for differences in socioeconomic status and wealth, African Americans live in neighborhoods that are markedly less affluent and more segregated than those occupied by whites of similar status.[30] In other words, African Americans do not live apart from whites purely because they have lower income or fewer assets—even after considering these factors, blacks continue to live in the most economically depressed, violent neighborhoods of any American racial or ethnic group. There is a consistent set of findings in sociological studies pointing to a racial and ethnic hierarchy in American neighborhoods, where whites live in the most advantaged neighborhoods after accounting for socioeconomic status, followed by different groups of Asian-Americans and Latinos, and finally by African Americans.[31] What this pattern makes clear is that the traditional literature on inequality, which focuses primarily on income, occupation, and education, is not sufficient for describing inequality in the places that people occupy. By studying neighborhoods and communities we see a different dimension of inequality, and a more severe brand of racial inequality.

The focus on neighborhoods and communities is not particularly novel within the discipline of sociology; what is unique about this book is the effort to fully integrate the study of neighborhoods with the broader literature on inequality and mobility, to think about and study neighborhoods and communities as one of the core dimensions of stratification, and to attempt to understand the persistence of neighborhood inequality across generations of American families, in the same way as has been done with the other prominent measures of inequality—income, wealth, occupation, and education.

Ecological perspectives on communities and inequality in America have always occupied a central place in the discipline, with a legacy in the United States dating back to the work of W. E. B. DuBois in Philadelphia and the research of the Chicago School of urban sociology.[32] This tradition has seen a resurgence since the late 1980s, generated, in large part, by William Julius Wilson's work on the concentration of poverty in America's cities, Douglas Massey's research on the persistence of segregation, and the advances that researchers like Robert Sampson and others have made in applying sociological theory to describe and explain the mechanisms underlying the changing patterns of stratification in urban neighborhoods.[33] In the two decades since these researchers began to refocus scholarly attention on urban neighborhoods and ghetto poverty, numerous studies have documented in great detail the prevalence of high-poverty neighborhoods and explicated the mechanisms producing change in neighborhood conditions,[34] and a mountain of research has demonstrated the ways in which neighborhood structural disadvantage and social organization affect individual and collective social outcomes.[35]

Despite this recent attention to urban neighborhoods, research on the spatial concentration of advantage and disadvantage still has not been brought into line with research on other dimensions of stratification in American society.[36] Basic questions about the extent of neighborhood disadvantage experienced by individuals over their lifetimes and over generations of family members, and the processes by which neighborhood inequality is generated and maintained, remain unanswered. To put it differently, we know very little about what I will refer to as "contextual mobility."

Contextual Mobility

When I use the term "contextual mobility" I am referring to the overall degree of movement in U.S. society across neighborhoods that are characterized by differential levels of economic resources and status. Before expanding on this definition, it may be helpful to step back and clarify what I mean with the use of terms like "context" and "environment," which will appear throughout the text. I am using the terms environment and context, interchangeably, to refer to social, economic, and physical aspects of individuals' residential settings, or their neighborhoods. For my purposes, one's environment or context refers to what individuals see and hear and breathe and experience around them when they engage in public life outside the home, along with the political, economic, and social forces that affect individuals on the basis of where they live. The neighborhood thus encompasses the people that occupy a residential area (i.e., one's neighbors and peers), the institutions that are prominent in the lives of residents (e.g., schools and health centers), the public officials representing the area and the political forces that affect the area (e.g., the mayor, police, city council representatives, the local school board), amenities in the area (e.g., parks, grocery stores, shopping outlets), the physical, geographic, and built environment (e.g., the level of air pollution, lead in the soil, layout of buildings, walkable space), and the opportunities available to residents (e.g., the presence of jobs, varying types of industry). In practice, all of these dimensions of a neighborhood are difficult to capture, especially with quantitative data from the census or other surveys. But because most of these spatial advantages and disadvantages come bundled together, it is possible (though of course not ideal) to use data on the racial and economic composition of neighborhoods, available at the level of the census tract at each decennial census, as a stand-in for the aspects of a neighborhood that might matter for families.[37]

Contextual mobility refers to the movement of individuals and families across neighborhoods that are more or less advantaged according to some measurable dimension of resources, status, or desirability. I use the term "mobility," rather than a term such as "change," to link the contextual mobility concept with the literature that has developed around other dimensions of inequality—for example, there is an extensive tradition of research on income mobility within economics and on occupational mobility within sociology. The idea of mobility suggests a process of transmission of advantages and disadvantages that results in the reproduction or dissolution of inequality over time. Mobility research tells us how much movement there is across the distribution of income in a society, for example, or how fixed individuals' economic positions are. Mobility research asks whether the rich tend to stay rich and whether the poor tend to stay poor, whether the children of laborers tend to be laborers themselves or tend to advance into white-collar occupations. In this book, I ask whether families in rich neighborhoods tend to stay in rich neighborhoods and whether families in the ghetto tend to remain in the ghetto.

From a conceptual standpoint it is also important to recognize the distinction between *contextual mobility* and related concepts such as *geographic* or *residential mobility*. Whereas geographic mobility refers to a change in geography (e.g., migration from one state to another), and residential mobility to a change in residence (e.g., a move across town), contextual mobility does not necessarily entail a change in residential location. Advancement in an individual's or a family's neighborhood environment can occur through a residential move, but it can also occur when the family remains in a neighborhood that is changing around it. In this sense, contextual mobility implies a change in the status of one's neighborhood, no matter the source of that change.

Why should we care about contextual mobility? Social mobility, measured along any dimension, is often thought of as the extent to which the advantages of one generation are passed on to the next, and is thus fundamental to our understanding of the type of society in which we live and how it works. Americans seem to believe firmly that systems of stratification are acceptable and necessary, as long as every member of society has a chance to rise in status or to pass on that opportunity to their children.[38] The same might be said of the neighborhoods we occupy. That is, the issue of ghetto poverty might not be seen as a particularly important problem if residents of urban ghettos commonly experience life in a disadvantaged environment for only short periods of time before moving on to more diverse neighborhoods. If residents typically remain in a disadvantaged setting for long periods of time, however, then there is greater potential for the environment to exert pernicious effects, and there is greater potential for a segment of society to become socially isolated from the opportunities, resources, and value systems that are common outside of extremely disadvantaged areas.[39]

The problem is that we know very little about how neighborhoods are experienced by individuals and families over long periods of time. This type of knowledge, on continuity and change in individuals' and families' neighborhood environments, is central to developing an understanding of how neighborhoods influence the trajectories of individuals. For instance, a child who is enmeshed in the social life of her neighborhood, who attends school with neighborhood peers, and who has lived in only one neighborhood throughout childhood would more likely be influenced by the environment around her than one who lived in the same neighborhood for a short period before moving on. The child would be even more likely to be influenced by the norms, attitudes, and opportunities in the neighborhood if her own mother had spent much of her life in a similar environment.

If the neighborhoods that individuals occupy are important elements of individual lives, it is likely that the cumulative exposure to different neighborhood environments, over individual lifetimes and across generations, matters most. This line of reasoning suggests that the role of neighborhoods in the life course can be captured only with a long-term analysis of the types of environments occupied by individuals and families. It is not enough to know whether an individual lives in a very poor neighborhood at a given point in time; instead it is essential to know what types of role models, resources, and risks are present in a child's neighborhood at various points in his/her development. It is essential to know how enmeshed the individual is in the social networks and the public life of the community and to know the types of residential environments that the individual and his/her family members have occupied over lifetimes and generations.

This book proposes two shifts of thinking with regard to the literature on inequality and mobility in America. The first is a shift from a pure focus on social or economic status within the family or the individual to a broader focus on the social environments surrounding families. While there now exists a vast literature on neighborhood poverty and community social organization, the neighborhood has not been conceptualized or studied in the same way as other dimensions of stratification. To be sure, various studies have described the stratification of places and processes of neighborhood mobility over short intervals, and recent work has begun to systematically integrate neighborhoods and places into the broader literature on stratification and mobility.[40] However, research on neighborhoods has rarely moved beyond a focus on the low end of the distribution of neighborhoods, and we know little about the degree of movement across that distribution over time—the *rigidity* of neighborhood inequality as experienced by individuals and families.

This latter point is related to the second proposed shift of thinking, which involves moving from a static view of neighborhood disadvantage and advantage at a given point in time to a dynamic view of neighborhood stratification that considers mobility across the distribution of neighborhoods over individual lifetimes and across generations of family members. More succinctly, I am arguing for the need to fully incorporate both *place* and *time* into the literature on racial inequality in America.

In emphasizing the importance of contextual mobility I am not suggesting that residential contexts are unrelated to other dimensions of stratification. Indeed, an additional justification for studying the stratification of residential contexts is that developing a clear understanding of persistence and change in individuals' neighborhood environments may be essential to understanding mobility across multiple dimensions. Despite the common conception of America as a nation where every man and woman can become a success no matter their origins, the most rigorous recent work on economic mobility in America suggests that "rags to riches" stories are much less common than one might think—and "rags to rags" or "riches to riches" stories are the norm.[41] There is a growing consensus in the literature that the idea of America as a uniquely mobile nation is overstated or incorrect. However, evidence on the mechanisms leading to the persistence of wealth and poverty across generations is still sparse.[42] Though they are overlooked in the literature on economic mobility, I argue that residential contexts may play a prominent role in the reproduction of social and economic status across generations.

I am not the first to raise this as a possibility. A common theme in many of the classic sociological texts on urban poverty is that the reproduction of economic status from one generation to the next is closely related to the lack of opportunities found in the urban ghetto.[43] More recently, the work of William Julius Wilson, Robert Sampson, and their colleagues has focused attention on the ways that structural disadvantage and aspects of social organization within neighborhoods can influence patterns of behavior within the boundaries of the neighborhood, thereby influencing the life course trajectories of neighborhood residents.[44]

The analyses in this book examine this hypothesis by explicitly integrating social environments into the broader literature on economic and social mobility—in other words, by examining the role that neighborhoods play in the reproduction of racial inequality over time. This approach recognizes that residential contexts do not only represent an important dimension of stratification but also may serve as an important pathway by which the economic circumstances, the social ties, and the cultural norms and practices of one generation are transmitted to the next. In this sense, information on continuity of residential conditions, in addition to economic status, may be especially relevant to the study of continuity and reproduction of social inequality.

Outline of the Book

The book proceeds in three parts. The first part of the book (chapters 2 and 3) presents empirical evidence on the persistence of neighborhood inequality across generations. Chapter 2 describes the overall degree of continuity and change in families' neighborhood environments and then focuses attention on the prevalence of upward and downward mobility across the distribution of neighborhoods among blacks and whites. This chapter provides the empirical foundation for the remainder of the book, as it shows how little progress African Americans have made in advancing out of the ghetto. The analysis then expands on this evidence and asks why racial inequality in America's neighborhood environments has been so persistent, and why the same families have remained in the ghetto for multiple generations.

After considering a wide range of family and individual-level factors that might explain the low rates of contextual mobility, I conclude that the persistence of the ghetto is *not* attributable primarily to factors that lie within the home or within the individual. In other words, the reason children end up in neighborhood environments similar to those of their parents is not that their parents have passed on a set of skills, resources, or abilities to the children that result in their ending up in similar neighborhoods. Instead, parents pass on the place itself to their children. Accounting for all of the individual or family characteristics that are measurable in the data, I find that children that grow up and remain in the same place—in this case, the same county—exhibit, by far, the lowest rates of contextual mobility.

For African American families, this evidence suggests that the inability to advance out of the ghetto appears to be closely related to individuals' attachments to specific places—cities and metropolitan areas—that have fared poorly in the post-industrial economy. Chapter 3 examines the set of forces—demographic, economic, and political—that have served to maintain the residential structure that is present in urban America, with a particular focus on four trends and forces that are crucial to explaining why inequality in urban neighborhoods has been so persistent: (1) the failure to complete the progression toward full civil rights; (2) the enactment of a diverse set of policies, informal strategies and institutional mechanisms used to maintain racial inequality in urban areas; (3) the restructuring of urban labor markets; and (4) the destructive response to economic dislocation in America's cities. I argue that the combination of structural shifts to urban economies and the federal government's erratic and sometimes destructive responses to deindustrialization helps to explain why African Americans have made virtually no progress in residential America.

The second part of the book (chapters 4 and 5) examines the consequences of multigenerational neighborhood disadvantage for African Americans. In these chapters I assess whether the persistence of severely unequal neighborhood environments has played a role in perpetuating racial inequality in economic status, educational attainment, employment and occupational status, and wealth. Whereas a substantial academic literature has assessed the impact of neighborhood environments on a wide range of outcomes, virtually all research on "neighborhood effects" ignores the history of advantage and disadvantage that families experience over time and across generations. These chapters in the second part show that when we consider the environments in which families live over long periods of time, we get a very different picture of the influence of neighborhoods.

Chapter 4 shows that neighborhood disadvantages experienced during childhood play a large role in explaining African Americans' low rate of economic mobility relative to whites in the post civil rights era. The relationship is particularly strong when we consider why African Americans have experienced such high rates of downward economic mobility in this era. The sociologist Mary Pattillo has argued that middle-class status is precarious for African Americans in part because even middle-class blacks often live in neighborhoods with much higher poverty than middle-class whites, and because middle-class blacks often live in neighborhoods that are linked, geographically and socially, with the black ghetto. Consistent with this research, I find that measures of childhood neighborhood poverty are an important part of the reason why African Americans in the middle class experience so much more downward economic mobility relative to whites. Neighborhood poverty plays an important role in explaining black/white gaps in income mobility and wealth mobility, but it appears less important in explaining gaps in educational mobility or occupational mobility.

Chapter 5 demonstrates how the neighborhood environment in one generation lingers on to affect the life chances of the next generation. The results from analyses in this chapter show that neighborhood disadvantages experienced by children do not fade away as they move into adulthood, but continue to have an impact on their own children's development, a generation later. This finding is consistent with the idea that individuals' childhood neighborhoods have a lingering influence on various aspects of their adult lives, including their schooling, their romantic partners, their occupational trajectories, and their adult income and assets. All of these aspects of parents' adult lives, in turn, influence the environment in which they raise their children and the resources they devote to child rearing. In this way, the full impact of the neighborhood environment is not felt in only a single generation, but persists over time and affects the next generation through multiple pathways. This finding reveals the way in which the social environments of previous generations form what I refer to as a "legacy of disadvantage" that continues to be felt in subsequent generations.

Having considered the persistence of neighborhood inequality and the consequences for African Americans, the third part of the book (chapters 6 and 7) considers strategies for reducing the concentration of disadvantage in America's neighborhoods and for halting the reproduction of racial inequality across generations. Chapter 6 examines, first, the two most prominent policy approaches for dealing with concentrated poverty—residential mobility programs designed to offer residents of disadvantaged neighborhoods the chance to "move to opportunity," and alternative approaches that focus on investing directly in urban neighborhoods in an attempt to deconcentrate disadvantage without moving residents out. My review of the residential mobility approach assesses evidence from a number of experimental and quasi-experimental programs that have been conducted in the past three decades and summarizes what these programs tell us about the prospects for relying on mobility to confront the problems of urban neighborhoods. Because there is not equivalent evidence with which to evaluate the second approach, I conduct an original analysis designed to generate sound empirical evidence on the question of whether intervening to reduce the concentration of disadvantage, without resorting to moving residents out, is likely to have benefits for children living within the most disadvantaged neighborhoods. Using a newly developed method designed to generate estimates of the causal impact of neighborhood change, I find that positive changes in the most disadvantaged communities—the deconcentration of disadvantage—leads to substantial economic benefits for African American children.

With these hopeful results in mind, I conclude by laying out a set of principles for a policy agenda focused on confronting the problem of the inherited ghetto. Any approach to addressing the problems arising in neighborhoods of concentrated poverty must begin with the recognition that the social problems that characterize poor, segregated urban neighborhoods have not arisen because of any character deficiencies of low-income African Americans or other ethnic minorities. These problems have emerged due to a combination of economic and political disinvestment in urban neighborhoods, along with social policies that have served to exacerbate the challenges of economic dislocation faced by poor communities. The pattern of disinvestment and punitive social policy has persisted for long periods of time, and the impact of this disinvestment will not be reversed with anything but a sustained investment in America's urban neighborhoods.

The implication is that good policy ideas are not sufficient to produce sustained change in the lives of families or communities. What is needed is *durable* urban policy, meaning policy with the capacity to create changes that persist across generations of families, and policies that are less vulnerable to the changing political mood in Washington or to the fluctuations of the business cycle. The concluding chapter offers a set of ideas for policies that fit the criteria for durable urban policy—the true challenge, however, is generating the types of political coalitions and political will to sustain the commitment to these policies over time.

Chapter 2 | The Inheritance of the Ghetto

In his book *The Truly Disadvantaged*, published in 1987, William Julius Wilson put together a theory that made sense of what Americans were seeing on the nightly news as they turned on their TV sets in the 1980s.[1] They were seeing violence that was concentrated in specific segments of America's cities to a degree that had not existed since the riots of the 1960s. They were seeing urban blight that left areas of the city empty and abandoned. They were seeing crack addicts and the homeless strewn across urban streets. And most of the faces they saw in these images were black. When Americans read the morning newspaper they saw statistics about the deterioration of the two-parent family structure, the rising dropout rate, failing urban schools, and the rising incarceration rate—and all of these trends were most pronounced among African Americans.

Some of what the nation saw and read was a product of sensational journalism and subtle racism—the images and stories of violence and desperation did not represent the large majority of black neighborhoods.[2] Even so, the statistics on poverty, crime, and violence confirmed the emergence of a new type of urban poverty. Wilson's book laid out a theory to explain the transformation of urban neighborhoods that has been repeated so frequently that it almost seems obvious in hindsight. In his book Wilson documented how the manufacturing base in northeastern and midwestern cities had begun to evaporate, leaving minority populations that had relied on stable, working-class jobs since the Great Migration without an employment base. With the decline in manufacturing jobs within central cities, joblessness skyrocketed and there were fewer "marriageable" black men who could support a family and play the role of breadwinner—the rate of families headed by a single parent rose sharply, as did the rate of welfare receipt. In addition to the transformation of urban labor markets, Wilson demonstrated how civil rights legislation allowed middle-class blacks to expand the boundaries of urban ghettos, or to leave them altogether, a process that had the unanticipated consequence of removing the "middle-class buffer" from black neighborhoods. When the middle class left, the community institutions they left behind, including the church and the schools, deteriorated rapidly.

The result of these and other, subtler changes was a concentration of poverty in the urban ghetto that was associated with an array of social problems, including violence, homelessness, joblessness, rising rates of families headed by single women, and welfare receipt. Whereas the ghetto of the 1940s was a place where all classes of African American families were forced to live, the ghetto of the 1980s was a place where the most impoverished African Americans had been abandoned. Americans saw the consequences of this concentration of poverty when they made forays into central cities or when they turned on their TVs and witnessed the everyday blight and bloodshed that characterized the urban ghetto of this period.

The second major work on urban poverty that was published during this period came from Douglas Massey and Nancy Denton, who wrote *American Apartheid* several years after the publication of Wilson's book.[3] Massey and Denton's argument did not challenge the accuracy of the theory put forth by Wilson, but they argued that Wilson's book overlooked the "missing link" underlying all of the changes that he had documented: the persistence of racial segregation. In *American Apartheid* and in subsequent works, Massey and his co-authors described how the changes in the labor markets of urban areas and the increase in black poverty that Wilson documented would not have had such serious consequences were it not for the rigid segregation in America's urban neighborhoods.[4] The core empirical finding underlying Massey's claims was this: despite the major advances made in civil rights in the late 1960s, racial segregation had barely declined in the post civil rights era. Decades after the Fair Housing Act of 1968, many of America's largest cities remained "hypersegregated," to use a term coined by Massey and Denton to describe areas characterized by the isolation and concentration of minority populations. Severe racial segregation was a necessary condition for the concentration of urban poverty and all of the social problems that emerged with it, they argued.

If one is willing to simplify the complex set of theories and analyses put forth by Wilson and Massey and their co-authors, there are two crucial observations about urban poverty that stood out from their work. The first, from Wilson, is that ghetto poverty transformed in the post World War II period, so that urban ghettos were increasingly characterized by the concentration of poverty and related social problems. The second, from Massey, is that racial segregation has persisted in the post civil rights era, and the segregation of urban neighborhoods by race has allowed for the concentration of poverty and other problems that Wilson described. The way that scholars have studied the sources of neighborhood inequality, the consequences of neighborhood inequality, and the persistence of racial inequality in America has been shaped by these two complementary observations about the persistence of racial segregation and the concentration of poverty in America's cities. In the wake of this research from Wilson and Massey, poverty has increasingly come to be thought of not only in individual terms but also in terms of how it is distributed across space and across communities.

This chapter presents evidence in support of an additional observation that provides a new perspective for scholars and policy makers attempting to understand and respond to concentrated poverty. The problem of urban poverty in the post civil rights era is not only that concentrated poverty has intensified and racial segregation has persisted *but that the same families have experienced the consequences of life in the most disadvantaged environments over multiple generations.* It is not just that the ghetto has persisted, but that the ghetto has been inherited. The problems and challenges of life in the urban ghetto are problems experienced by parents and then passed on to children—multiple generations of family members have been taught in the nation's worst schools and have been exposed to the nation's most unhealthy and most violent environments. This observation complicates the way scholars understand urban poverty, but it also complicates the way policy makers think about addressing urban poverty—confronting the problems of the urban ghetto requires confronting problems that have been faced by generations of African American families. This is the problem of the inherited ghetto, and this chapter presents the initial evidence to document how severe a problem it is.

Neighborhood Poverty in Black and White, Past and Present

Before describing the transmission of neighborhood environments across generations, a process I refer to as contextual mobility, it is useful to begin by describing the overall degree of racial inequality in children's neighborhood environments both in the past and in the present. Figure 2.1 shows the distribution of neighborhood environments of white and black children born during two distinct periods: first, children born from 1955 through 1970, the first cohort of children raised during or just after the civil rights era; and second, children born thirty years later, from 1985 through 2000, a group that can be thought of as the current generation of American children and young adults.

As is visible from the figure, being raised in a high-poverty neighborhood is extremely rare for whites born in both periods, but is the norm for African Americans. Among children born from 1955 through 1970, only 4 percent of

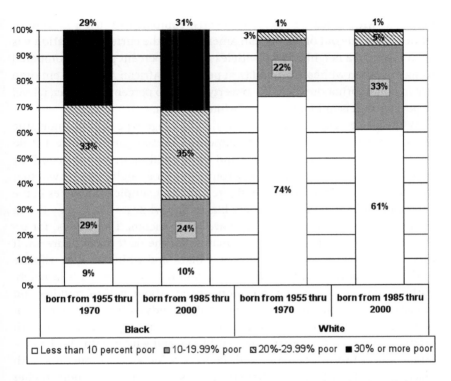

Figure 2.1. Neighborhood poverty levels among blacks and whites born in two periods: 1955–70 and 1985–2000.

whites were raised in neighborhoods with at least 20 percent poverty, compared to 62 percent of African Americans. Three out of four white children were raised in neighborhoods with less than 10 percent poverty, compared to just 9 percent of African Americans. Essentially no white children were raised in neighborhoods with at least 30 percent poverty, but three in ten African Americans were. These figures reveal that African American children born from the mid-1950s to 1970 were surrounded by poverty to a degree that was virtually nonexistent for whites.

This degree of racial inequality is not a remnant of the past, as the figures for children born thirty years later make clear. If there is any difference between children in the previous generation and in the current one, the degree of neighborhood disadvantage experienced by African American children has worsened in the current generation. Two out of three African American children born from 1985 through 2000 have been raised in neighborhoods with at least 20 percent poverty, compared to just 6 percent of whites. Only one out of ten African Americans in the current generation has been raised in a neighborhood with less than 10 percent poverty, compared to six out of ten whites. Even today, 31 percent of African American children live in neighborhoods where the poverty rate is 30 percent or greater, a level of poverty that is unknown among white children.

While the severity of neighborhood disadvantage experienced among the black population has been well documented, these figures provide a striking reminder of the fact that black and white children in America continue to be raised in entirely distinct environments. One might wonder whether the racial discrepancies visible in figure 2.1 reflect simple differences in the degree of individual poverty among blacks and whites—blacks may live in poor neighborhoods because they have lower income themselves, for instance. This is not an adequate explanation for the patterns in figure 2.1. If this figure is reproduced including only black and white families who are in the upper portion of the income distribution, the racial gaps in neighborhood poverty are even more pronounced. About half of middle- and upper-income blacks were raised in neighborhoods with at least 20 percent poverty, compared to 1 percent of whites. This finding is consistent with extensive research demonstrating that blacks and whites with similar economic status live in dramatically different residential environments, with blacks living in areas with higher crime rates, poor quality schools, higher poverty rates, lower property values, and severe racial segregation.[5]

Living amid such concentrated poverty does not mean simply that a child's neighbors have little money. In the American context, neighborhood poverty is fundamentally interwoven with racial segregation, with the resources available for children and families in the community, with the quality of local institutions like schools, with the degree of political influence held by community leaders and residents, with the availability of economic opportunities, and with the prevalence of violence. Living in a high-poverty neighborhood typically means living in an economically depressed environment that is unhealthy and unsafe and that offers little opportunity for success.

Figure 2.2 uses census data to provide a partial description of the different dimensions of disadvantage that come bundled together at the neighborhood level by examining characteristics of high-poverty neighborhoods in 1970 and in 2000, as compared to all other nonpoor U.S. neighborhoods. In both years, the most prominent racial or ethnic group in neighborhoods with at least 30 percent poverty was, not surprisingly, African Americans. In 1970, the poorest U.S. neighborhoods were 44 percent black, while neighbor-

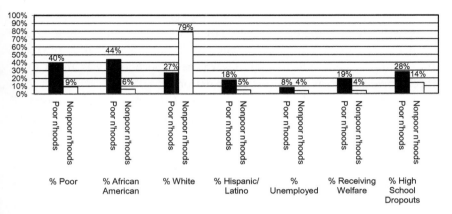

High-poverty neighborhoods compared to all other neighborhoods in 1970

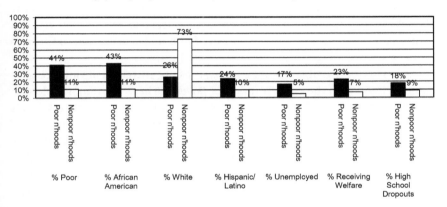

High-poverty neighborhoods compared to all other neighborhoods in 2000

Figure 2.2. Characteristics of high-poverty neighborhoods in 1970 and 2000.

hoods with less than 30 percent poverty were just six percent black, on average. In 2000, high-poverty neighborhoods were 43 percent black, compared to 11 percent black in the remainder of neighborhoods. In both periods, high-poverty neighborhoods had extremely high rates of joblessness and idleness. For instance, in 1970 high-poverty neighborhoods had 8 percent unemployment, 19 percent welfare receipt, and a high school dropout rate of 28 percent among youth aged 16–19. By 2000 these figures had changed somewhat due to the growing educational attainment of the population as a whole and the worsening economic climate in such neighborhoods—in 2000, high-poverty neighborhoods had unemployment rates of 17 percent and welfare receipt rates of 23 percent, while 18 percent of youth aged 16–21 were high school dropouts. Compared to the rest of the nation, these neighborhoods featured a remarkable concentration of jobless adults—in 2000, the unemployment rate in high-poverty neighborhoods was more than three times as high as in the rest of the nation.

Even these figures do not capture some of the most salient aspects of high-poverty neighborhoods, such as the prevalence of violence. Data on crime and violence at the level of neighborhoods are not available for the nation as a whole, but it is possible to provide a more vivid description of what it means to live in an area of concentrated disadvantage by narrowing the focus to a single city with available data, in this case Chicago, and to a single dimension of violence, in this case homicides. The maps in figures 2.3 and 2.4 show census tracts in Chicago in 1970 and 2000, respectively, and are shaded by the degree of neighborhood poverty in the census tract, with the darkest shaded tracts indicating those with at least 30 percent poverty. The maps also show the spatial distribution of homicides occurring in Chicago from 1966 through 1970 and then from 1996 through 2000.[6]

As is strikingly visible from the maps, the concentration of violence goes hand in hand with the concentration of poverty. There is a remarkable spatial clustering of homicides in and around neighborhoods with high levels of poverty, a pattern that is most striking in 1970 when the vast majority of homicides were clustered in the most disadvantaged sections of the city, the primarily black, high-poverty neighborhoods of the west and south sides. By 2000, poverty had spread as the traditional black ghetto widened to include a broader area stretching further south and further north and west. The spatial distribution of homicides widened accordingly, stretching into the same new high-poverty neighborhoods. In both periods, there are entire sections of this violent city where the most extreme form of violence, a local homicide, is an unknown occurrence. There are other neighborhoods where homicides are a common feature of life. Several neighborhoods on the south and west sides of the city experience the shock of a local homicide on a regular basis, almost once a month on average.

Not every city is as segregated by race and income as Chicago is, and not every city is as violent. Still, these maps provide perhaps the most vivid portrait of what living in areas of concentrated poverty can mean in America's cities. The neighborhoods shaded darkest in the maps, where the dots representing homicides are most densely clustered, are the types of neighborhoods in which three out of ten black children from the current and previous generations have been raised in America. These are environments that

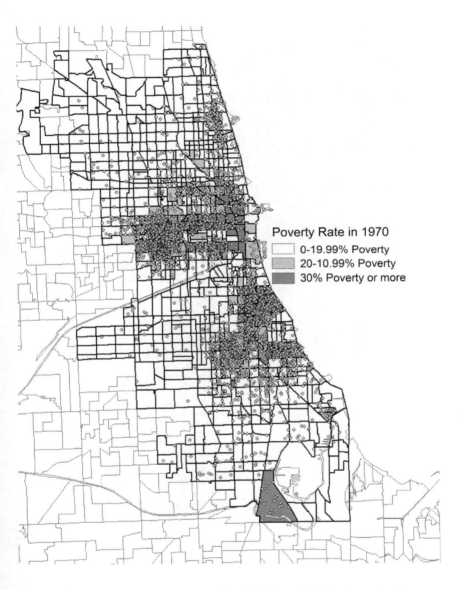

Figure 2.3. Homicides in Chicago from 1966 to 1970, by neighborhood poverty rate.

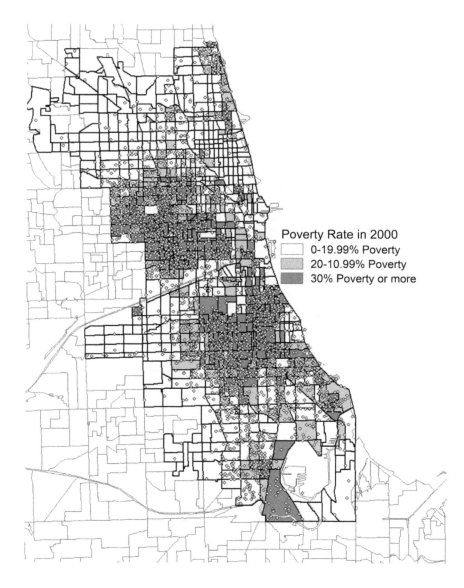

Figure 2.4. Homicides in Chicago from 1996 to 2000, by neighborhood poverty rate.

are unknown among whites, whether they were born in the late 1950s or the late 1990s.

While the figures and maps presented to this point reveal the severity of racial inequality in America's neighborhoods, this evidence does not reveal how neighborhood inequality has been experienced by families over time. Numerous scholars have examined the degree of disadvantage at a given point in time or as experienced by a given birth cohort. But these studies have not considered how advantaged and disadvantaged neighborhoods have been transmitted from parents to children, or the degree of *multigenerational* exposure to neighborhood poverty. The remainder of the chapter turns to these issues by examining intergenerational *contextual mobility*.

The Intergenerational Transmission of Neighborhood Environments
In beginning to think about the degree of contextual mobility in the post civil rights era, it is necessary to consider first a more abstract question about intergenerational transmission: why is inequality, along any dimension, transmitted across generations? Much of the recent literature on economic mobility approaches this question inductively by examining how much of the similarity in adult income between parents and their children can be explained by other aspects of their lives—their occupations, for instance, or their educational attainment. This same approach can be used to better understand contextual mobility, and later in the chapter I test whether continuity across generations of family members is explained by various aspects of family background, human capital, or economic resources that parents pass on to their children.

However, there are also unique reasons why successive generations of family members may end up in very similar neighborhood environments, reasons that are independent of families' human capital or financial resources. The most obvious reason is that people develop ties, both social and psychological, that connect them with specific places.[7] A child who is raised in a working-class neighborhood, for example, may continue to live in such a neighborhood even if he lands a job in a white-collar occupation and could afford to live in a more affluent neighborhood. The attachment to the neighborhood in which he was raised, the sense of "belonging" that he feels in a working-class area, may be more important than the desire to move to a new environment.

But while ties to places are likely to be important for all groups, there are several mechanisms that facilitate or constrain the mobility of white and nonwhite racial and ethnic groups in very different ways, leading to the reproduction of racial inequality in neighborhood environments over time. Discrimination in the housing market is one obvious example of an explicit and effective mechanism by which racial inequality was maintained through the 1960s and beyond.[8] Although discrimination in the housing and lending markets was made illegal with the passage of the Fair Housing Act of 1968, there is strong evidence that racial discrimination in rental housing and home mortgage lending remains prevalent in American cities.[9] In addition to blatant discriminatory practices, the residents of a neighborhood may use informal intimidation or violence to "defend" their neighborhood from encroachment by members of other racial or ethnic groups,[10] while other actors like real estate agents and local politicians may take informal or formal action to restrict blacks to specific sections of urban areas and to maintain boundaries between minority ghettos and white neighborhoods.[11]

It is also possible, of course, that individual preferences and mobility decisions have played a role in maintaining the rigid segregation in America's cities. Part of the reason why preferences for neighborhood composition have garnered increasing attention as an explanation for residential patterns in urban areas is the realization that despite the declines in organized discrimination following the 1960s, America's cities continue to be remarkably segregated by race and ethnicity.[12] Some have argued that different racial groups' preferences help to explain why segregation is so persistent—for instance, one very consistent finding from this literature is that African Americans are the most open of any racial or ethnic group to living in integrated neighborhoods, yet this group is ranked as the least attractive neighbors by all other racial and ethnic groups.[13] Even this claim is complicated, however, because of the possibility that individuals' stated preferences about their desired neighborhood racial composition may reflect more general desires to live among high-status neighbors or in neighborhoods with low crime rates and high property values.[14] In a nation with severe racial inequality, the racial composition of a neighborhood may serve as a proxy for these diverse neighborhood attributes that affect where white and black Americans choose to live.[15]

Researchers have made little progress in sorting out the relative importance of each factor that plays some role in maintaining rigid segregation in urban neighborhoods. But the larger point is that all of the factors I have discussed—social and psychological ties to places, discrimination, informal intimidation, and individual preferences—provide unique explanations for why neighborhood advantages and disadvantages are particularly likely to linger on over time and to be passed on from parents to children. In other words, these factors support the hypothesis that neighborhood inequality may be one of the most rigid dimensions of inequality in America, and they help to explain why mobility out of the poorest neighborhoods may be even less common than mobility out of individual poverty.

Only a few studies have examined the degree of continuity and change in families' neighborhood environments over time, however. The small number of studies that have examined patterns of continuity and change have reached a common conclusion: blacks from all income groups are much less likely than whites to exit from poor neighborhoods, and are more likely to experience downward contextual mobility (e.g., moving from a middle-income neighborhood to a poor neighborhood) than upward mobility, at least when mobility is measured over a small number of years.[16] In fact, African Americans have repeatedly been found to be much less likely to move out of high-poverty neighborhoods than whites, even after accounting for other individual differences.[17]

These studies suggest substantial differences in the degree of persistent neighborhood disadvantage experienced by blacks and whites, but the studies are limited because they typically focus on short intervals in a child's life, providing only a brief glimpse into the patterns of continuity and change across the life course. The remainder of this chapter represents the first effort to provide evidence on the overall persistence of neighborhood economic status across the full distribution of neighborhoods and from one generation of family members to the next.

An Initial Look at Contextual Mobility

To what extent are neighborhood conditions passed on from parents to children? To generate the first piece of evidence addressing this question, I begin by using standard tools from the research literature on intergenerational economic mobility to describe the strength of the relationship between the neighborhood environment in one generation and the neighborhood environment in the next generation, giving a simple description of the degree to which parents pass on their neighborhood advantage, or disadvantage, to children. To obtain these estimates I follow the most common methods developed to estimate the strength of the relationship between a parent's income and her child's income, a generation later—but instead of examining income mobility I examine neighborhood income mobility. The results tell us how well the neighborhood environment in which a child is raised predicts the type of neighborhood in which that child will end up as an adult—or the strength of the relationship between one's neighborhood origins and destinations. If there is a perfect relationship between parents' and children's neighborhood environments, meaning the parent's neighborhood predicts the child's neighborhood perfectly, this estimate would be 1.00; if there is no similarity between parents' neighborhoods and their children's neighborhoods, this estimate would be 0.00.

Among the full sample of whites and blacks, I estimate the strength of the relationship between the average income in parents' neighborhoods and in their children's neighborhoods to be .67, meaning a 10 percent change in the parent's neighborhood income is associated with a 6.7 percent change in the child's neighborhood income as an adult.[18] In relation to similar estimates in the literature on economic mobility, this figure is extremely high and tells us that the neighborhood conditions of parents and their children are remarkably similar.

To make the result less abstract, we can think about what this estimate would imply for a hypothetical family living in the United States beginning sometime in the 1970s. Imagine that this family lives in a very poor neighborhood in 1970 in "generation one," when we first begin to track the residential environments in which the family lives. In 1970, the average income in the family's neighborhood is half of the national average for all U.S. neighborhoods. If the typical neighborhood in the United States had an average income of $50,000, our family lived in a neighborhood with an average income of $25,000—in other words, the family is starting in a very poor neighborhood. Based on the estimate of intergenerational persistence, it is possible to simulate how this family's neighborhood environment would be expected to change with each passing generation. For simplicity, I will assume that the rate of intergenerational mobility remains the same in the future. Figure 2.5 shows the results from this simulation.

In the second generation the children in our hypothetical family could expect to live, as adults, in a neighborhood where the average household income among all neighbors is about a third lower than the national average. If the typical American neighborhood still had an average income of $50,000, a son or daughter of our original parents could expect to live in a neighborhood with an average income of about $33,500. In the third generation the grandchildren of our original parents could expect to live in a neighborhood that is about 22 percent less affluent than the average American neighborhood. This is the pattern that is depicted in figure 2.5—with each passing generation, the children are moving closer to the national average, but they remain in relatively poor neighborhoods. It is not until the fifth generation that the great-great grandchildren of our original parents can expect to live in a neighborhood where the average income is within 10 percent of the national average.

If each generation lasts roughly twenty-five years, this means that a full

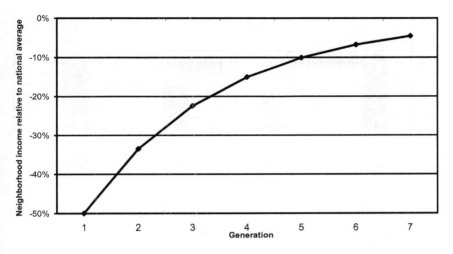

Figure 2.5. Neighborhood economic status of a hypothetical family over seven generations.

century will pass before the descendants of a family starting in a very poor neighborhood can expect to live in a neighborhood where the distribution of residents' incomes is similar to that found in the typical American neighborhood. Thus, the family that we first observed in a poor neighborhood in 1970 would continue to live in a relatively poor neighborhood, on average, until the year 2070 if the patterns that have existed over the last few decades do not change in the future. This exercise, although hypothetical, provides perhaps the clearest illustration of how persistent neighborhood advantages and disadvantages are across generations of family members. While inequalities that exist at a given point in time typically fade away as generations pass, they fade extremely slowly.

What do these findings mean for families that are not hypothetical? They mean that the inequalities that existed among families a generation ago, in the 1970s, have been passed on to today's families, with little change. They mean that the type of residential environment in which American families now live has been inherited from the previous generation.

Even this depiction of continuity across generations is incomplete, however, because it suggests that the process of contextual mobility works in the same way for all groups within a society. An alternative way of examining these dimensions of mobility is to take all of the families beginning in the poorest (or richest) segment of U.S. neighborhoods—I will look at the

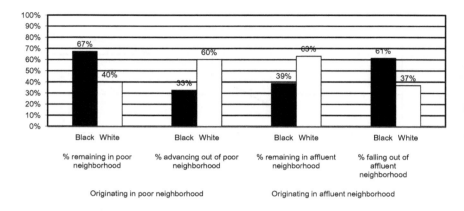

Figure 2.6. Intergenerational mobility out of the poorest and most affluent neighborhoods among blacks and whites.

poorest and richest quarter of American neighborhoods—and examine the proportion that remains or moves out of the poorest (or richest) quarter of neighborhoods over a generation. This analysis gives a very clear sense of how intergenerational mobility out of the poorest and richest neighborhoods differs for African Americans and whites.

The first two columns from figure 2.6 show the proportion of black and white families beginning in the poorest U.S. neighborhoods that remain in the poorest neighborhoods a generation later, and the second pair of columns shows the proportion that advance out of the poorest neighborhoods over a generation. Among African Americans beginning in the poorest quarter of U.S. neighborhoods, two out of three remain in the poorest quarter of neighborhoods in the next generation, and one out of three advance upward into a neighborhood with less poverty. The figures for whites present a very different story. About 40 percent of whites originating in the poorest American neighborhoods remain there in the next generation, and 60 percent move upward. So if one were to pick out ten white children living in a poor neighborhood in 1970 and track them into adulthood, we would find that just four of them are now raising their own children in neighborhoods with similarly high levels of poverty. The other six could now be found raising their own children in a neighborhood that is much less poor than the one in which they were raised, a neighborhood that is closer to the typical American neighborhood.

Just as African Americans are less likely to advance out of the poorest U.S.

neighborhoods, they are more likely to fall downward over a generation. The third pair of columns in figure 2.6 shows the proportion of black and white families originating in the most affluent quarter of U.S. neighborhoods who remain in the most affluent neighborhoods a generation later, and the last pair of columns shows the proportion that move downward into a less affluent neighborhood. Among the small number of black families who lived in the richest quarter of U.S. neighborhoods a generation ago, only 39 percent remain there in the next generation. If one were to again select ten black children in 1970, this time from the richest U.S. neighborhoods, four of them would still be found in an affluent neighborhood a generation later, while the remaining six would now be raising their children in neighborhoods that are less affluent than those in which they were raised. If one also selected ten white children in 1970, at least six of them would still be found in the nation's most affluent neighborhoods a generation later.

In essence, when white families live in a poor neighborhood, they typically do so for only a single generation; when they live in a rich neighborhood, they usually stay there for multiple generations. The opposite is true for African American families: Neighborhood affluence is fleeting, and neighborhood poverty is most commonly *multigenerational*.

This pattern becomes more apparent from figure 2.7, which shows the proportion of all African American families and white families that have

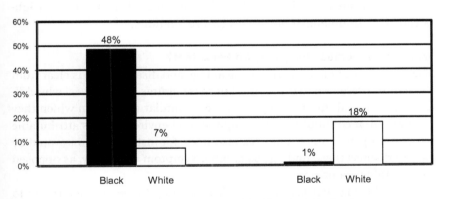

Figure 2.7. Multigenerational exposure to neighborhood poverty and affluence among blacks and whites.

lived in the poorest and the most affluent US neighborhoods over consecutive generations. Over the past two generations, 48 percent of all African American families have lived in the poorest quarter of neighborhoods *in each generation*. The most common experience for black families since the 1970s, by a wide margin, has been to live in the poorest American neighborhoods over consecutive generations. Only 7 percent of white families have experienced similar poverty in their neighborhood environments for consecutive generations. By contrast, persistent neighborhood advantage is virtually nonexistent for black families. One out of every one hundred black families in the United States has lived in affluent neighborhoods over the past two generations, compared to roughly one out of five white families.

These same patterns emerge no matter how one wishes to examine the data, and the racial disparities in multigenerational neighborhood disadvantage become increasingly severe when one examines the extremes of the distribution of neighborhoods. For example, one quarter of all African American families have lived in the poorest 10 percent of all U.S. neighborhoods in consecutive generations, compared to just 1 percent of whites. Thus, the true depth of racial inequality in neighborhood environments becomes even more pronounced when we consider the neighborhoods where poverty is most concentrated. It is not uncommon for successive generations of black family members to live in America's poorest neighborhoods, while persistent exposure to the poorest neighborhoods is virtually nonexistent among whites. This is the reality of racial inequality in America's neighborhood environments over the past two generations.

Why Is Neighborhood Inequality So Persistent?

The persistence of neighborhood advantage and disadvantage is clear from the figures presented to this point, but these figures do not reveal why children tend to end up in settings that are so similar to those in which they were raised. If continuity in the neighborhood environment is attributable to continuity in families' financial resources, for instance, then it would be easy to dismiss these findings as another symptom of poverty, as opposed to something about *places*.

The following analysis assesses this possibility. To begin, we'll return to the estimate of the overall strength of the intergenerational association in neighborhood income, which is .67, as noted above and as shown again in the first column of figure 2.8. As a reminder, if all parents and their children lived in identical neighborhoods, then we would get an estimate of 1.00, and if there was no relationship between parents' neighborhoods and their children's neighborhoods whatsoever we would get an estimate of 0.00. The

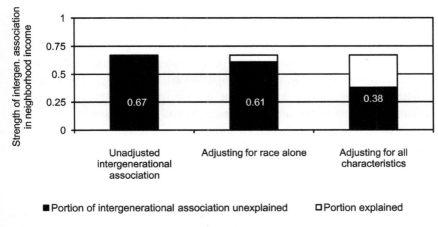

Figure 2.8. Decomposition of the intergenerational association in neighborhood income.

.67 estimate tells us that parents and their children live in extremely similar neighborhood environments, but this is before we consider any other characteristics of parents and their children that might explain this similarity.

The second column of figure 2.8 "adjusts" this estimate to consider the family's race alone. The results from this model allow for an assessment of the possibility that parents and children may live in similar neighborhoods simply because they are of the same race and because race is an important determinant of the type of environment in which an individual lives. There is some truth to this argument, as race explains a small part of the association between parents' and children's neighborhood environments—in the second column the strength of the intergenerational association is down to .61, instead of the original estimate of .67.

But the real test is in the third model, which expands beyond race to adjust for a range of characteristics of the child and his family. The last column of figure 2.8 shows the strength of the relationship between neighborhood economic status across two generations after statistically adjusting for parents' and children's income, their educational attainment, the "status" of their jobs, whether they own their homes, receive welfare, or reside in public housing, and their marital status. The full results, which are shown in an online appendix to the book ("*Stuck in Place*: Methods Appendix"),[19] indicate that children with parents who have high-status jobs and high income end up in more affluent neighborhoods as adults, while children who obtain more education, have high income, and have high status occupations find themselves in higher-income neighborhoods as adults. Children who own their own home, have more kids, or live in public housing end up in less affluent neighborhoods, conditional on all of the other characteristics in the model. A few of these relationships are somewhat counterintuitive, but the fact that income, education, and occupation are the strongest predictors of neighborhood economic status is not at all surprising. What is surprising is that all of these characteristics of parents and children explain less than half of the association between parents' and children's neighborhoods. In other words, most of the similarity between parents' neighborhoods and their children's neighborhoods is not attributable to the resources or human capital that parents and children bring with them to the housing market.

This leaves us with a challenging question: if it is not individual resources or education that explains the continuity of neighborhood advantages and disadvantages across generations, then why do parents and children end up in such similar environments? One potential answer lies in the *places* that parents and children occupy. That is, it could be that in addition to passing on resources or a mindset focused on the future, parents may pass on a place to their children, a hometown in which children are raised, a neighborhood in which children feel comfortable, a city that children remain in as they approach adulthood. It is possible to test this idea by examining the strength of the similarity in children's origin and destination neighborhoods for children who remain in the same place in which they were raised and for children who move on to a different place upon reaching adulthood. Because not all children in the sample live in a metropolitan area, I use residence in the same county as a child and as an adult to define the group of children who remain in place from childhood to adulthood.

The first two columns of figure 2.9 show the intergenerational association in neighborhood income for the two groups of children, those who stay close to home when they reach adulthood and those who leave their origin county. There is a substantial difference between the two groups. If children grow up and remain in the same county in which they were raised, the strength of the association between their adult neighborhood and that of their parents is .79, which indicates remarkable similarity in the neighborhood environments of parents and children. If they move on to a different county, it is only .49—still a strong relationship but not nearly as strong as that for children who remain in the same county. Connections to specific places appear to be an important part of the reason why parents and their children live in such similar neighborhoods.[20]

The remaining columns in the figure explore this finding in a bit more depth. One possible explanation for these findings is that children may grow

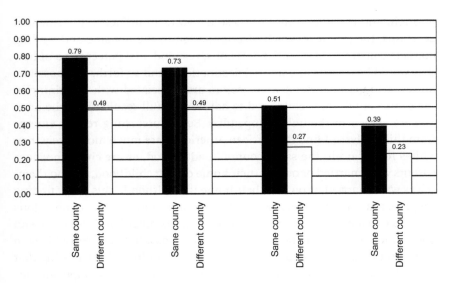

Figure 2.9. Intergenerational association of neighborhood income for children who remain in same county and for children who move to different county in adulthood.

up and live in the same actual neighborhood in which they were raised. This does not seem to explain the initial findings—the third and fourth column of the figure show the same results, after removing from the sample all children who end up in the same actual neighborhoods as adults. Even after this group is removed, the strength of the relationship between parent's and children's neighborhoods is extremely strong if the child remains in the same county. The subsequent columns in figure 2.9 go one step further and show the same results after adjusting for all of the characteristics of parents and children, as described above. While these characteristics do explain part of the similarities in neighborhood environments, much of the association remains unexplained. More important, the difference between children who remain in the same county as adults and those who move on is still pronounced.

I should note that this analysis does not help us sort out the mechanisms leading respondents to remain in the same places over time or to depart their hometown for a new destination. To do so would require extensive information on respondents' decision-making processes as they decide upon a geographic destination and a neighborhood within that destination, including the strength of their social networks in their neighborhood or city of origin and the importance of these networks in influencing residential decisions, the extent to which discrimination in the housing and lending markets constrains residential decisions, respondents' perceptions of how they would be treated in potential destinations, and so forth. It is possible, however, to get a sense of what factors are associated with remaining in the same county from childhood to adulthood (full results from the analysis are shown in the online appendix). Some interesting results emerge from this analysis: I find that African Americans are much more likely than whites to remain in the same county in adulthood, as are children whose parents were married or owned their home during childhood, or who themselves were married or owned their home in adulthood. This latter finding suggests that home ownership and being married may create connections to a place that endure across generations. On the other hand, children who obtain more education and earn more income as adults are more likely to move on to a different county when they reach adulthood, suggesting that education may broaden the horizons of youth or provide new opportunities in different places.

The subtler factors that lead children to stay in place are more difficult to capture in data from a survey. The larger point, however, is that connections to places—whether the result of constraints on mobility, the strength of social and familial ties, or some combination—play an extremely important role in leading to continuity in the social environments surrounding families and thereby reproducing neighborhood inequality.

This finding raises several intriguing questions about how places have affected trends in racial inequality over the last several decades. Considering how common it is for children to grow up and remain in the same community, a natural question to examine is how individuals' economic prospects are linked to the fortunes of their neighborhoods or hometowns. For example, what do strong connections to places mean for black families who migrated to rust-belt cities that have experienced substantial declines in manufacturing employment over the last several decades? To answer this type of question requires moving beyond the family-level data available through a sample survey and examining the forces that affect urban communities as a whole, which is what I attempt in the following chapter.

The Inherited Ghetto

The overriding conclusion from this chapter is that neighborhood environments, along with all of the advantages and disadvantages that go with them, tend to be passed on from parents to children—and this pattern has not changed much in the post civil rights era. Inequalities in families' neighborhood environments that exist at one point in time do fade slightly as one generation passes to the next, but they fade away extremely slowly. The primary consequence of this pattern is that the stark racial inequality that existed in the 1970s has been transmitted, in large part unchanged, to the current generation. Two out of three black children who were raised in the poorest quarter of neighborhoods continue to live in the poorest quarter of neighborhoods as adults, and about half of black families have lived in the poorest quarter of neighborhoods over consecutive generations. These findings indicate that the concentration of African Americans in today's poorest urban neighborhoods represents a continuation of disadvantage that has persisted since the 1970s.

This conclusion becomes most apparent when we consider the intersection of race and class in urban neighborhoods, a connection that is encompassed in the concept of the urban ghetto. In the introductory chapter I provided a highly theoretical definition of the term "ghetto" as the spatial expression of a variety of social processes leading to the concentration of disadvantaged groups in residential areas; to conclude this chapter I will operationalize this concept in a more transparent, concrete manner, by identifying ghetto neighborhoods as those that are majority black and among the poorest quarter of all American neighborhoods. Defined in this way, I find that about 72 percent of black adults living in today's urban ghettos were raised by parents who also lived in the ghetto a generation earlier. In other words, almost three out of four black families living in today's most segregated, poorest neighborhoods are the same families that lived in the ghettos of the 1970s.

This finding provides the clearest reflection of what I mean when I refer to the inherited American ghetto. More than any other finding I will present, this statistic reveals something about racial inequality that is hidden even in the most rigorous academic studies and the best journalistic accounts of life in the most disadvantaged neighborhoods. Inequality in America's neighborhood environments is a phenomenon that is not experienced at a single point in time; it is a phenomenon that is experienced continuously, that lingers on within families as time passes. The problem of the urban ghetto is not simply that it has persisted over time, but that the same families have experienced the disadvantages associated with life in the ghetto over multiple generations. The violence that children in the most dangerous urban neighborhoods see around them is familiar to their parents, even if the intensity or character of the violence may change. The schools these children attend are similar to the schools their parents attended a generation earlier, even if funding is invested in some periods and then withdrawn in others.

As I will demonstrate later in the book, it is the *cumulative* effect of living in concentrated disadvantage, over generations, that is particularly severe. When families live in disadvantaged neighborhoods over multiple generations, children show substantially worse developmental outcomes when compared to families that live in poor neighborhoods in a single generation, and this remains true even after we account for everything else about a family that might affect children's development.

This reality complicates how policy makers approach the problem of the urban ghetto. We cannot think about the social problems in areas of concentrated poverty, or the disadvantages faced by residents in such areas, as distinct from their historical context. To confront concentrated poverty and to provide opportunities for residents of the poorest urban ghettos, we must confront disadvantages that have been handed down over generations.

Chapter 3 | **A Forty-Year Detour on the Path toward Racial Equality**

Considering the momentous social changes that have occurred since the peak of the civil rights movement, how is it that the generation of children who should have benefited most from that movement has made so little advancement in residential America? The results from chapter 2 provide the first part of an answer. African Americans' lack of progress in residential America is *not* primarily a product of accumulated deficits in individual human capital that might be thought to explain why, as a group, they remain concentrated in the nation's poorest neighborhoods. This is not to say that racial inequality in schools or in the labor market is trivial or has faded away over the past four decades, but rather that African Americans' educational attainment, economic circumstances, and occupational positions cannot explain why they continue to live in such disadvantaged neighborhoods.

Instead, the results suggest that the transmission of neighborhood advantages and disadvantages is driven primarily by the transmission of *places* from parents to children. A large part of the reason that African Americans continue to live in the nation's most disadvantaged environments is that they have remained within communities and cities that have borne the brunt of four decades of economic restructuring and political disinvestment. Connections and attachments to specific places, arising due to a combination of white discrimination, hostility and violence, housing and credit constraints, and social and familial ties, emerged in chapter 2 as a powerful explanation for the persistence of neighborhood inequality among the children of the civil rights era. To understand why these connections to places have limited mobility, however, we must move beyond the individual-level data and focus on broader trends and social policies that have served to maintain the unequal residential structure that is present in urban America.

In the introductory chapter I defined the concept of the urban ghetto as the spatial expression of social processes, including processes of social and economic exclusion, discrimination, and disinvestment. This chapter puts flesh to these abstract ideas, describing how the processes have played out over the past several decades, what forces are behind them, and what their consequences have been. To do so I draw on the research produced by urban scholars analyzing the forces at work in urban communities, research that describes in detail a set of changes that have affected the prospects of African Americans and African American communities since the civil rights period.

An inherent limitation of a national analysis such as this one is the tendency to ignore the importance of local politics, local policies, and local histories that have shaped the trajectories of individual neighborhoods, cities, and metropolitan areas. To complement the national analysis, I have included a series of historical case studies, interspersed throughout the chapter, that focus on the specific forces at work within individual cities, the local political structures, and the key policies that have shaped the trajectories of neighborhoods within each city.[1] The cities that I selected are all places where a substantial number of African American and white families from the PSID sample originated, allowing for a closer look at what has happened to the specific communities of the families that form the sample of the PSID.

While acknowledging the unique trajectories of individual cities and the neighborhoods within them, there is nonetheless a consistent and overarching conclusion that emerges from the analysis in the chapter: African Americans have not made substantial progress in residential America since the 1970s largely because of a multifaceted set of economic shifts, demographic trends, and social policies that have served to maintain residential segregation in urban neighborhoods, by income and by race, and to limit black upward mobility in the post civil rights period. This process has consisted of several overlapping elements, but I identify four components that are crucial to understanding why inequality in urban neighborhoods has been so persistent: (1) the failure to complete the progression toward full civil rights; (2) the implementation of a diverse set of policies, informal strategies, and institutional mechanisms used to maintain racial inequality in urban areas; (3) the restructuring of urban labor markets; and (4) the destructive response to economic dislocation in America's cities.

In highlighting the importance of these four factors, it is important to make clear that the residential trajectories of African Americans and other groups are not *determined* by policies or actions taken by external groups or by forces that lie outside the individual families making decisions about where to live. Individuals' and families' connections to places arise from an array of factors, from social and familial networks to psychological attachments to a place.[2] Without denying the importance of these factors and the role of individual agency, it is also crucial to analyze how these choices have been constrained in different ways for blacks and whites, and how these choices have come to have different implications due, in large part, to local, state, and federal urban policy. As a consequence of the range of policies and economic shifts that I will describe, African Americans have remained tied to places where poverty has become increasingly concentrated, where opportunities for economic advancement have declined, and where the risk of going to prison has become more prevalent than the hope of going to college. This chapter documents how these processes have played out across the country. The chapters that follow analyze the consequences of these processes for the persistence of racial inequality.

UNEQUAL PROSPERITY: THE CASE OF ATLANTA

I begin the tour of five case studies by considering the City of Atlanta. In one sense, Atlanta can be seen as a story of a region's successful adaptation to the post-industrial urban economy. As a whole, the Atlanta metropolitan area has fared well since the 1960s, with substantial population growth, growth of jobs in the service sector, rising average income, and rising employment. But lying beneath the impressive figures on overall economic growth is a story of severe inequality within the region.

This story begins to emerge when one considers the fortunes of the city in contrast to the fortunes of the metro area surrounding it. From the early 1970s to the middle of the 1990s, the Atlanta metro area population approximately doubled—but the population within the city limits declined. Over a similar time frame, average income in the metro area rose substantially—but again, average income declined within the city. This pattern reflects the divergent fortunes of the city itself and the suburbs surrounding it—but the pattern also reflects a severe form of racial inequality that maps onto the central-city/suburban distinction.[3]

The Atlanta metropolitan area has seen an explosion of growth in the population of African Americans over the past several decades. But back in 1970, fully 82 percent of the Atlanta metro area's black population lived within the city limits. This concentration of the region's black population within the city is reflected in the location of PSID sample members—among first-generation sample members living in the Atlanta region, virtually every black family originated within the city limits. The neighborhoods that were passed on from African American parents, a generation ago, to their children were neighborhoods that were located within the city of Atlanta. What has happened to those neighborhoods over time, and why have they seen such divergent fortunes relative to neighborhoods in the city's suburbs?

An extensive literature on Atlanta's recent political and economic history suggests that the trajectories of change in the neighborhoods of Atlanta and the surrounding suburbs can be characterized by an overarching political climate emphasizing unfettered economic growth, a focus on policies promoting competition and fragmentation within the metropolitan area, and the maintenance of rigid segregation in communities in and around the city despite rapid growth of the black middle and upper classes. These changes have been driven in large part by a powerful class of business elites with an interest in promoting economic growth while avoiding severe racial conflict within the city. Atlanta was the first large southern city to elect an African American mayor, as Maynard Jackson was elected in the same year (1973) that black mayors were elected in Detroit and Los Angeles for the first time. But in all of these cities, the election of an African American mayor did not lead to a substantial redirection of resources toward the cities' poor black community, as black mayors commonly were elected after forming coalitions with the city's business elite. In Atlanta, policies implemented under Maynard Jackson, and later under Andrew Young, resulted in an expansion of the black middle class through public sector employment, the promotion of downtown development, and the maintenance of an economic and political environment focused on economic growth.[4] The city's poor black communities remained severely neglected, which led to extreme inequality across Atlanta's neighborhoods and the wider metropolitan area.

All of the social policies and economic forces that have affected the city's neighborhoods have been implemented in a context of racial tension and hostility. As in many other cities, the racial segregation of Atlanta's neighborhoods was maintained through formal, intentional policy through the 1960s. The engineering of neighborhood change during urban renewal led to large-scale displacement of African Americans and a racialized reorganization of the city. Blacks were systematically moved from areas that bordered the downtown or predominantly white sections of the city, which reinforced the rigid color lines of the city.[5] With the expansion of civil rights and the forced desegregation of the public school system, whites began to leave Atlanta in large numbers in the 1970s—by 1990, the white population within Atlanta's city limits was about half the size of what it was in 1970. Efforts to link all parts of the city to the suburbs have met with fierce opposition from predominantly white suburban communities, making it difficult for African Americans to enter or commute into northern suburbs with strong job growth.[6]

Surveys of Atlanta residents suggest that racial tension continues to play a role in the rigid segregation of neighborhoods within the city as well as the segregation of communities throughout the larger metropolitan area. For instance, as of 2001 almost 90 percent of African Americans in the Atlanta metropolitan area indicated that discriminatory practices were believed to be commonly used by whites in the housing market. Most respondents, white or black, believed that whites in the northern, largely white suburbs of Atlanta would be upset if a black family moved into the neighborhood.[7]

Despite the persistent segregation of the Atlanta metropolitan area, patterns of migration into and out of the city have changed over time in ways very different from those of many cities across the country. First, Atlanta's suburbanization was not limited to whites. A large segment of the black middle class migrated beyond the city limits and into the south suburbs of Atlanta, and the metropolitan area as a whole has seen an explosion of growth in the African American population.[8] The area surrounding Atlanta contains some of the few predominantly black, middle-class suburbs in the country—but these suburbs are almost as racially segregated as neighborhoods within the city limits. Second, Atlanta is unique in that it has experienced a recent return migration of whites into the city, along with a new population of Hispanic and Asian Americans. Since 1990, the population of whites in Atlanta has grown by about thirty thousand. In combination with the growth of the Hispanic and Asian populations within the city, Atlanta has shifted from a predominantly black city to a racially and ethnically diverse city, albeit one where African Americans are still the largest racial group.[9]

Even so, Atlanta remains an extremely segregated city. African Americans represent just over half of the city's population, yet the

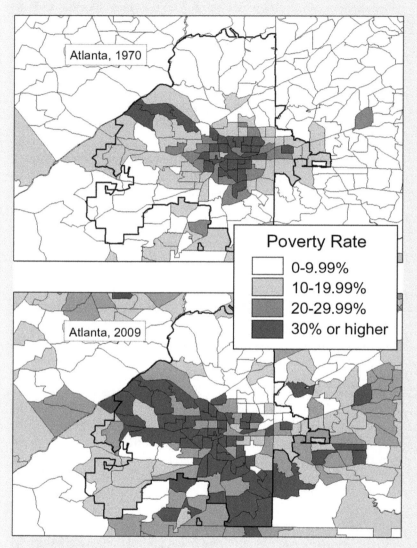

Figure 3.1. Neighborhood poverty in census tracts surrounding Atlanta in 1970 (top) and 2005–9 (bottom). Sources: Data from 1970 are based on the 1970 Census; data from 2005–9 are from the American Community Survey.

average black resident of Atlanta lives in a neighborhood that is 80 percent black. Atlanta once promoted itself as the "city too busy to hate," reflecting the long-standing focus on economic growth in the city.[10] Yet racial tension and hostility permeate much of the most salient public policy that has been implemented over the years and help to explain why the city's neighborhoods remain so segregated.

The Lingering Significance of Race

The tail end of the civil rights era again serves as a convenient point of departure for the analysis of the forces that have acted to limit mobility out of the ghetto. Specifically, I begin by returning to the passage of the Fair Housing Act in April 1968. After previous efforts met with failure, the 1968 Fair Housing Act made discrimination in housing illegal and banned practices such as redlining and racial steering. The legislation fell short of the broader goals of its proponents, however. For instance, the Kerner Commission, which was assembled by President Johnson to investigate the causes of the urban riots that ripped through America's cities over the previous summer, recommended both fair housing legislation and an active policy to promote the construction of affordable housing outside of the ghetto.[11] Only the former recommendation was implemented, and even this has never come close to ending or even substantially limiting the prevalence of discrimination. Part of the reason is that compromises made to secure passage of the legislation made it extremely difficult to prosecute claims of discrimination.[12] But even in the subsequent decades, as the procedures for prosecution were revised and fair housing groups proliferated, the overall impact of the antidiscrimination legislation remains questionable.[13]

One could argue that the Fair Housing Act was responsible for the elimination of the most blatant forms of institutional discrimination, but the best experimental evidence available demonstrates clearly that discrimination remains prevalent in America's residential markets and that it affects every aspect of individuals' search for housing. The evidence comes from a series of experimental "audits" of the real estate industry that have been conducted under the auspices of the federal Department of Housing and Urban Development (HUD) in 1977, 1989, and again in 2000.[14] The experimental procedures are straightforward. Pairs of individuals are matched, one of whom is white and the other a racial/ethnic minority, and are given matching fictitious information about their finances and assets, their employment history, and other personal circumstances that may come up in an interview with a real estate agent or a loan officer. After being provided this information and trained on how to approach the meeting, what questions to ask, and so forth, the paired home or apartment seekers are sent off to inquire about the same advertised units. It is the most basic, yet most effective, way to discern just how much racial discrimination still exists in the housing market.

For an assessment of the prevalence of racism we can turn to the 2000 Housing Discrimination Study, which was conducted in twenty metropolitan areas nationwide.[15] If there were any doubts about whether racism remains a major presence in the lives of racial and ethnic minorities, the results from this study should dispel them. The audit study showed that in 17 to 25 percent of cases African Americans and Latinos are "consistently" treated unfavorably when compared with their white counterparts. What, exactly, does it mean to be consistently treated unfavorably? According to the evaluators of the report: "Whites were more likely to find out about available houses and apartments, more likely to be given the opportunity to inspect these units, more likely to be offered favorable financial terms, more likely to be steered toward homes for sale in predominantly white neighborhoods, and more likely to receive assistance and encouragement in their housing search." In virtually every aspect of the search for a home, whites are treated more favorably than nonwhites.

These findings do not only confirm the continued existence of discrimination; they reveal a new, more "subtle" form of discrimination in America's residential markets. While blatant acts of discrimination and intimidation undoubtedly still occur, the dominant form of discrimination in residential markets is one where home seekers are steered toward or away from apartments, houses, and neighborhoods in ways that reproduce racial segregation and constrain the housing options of racial and ethnic minorities.[16] It is possible, in theory, for every eligible citizen to obtain financing and buy a home, or rent an apartment, in any neighborhood within any community—there are no formal rules barring minorities from living wherever they wish. But in practice, housing options remain constrained for racial and ethnic minorities and for all low-income populations because of the subtle practices that continue to pervade the real estate industry.

One must keep in mind that these studies focus on only one aspect of the residential market—real estate agents. Equivalent evidence from audit studies of the mortgage lending process shows similar results, with African American and Hispanic loan applicants receiving less information, less time with officers, and fewer loan offers than whites with the exact same qualifications.[17] Further, these studies do not consider the role that subtle or even blatant hostility from potential landlords and neighbors may play in influencing families' residential choices. It is unclear exactly how much of an impact these types of continuing discrimination have on current residential patterns, but it is clear that this is a problem that has not been resolved.

A GLOBAL CITY IN MORE THAN ONE SENSE: THE CASE OF DALLAS

Perhaps more than in most other cities, the fortunes of Dallas's neighborhoods have risen and fallen in tandem with the fortunes of the local economy. Poverty across the city rose in the wake of the drop in oil prices and the collapse of the banking industry in the mid-1980s, leading to the proliferation of high-poverty neighborhoods within the city. In the 1990s, this pattern reversed as the Dallas metropolitan area experienced strong economic growth in the service sector, in finance, and in technology. Concentrated poverty declined sharply over the decade—however, new figures from the latter half of the 2000s indicate that the decline was temporary. The primary change occurring from 1980 to 2009 is that concentrated poverty has spread over a wider area of Dallas and its surrounding suburbs. There are many "newly" poor neighborhoods in and around Dallas, most in the south of the city but some in sections of the north as well.

Local economic conditions affect the trajectories of urban neighborhoods in every city, but the vulnerability of communities in Dallas is particularly pronounced. For much of the past half century, local planning and local politics have been dominated by the city's business elite.[18] Whereas the Ku Klux Klan had been active in Dallas politics prior to the 1930s, a new class of businessmen came together to control local politics in subsequent decades, guided by the goal of making the city conducive to commerce and economic growth.[19] The dominance of the business class in Dallas politics has had several important implications for the trajectories of the city's neighborhoods. First, it helps explain why Dallas was not a center of activity and unrest during the civil rights era. The Dallas elite feared resisting integration because they were concerned about the instability associated with racial violence and the possibility of losing investment from the north.[20] They appeased African American leaders within the city with symbolic gestures and small-scale concessions, and they were never threatened at the polls because blacks made up only about 30 percent of Dallas's population. Second, the dominance of the business elite helps to explain the trajectory of public policy and local planning in Dallas and beyond, which was geared toward economic growth and largely ignored the needs of working-poor and minority communities within the city. For instance, in the 1950s a large segment of the city's black community was relocated into the south part of the city when their neighborhood was cleared and the Central Expressway was built.[21] This type of infrastructure project, which was implemented as part of a concerted effort to make Dallas a hub of regional commerce, is one example of a way that local policy was used to promote the dual goals of generating economic growth while constricting the city's black population to a small area within the city.

The focus on making Dallas attractive to business has persisted over time, through periods of strong growth and through periods of economic crisis. This approach to urban planning and policy has contributed to making Dallas a "global city," hosting the headquarters of several Fortune 500 companies and serving as a center for regional and international finance and technology.[22] As with many other global cities, efforts to lure corporations and businesspeople from around the world come at the expense of services and amenities targeting the needs of a city's own residents and communities.[23] This has certainly been the case with Dallas's black community. While neighborhoods across the city have seen poverty rise and fall over time, the most severe concentration of poverty has been located in the same set of neighborhoods on the south side of the city for the past forty years. These are the same neighborhoods where the city's African American population is concentrated, and these are the neighborhoods where virtually all of the African American families in the PSID sample originated. They are neighborhoods that have lost jobs over time, that have experienced consistently high rates of violence, and that have remained highly segregated.

Some of the second-generation African American PSID sample members remained in the southeast section of the city into adulthood, and it is not hard to understand why their adult neighborhood environments look so similar to their childhood environments. But others have moved on to different neighborhoods within the larger Dallas metropolitan area, which has become remarkably diverse over time.

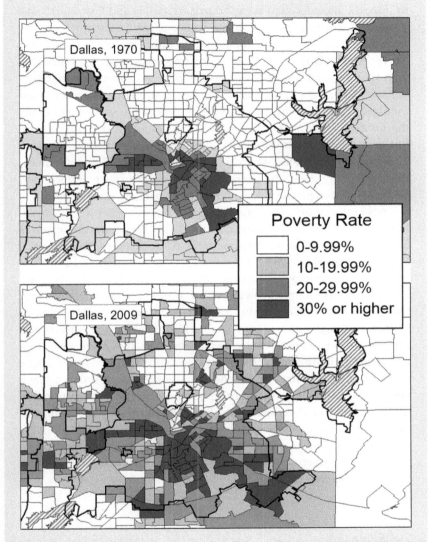

Figure 3.2. Neighborhood poverty in census tracts surrounding Dallas in 1970 (top) and 2005–9 (bottom). Sources: Data from 1970 are based on the 1970 Census; data from 2005–9 are from the American Community Survey.

In 1980, the metropolitan area comprising Dallas and Fort Worth was 76 percent white, 15 percent black, and 8 percent Hispanic.[24] Thirty years later, only half of the population is white, the black population has remained stable, and the immigrant population has exploded: the metropolitan area is now 28 percent Hispanic, with a new population of Asian Americans (6 percent). This new ethnic diversity has eroded the rigid segregation of the area's black population—whereas in 1980 the average African American lived in a neighborhood where two-thirds of the residents were black, now the average African American lives in a neighborhood where just 35 percent of residents are black. Within the city itself, the average African American's neighborhood changed from 75 percent black in 1980 to 50 percent black in 2010.

Looking back over the past two generations, the white and black families that originated in and around Dallas have found themselves in an urban area that has become "global" in two very distinct ways. First, they find themselves in a city that is an international center of finance and technology. While this location in the global economy has led to recent economic growth in and around Dallas, it comes with the danger that local communities will become increasingly neglected as local and regional leaders focus their attention on the needs and interests of the international elite. Second, they find themselves in a diversifying city in which Hispanics now represent the largest single racial or ethnic group. While the neighborhoods of Dallas's black ghetto have remained consistently poor and segregated over time, the traditional black/white dichotomy has been blurred by the explosion of growth in the city's Hispanic population. Whether this "globalizing" city leads to newly integrated communities or growing stratification within the metropolitan area is a question that will be resolved in the coming decades.

The Role of Informal and Formal Policies
in Maintaining Racial and Economic Segregation

The persistence of discrimination reflects a broader conclusion about racial inequality after the 1960s. While African Americans did make substantial gains in basic freedoms during the 1960s, the basis for continuing racial inequality was not eliminated but simply shifted. Prior to the civil rights era, racial inequality had been tacitly or explicitly supported by law. In the post civil rights period racial inequality has been maintained by a combination of informal actions of individuals, organized collective action, and political efforts and public policies designed to maintain and reinforce racial and class inequality in urban neighborhoods.

Among the key elements of this effort is the massive subsidization of white outmigration from central cities, combined with a concerted effort to consolidate black urban populations within centralized public housing.[25] In both cases, the federal government has played a central role. Beginning with the establishment of the Home Owners Loan Corporation (HOLC) in the 1930s, the federal government has taken a direct role in subsidizing home ownership by guaranteeing or providing mortgages to home owners. The HOLC was created as a means to provide low-interest refinancing to families in danger of losing their homes during the Depression, while also funding loans to allow some families to reacquire homes lost to foreclosure.[26] Instead of using its role in the home mortgage industry to promote home ownership for all groups, the federal government adopted a set of standards set by the real estate industry to rank the riskiness of potential loans. Homes in racially homogeneous neighborhoods were ranked highest, and homes in primarily black or racially mixed neighborhoods, or even neighborhoods *near* black neighborhoods, were ranked lowest and were largely excluded from the program. The practice of "redlining" emerged from the ranking system the HOLC used to determine the areas eligible for loans—predominantly black communities were outlined in red in the HOLC maps to signify that they had received the lowest rankings and were thus ineligible for loans. These maps, and the practice of ranking communities based on their racial composition, spread throughout the banking industry.

The precedent set by HOLC was then extended to subsequent home mortgage programs that were much larger in scale, run through the Federal Housing Administration (FHA) and, later, the Veterans Administration (VA). Together, the FHA and VA made possible the rapid expansion of home ownership in the postwar years by providing government backing for loans made by private lenders and thus allowing lenders to offer low-interest loans with the knowledge that these loans were guaranteed by the federal government. When demand for housing exploded after World War II, these programs made home ownership possible on a broad basis for the first time in U.S. history—for instance, in the 1950s a third of all private housing was financed with FHA or VA loans.[27]

While broadening access to home ownership, the programs also played a major role in facilitating the racial inequality that has come to characterize urban and suburban communities in the postwar era. Because the FHA was initially designed to stimulate the construction industry, the program favored the construction of new homes, primarily in the suburbs, as opposed to the rehabilitation of homes within cities. The program thus represented a tacit shift in national housing policy, one that moved the nation away from the development of affordable rental housing and toward the development of newly constructed single family homes. One can argue that Americans have always yearned for the open space of the suburbs as opposed to the dense cities, but it is crucial to note that it was federal intervention into the housing market that made outmigration to the suburbs possible for large segments of the population. Federal backing of home mortgages, combined with generous subsidies for home ownership (such as the home interest mortgage deduction), provided incentives for white families to move to the suburbs and become home owners no matter their residential preferences. The federal investment in suburbanization was a *restricted* investment, in the sense that it was not available to minority groups like African Americans.[28] The official FHA guidelines discouraged loans to racial minorities and prohibited loans that would lead to racially or economically integrated neighborhoods. In an effort to maintain "neighborhood stability," loans were to be made to families that would maintain homogeneous communities. The FHA manuals actually encouraged the use of restrictive covenants as a means of ensuring the stability of the neighborhood.[29] As a consequence, the home ownership boom never reached nonwhite populations in America's cities.

Public initiatives designed to reinforce segregation were not limited to mortgage lending. In the early part of the twentieth century, "racial zoning" plans that excluded individuals from designated residential areas based purely on race were overturned and deemed unconstitutional. The same cannot be said, however, for efforts to exclude individuals based on their income or assets. Indeed, interventions into the housing market that result in *economic segregation*, most notably the use of exclusionary zoning, have been upheld repeatedly in the courts.[30] Local zoning ordinances, which throughout the past century have been encouraged by the federal government and the states, have provided municipalities with the opportunity to indirectly exclude unwanted neighbors by limiting the types of housing that can be built in a given area—for instance, by setting minimum lot sizes for new housing or prohibiting the construction of apartment housing in areas of single family homes—and thus limiting the types of families that can afford to live in the community.[31] The discretion given to localities to place restrictions on the use of land is unique to the United States, and it has given local governments enormous power to engineer economically exclusive communities.[32] The consequences are not limited to the separation of the rich and the poor, but also create unnatural inefficiencies in the housing market. Zoning and other forms of local land use regulation are one of the primary contributors to the steep decline in affordable housing available for low-income Americans, a group that has seen its housing cost burden rise sharply since 1960.[33]

Exclusionary zoning can be thought of as the living descendant of the previous generations' most widely used methods of maintaining residential inequality in cities where black populations swelled and threatened to encroach upon white neighborhoods. In the past, formal agreements that prohibited home owners from selling to African Americans and other groups, or "restrictive covenants," were used to enforce racial segregation in urban neighborhoods (and were condoned by local governments). "Neighborhood improvement associations" were established to develop such covenants, while also administering informal intimidation and violence in an attempt to keep blacks from entering white neighborhoods.[34] Discriminatory lending practices, which used the racial composition of a neighborhood as a means of distributing federally financed loans, were used to maintain this racial inequality. While it is a less explicit form of discrimination, handing over control of land use to localities is an effective substitute that offers a way of ensuring that segregationist tendencies or preferences are not obstructed.[35]

During the same period in which the federal government was investing heavily in white, suburban neighborhoods, it was also acting to consolidate and centralize black populations within cities. From World War II into the 1950s and 1960s, the flow of African Americans into northeastern and midwestern cities continued, resulting in urban blacks living in overcrowded, slum conditions within the rigid boundaries of the ghetto. The growing demand for housing among urban African Americans, combined with whites' desires to "protect" communities that were threatened by the prospect of racial integration, led to the passage of what is known as "urban renewal" as part of the Housing Acts of 1949 and 1954. The two housing acts provided funds to be used by the federal government to acquire, clear, and redevelop entire segments of the city composed of slum housing. While some of the "blighted" areas that were razed were rebuilt into residential areas, the more common usage was for nonresidential development. Redevelopment was carried out largely by private contractors, and original residents were typically forced to relocate into new communities—as numerous scholars have documented, urban renewal was more a policy for economic revitalization than for housing, and the true benefits of urban renewal went to private developers.[36]

The new public housing projects being built through urban renewal were typically located either in the black ghetto or on its periphery, thus reinforcing the racial segregation that was already prevalent in most cities and concentrating poor residents within the neighborhoods in which projects were located.[37] The location of public housing high-rises provides another example to refute the idea that the persistence of racial segregation and the urban ghetto can be explained as the product of unfettered market forces sorting individuals with different preferences and resources into different communities. The concentration of poverty in specific neighborhoods within central cities was a direct product of political battles in which competing interests exerted differential influence on the political process, resulting in areas that had little political clout and severe social problems being forced to absorb the challenges associated with the concentration of residents with few resources, minimal external support, and blocked opportunities for advancement.

Urban renewal led to a shift in the urban landscape from decentralized slums to centralized public housing complexes and brought about an entirely new level of segregation in urban neighborhoods, by race and by class. As Doug Massey and Nancy Denton note in *American Apartheid*, the segregation that arose from this period of urban redevelopment was "the direct result of an unprecedented collaboration between local and national government."[38]

One might conclude that the methods used to maintain racial inequality in urban neighborhoods became less blatantly discriminatory in the post civil rights era, as many of the original tactics were made illegal—including racial discrimination, restrictive covenants, and redlining. But a new set of tactics emerged. Some were subtler versions of old practices, such as the persistence of racial discrimination in housing and lending. Others were institutional responses designed to maintain residential inequality within the legal context of newly established civil rights, such as federal home mortgage lending programs and the use of exclusionary zoning. Finally, the post civil rights period saw reincarnations of tactics that are as old as the nation itself, such as violence and intimidation tacitly supported by local officials.[39] Together, these formal and informal policies have been remarkably effective in reinforcing the walls of the urban ghetto even after the advances made in the civil rights period. When combined with the transformation of urban labor markets, the effects of these policies have been destructive for African American communities.

THE NEW AMERICAN CITY: THE CASE OF LOS ANGELES

As noted in the introductory chapter, one of the limitations of the data set used throughout this book is that it allows for an analysis of whites and African Americans only. Nowhere is this limitation more glaring than in the study of Los Angeles. In L.A., the number of whites and African Americans living in the city has declined steadily over time; but unlike many other cities, the overall population has grown substantially due to an influx of Hispanic and Asian Americans.[40] The dominant ethnic group in Los Angeles is now Hispanics, who compose almost half of the city's population. The ethnic diversity within L.A.'s city limits has changed the character of the city and its neighborhoods, transforming communities that were once racially segregated black neighborhoods into multiethnic spaces. In 1980, the average African American resident of Los Angeles lived in a neighborhood that was two-thirds black; now, due to the flood of immigrants into the city, the average African American lives in a neighborhood that is just 30 percent black, with a greater number of Hispanics than blacks.

Despite the diversity that has come to characterize Los Angeles, the city's nonwhite neighborhoods have faced many of the same challenges as communities in Detroit, Philadelphia, and New York. The processes that are most central to the trajectories of L.A's nonwhite communities are quite different from those that have affected the major northeastern and midwestern cities, however. Since the 1980s, urban scholars on the west coast have documented the discrepancies between the way that urban growth and neighborhood change operate in cities like Chicago and New York and the way that they operate in Los Angeles. Whereas patterns of growth and change in Chicago and New York are driven in large part by a powerful mayor and a centralized planning process, L.A. represents an alternative model featuring decentralized planning and governance, a weak mayor and powerful council.[41] Whereas classic research from the Chicago School of urban sociology envisioned neighborhood change emanating out from the center of the city, researchers studying L.A. observed a fragmented, decentralized metropolitan area in which the growth of neighborhoods, suburbs, and "edge cities" is driven by private forces operating with minimal regulation from any centralized government.[42] As the city has increasingly become a hub for global business, urbanists studying L.A. argue that the primary goals driving development are to create physical spaces that cater to the global elite while barricading off poor or ethnic minority communities.[43]

Despite these different political structures, the neighborhoods of Los Angeles have been affected by many of the same forces that have structured the trajectory of changes in urban neighborhoods in cities across the country. However, Los Angeles has experienced these changes in different ways, and at different times. For instance, the industrialization of L.A. and the migration of African American families into the city occurred later than in the northeastern and midwestern cities, arising in large part as a response to the demand for labor during and after World War II. The decline in wartime manufacturing employment within Los Angeles was more pronounced and more sudden than in cities across the country.[44] Over time L.A.'s economy became increasingly bifurcated, with growing opportunities for high-skilled, white-collar professionals as well as menial jobs that have come to be dominated by low-skilled immigrants. This growing inequality within the urban economy had several consequences. There was rapid growth in the city's black middle class in the 1950s and 1960s, accompanied by substantial outmigration into L.A.'s suburbs. At the same time, poorly educated African Americans, particularly men, have fared poorly as blue-collar jobs have declined and employment opportunities have disappeared.

Just as in many other cities across the country, racial and ethnic tensions in Los Angeles played a central role in driving housing policy and structuring the trajectories of communities. In the 1950s and 1960s explicit policies were adopted by the L.A. Realty Board to protect the "racial integrity" of white communities within the city, and these policies were reinforced by private developers' efforts to restrict new developments to white buyers and by the restrictions on federally backed mortgages, which were rarely given to minority homeowners.[45] After World War II, opposition to the construction of new public housing projects led to the siting of several projects in the Watts section of the city, reinforcing existing lines of racial segregation and concentrating poverty within this section of Los Angeles. Tension between the black community and the police has been even more intense in L.A. as compared with other cities, culminating in the Watts riots of 1965 and the Rodney King riots of 1992.[46] The Los Angeles Police Department responded to the 1992 riots by further militarizing their operations, and it was only years later that the department was forced to implement reforms to rein in the autonomy of L.A.'s police, which had become known for brutality, corruption, violations of rights, and a relative lack of oversight from the mayor's office.[47]

The unique timing of changes in the area's labor market, demographic composition, and social and political history has meant that trends of change in the city's and the metropolitan area's neighborhoods look very different from trends of change in other cities across the country. Whereas most cities saw a decline in the degree of concentrated poverty over the 1990s, the metropolitan area that includes Los Angeles and Long Beach experienced the largest *increase* in high-poverty neighborhoods in the nation over the same time period. Paul Jargowsky proposes three potential explanations for this anomalous pattern of change: (1) the response to the Rodney King riots led to greater levels of migration away from Los Angeles among white residents and more affluent nonwhite residents; (2) continuing immigration into the area from South and Central America brought a new population of low-income immigrants into the area; and (3) the economic recession of the early 1990s hit the area particularly hard.[48] To make matters more complicated, newly available data from the end of the 2000s suggest that concentrated poverty has subsequently declined somewhat in the Los Angeles metropolitan area, contrary to trends in other parts of the country.[49]

The trends visible in Los Angeles shed light on an important insight that is easy to overlook in any national analysis of urban change: Even if cities across the country are affected by a similar array of social, political, and economic forces, there is tremendous variation in the way that these forces operate within local contexts that feature unique political structures, populations, and histories.[50] This book is national in scope, meaning that much of the variation in the trajectories of cities across the country is neglected or obscured in favor of broad trends that have affected many cities throughout the country. But the research on the recent history of Los Angeles makes it clear that racial and ethnic inequality in the city's neighborhoods has been maintained through very different processes than in cities in the northeast and midwest. Differences in political structure and planning, in the history of the urban economy, and in patterns of migration into and out of the city have resulted in very different trajectories of change

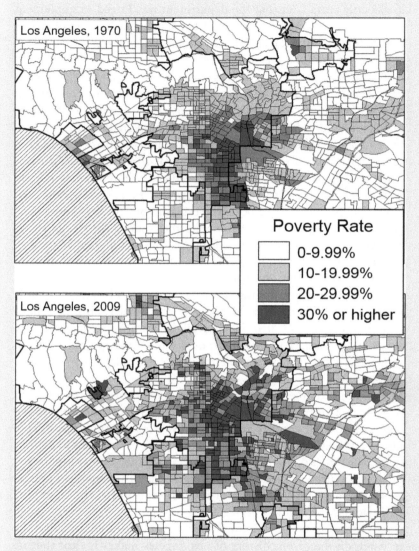

Poverty Rate
0-9.99%
10-19.99%
20-29.99%
30% or higher

Figure 3.3. Neighborhood poverty in census tracts surrounding Los Angeles in 1970 (top) and 2005–9 (bottom). Sources: Data from 1970 are based on the 1970 Census; data from 2005–9 are from the American Community Survey.

in L.A.'s neighborhoods when compared with neighborhoods in Chicago, Philadelphia, New York, Detroit, and other big cities in the midwest and northeast. At the same time, just as in these other cities, Los Angeles' minority neighborhoods have been the object of severe disinvestment over time, joblessness has become a pronounced social problem as the city's economy has transformed, police/resident relationships have exploded in major riots, and concentrated poverty has risen over time. In these ways, the forces that have structured trajectories of change in Los Angeles' neighborhoods look quite similar to the forces affecting minority communities across the country.

Urban Transformation and Economic Dislocation

The story of the transformation of urban labor markets, particularly in older rust belt cities of the northeast and midwest, is now well known. Beginning as early as the 1940s and 1950s in some cities like Detroit,[51] the industries that supported the mass urbanization of African Americans in the first half of the twentieth century began to deteriorate, shedding the stable working-class jobs that supported urban populations for decades.[52] The pace of deindustrialization was swift and the scale was massive. New York City lost almost 500,000 manufacturing jobs from 1969 to 1989, reducing the number of jobs in the industry by more than half.[53] In Chicago, Loic Wacquant and William Julius Wilson document how the shift of manufacturing positions out of the city brought about a rapid transformation of African Americans' labor force status within the urban economy.[54] From 1957 to 1982, Chicago's manufacturing industry, which had been a primary source of employment for the black community since the Great Migration,[55] began to shed jobs within the city even as the industry grew nationwide.[56] Whereas labor force participation among African Americans was similar to that among other racial and ethnic groups in 1950, by 1980 blacks had substantially lower rates of employment. The city no longer provided the jobs that supported the sizable black working class that emerged in Chicago and similar northern and midwestern cities, and joblessness and economic exclusion became dominant features of the urban ghetto.

While deindustrialization is often presented as a natural process of labor market adaptation to new technological realities, every step of this process bears the imprint of political forces that shaped its form and its impact. The shift of manufacturing jobs out of rust-belt cities was facilitated by the federal government's investment in roads and highways and its massive subsidies for suburban home ownership. America is unique in its consistent support for the construction of roads and highways, for its low gas taxes, and for its use of taxes and tolls to support the automobile industry and industries associated with highway construction—policy stances that have been driven in large part by the strong influence of the automobile and "highway" lobby. The United States is also unique in its *lack* of investment in public transportation within cities and in public options for movement across cities, such as Amtrak. Whereas national transportation policy could be used to provide city and suburban residents with multiple options that allow for convenient transportation within and outside the city, the policy choices that have been made over the past century frequently have torn urban neighborhoods apart while providing incentives for urban residents and businesses to depart the city.[57]

Just as housing and transportation policy has encouraged the mass suburbanization of white America, the shift of manufacturing jobs out of rust belt cities was facilitated by the federal government's sustained investment in roads and highways, along with its subsidies for suburban home ownership. All of these forces made it possible for workers to move to the suburbs and for firms to vacate central cities. Political scientist Peter Dreier describes in his research how the government worked directly with leading defense contractors to facilitate the exodus out of central cities, which gave these firms the opportunity to avoid the reach of big-city unions and politicians. Just as local housing decisions were the product of political forces operating in a highly unequal environment, the state played a central role in intervening to restructure urban labor markets, leading to disastrous consequences for urban populations.[58] The resulting inequality between cities and suburbs within the same metropolitan areas has had consequences that have become amplified over time. When cities are much poorer than their suburbs there is the potential for cleavages to sharpen and for further disinvestment to arise.[59]

William Julius Wilson was the first scholar of urban poverty to recognize and analyze the impact that economic transformation, in the form of deindustrialization, had on urban neighborhoods, especially in the former industrial centers of the northeast and midwest. As Wilson observed in his landmark book *The Truly Disadvantaged*, the decline in manufacturing jobs within urban centers created widespread joblessness and combined with the changing demographic patterns in America's cities to create a new kind of concentrated poverty. The new ghetto neighborhood was characterized by economic dislocation, the decline in traditional two-parent family structure, rising violence, and the deterioration of core community institutions such as the church and the schools.[60] Importantly, the deterioration of these and other institutions that are central to the economic functioning and social integration of any community have been driven not only by demographic and economic changes within the nation's central cities, but also by active decisions made across a realm of policy arenas that resulted in the abandonment of poor and nonwhite communities within the urban population. Using schools as an example, recent research has challenged the notion that drops in federal funding or overall urban decline can explain the deterioration of urban public schools. Instead, decisions surrounding the separation of city/suburban school districts, the distribution of students from different racial/ethnic groups across schools within urban school districts, and the allocation of resources to different schools and populations of students all combined with the broader economic and demographic changes in urban areas to result in the disastrous decline in the quality of urban schooling.[61]

Disinvestment in the educational experiences of African Americans reflects broader disinvestment in urban communities. Instead of responding to deindustrialization and large-scale urban transformation with ameliorative social policy, the federal government disengaged from urban issues and responded with punitive social policies that have exacerbated the problems faced by urban populations.[62] After federal aid to cities rose substantially from the end of World War II to the mid-1960s, it has been wildly erratic in the subsequent decades, especially in the realm of public and affordable housing.[63] The fluctuations in aid, combined with the efforts of several administrations to effectively incapacitate the federal Department of Housing and Urban Development, have made it difficult for local housing agencies to create sustained financial support for public housing projects, contributing to the rapid deterioration of projects in many central cities.[64]

This process was exacerbated by misguided policies that served to intensify the concentration of poverty among public housing residents. Until the post–World War II period, eligibility for entrance into public housing was based on families' ability to rent affordable housing within the private market. The income thresholds for eligibility were reduced in a series of shifts in policy designed to limit access to public housing to the neediest, leading to the eviction of families with low-to-middle incomes that were no longer eligible. But the unintended consequence of these policy shifts, combined with changes that made it more difficult for housing authorities to screen residents, was that public housing projects became the destination of last resort for urban families. Housing authorities also had fewer resources for operating costs as poorer families replaced the low- to middle-income families that were previously eligible for public housing, leading to lower levels of rent paid by families who had income well below the poverty line.[65]

There are numerous vivid accounts of how the deterioration of public housing projects has led to areas within cities that are characterized by violence, hopelessness, and urban blight.[66] An excellent example of a project that changed dramatically over time is found in Sudhir Venkatesh's history and ethnography of the Robert Taylor Homes housing project in Chicago, titled *American Project*.[67] Venkatesh chronicles how the Robert Taylor project, once a symbol of progress for blacks living in one of America's most segregated cities, was gradually abandoned by local police and the Chicago Housing Authority and allowed to deteriorate into a notoriously violent and gang-ridden complex. The project transformed into a symbol of the violence and poverty that characterized urban ghettos in the 1980s, but the process of federal and local abandonment that led to its demise is typically left out of this story.[68]

WHEN PEOPLE (AND WORK) DISAPPEAR: THE CASE OF DETROIT
Detroit has become the poster child for the burnt-out, abandoned, rust-belt city. The city population shrunk from over 1.2 million in 1980 to just over 700,000 in 2010, and most of those who left were white.[69] In 1980 there were over 400,000 whites living within the city limits, and by 2010 there were just 55,000 remaining. The number of African Americans in the city has dropped as well, from 775,000 in 1980 to 600,000 in 2010—but the relative presence of blacks has grown over this time, from 63 percent of the city's population to 84 percent. Detroit is the most racially segregated city in America—but the figures on segregation are little more than an abstract way of describing the reality of Detroit: it is a city where almost all whites have left, few immigrants have moved in, and only African Americans remain.

What happened to Detroit is the extreme version of what has happened to cities all across the country, with a few exceptions that have exacerbated the situation in Detroit. The city is unique in the degree to which its economy and its residents have relied on jobs in the manufacturing sector, in particular the automotive industry. When manufacturing plants started to leave the city, a process that began as early as the 1940s, Detroit began a gradual descent that has continued to the present day.[70] From 1960 to 1980, the percentage of jobs in the larger metropolitan area that were located within the city limits dropped in half, from 44 percent to 22 percent.[71]

But the story of Detroit's decline is not simply a story about a changing urban economy. In fact, the larger metropolitan area surrounding the city has fared quite well over time, with steady growth in employment and rising income.[72] Detroit's narrative is about the divide between the central city and its suburbs, and about a changing urban economy within a context of racial hostility and violence, political and demographic change, and unequal investment in populations and in places.[73] Racial conflict and competition have dominated social, political, and economic life in Detroit since the 1920s, when the first waves of African Americans began migrating north to work in the factories of cities in the midwest and northeast. In 1920 there were fewer than 25,000 African Americans in the Detroit metropolitan area. Thirty years later, there were over 350,000 African Americans living there, and thirty years after that, in 1980, there were more than 900,000. Detroit went from a white city to a black and white city rapidly, and the combination of racism, competition for jobs and space and political influence, and widespread discrimination created the conditions for severe racial conflict.

After numerous racially charged incidents of violence in the prior decades, the growing hostility between the city's police force and its black population combined to generate the conditions for the 1967 riot, in which over forty people were killed, over a thousand were injured, and over seven thousand were arrested.[74] Whites had already begun to leave Detroit in droves, but when Coleman Young was elected several years later as the city's first black mayor, the outmigration of whites accelerated rapidly and continued for the next several decades.

As Detroit lost residents, the city's tax base grew smaller. Federal aid to the city dropped precipitously over the same period. In 1980 Detroit received 26 percent of its budget, almost 400 million dollars, from the federal government. A decade later the city was receiving only 161 million dollars from the federal government, just 8 percent of its budget.[75] City services deteriorated, city taxes were high, housing was being demolished instead of rebuilt, and the city's neighborhoods were neglected as successive mayoral administrations focused their energies and resources on high-profile downtown development projects.[76] Further, immigrants were not pouring into Detroit like they were into other cities in the northeast, south, and west coast. Whereas many cities shifted to a service- and information-based economy and saw neighborhoods revitalized by immigrants, Detroit emptied out.

As dire as the circumstances in Detroit have been over the past several decades, the city experienced the nation's largest *decline* in concentrated poverty over the 1990s.[77] The automotive industry fared well over the decade, a few major companies relocated their headquarters to downtown Detroit, and many residents were put to work building stadiums like Comerica Park, home of the Tigers, and Ford Field, home of the Lions.[78] As in many cities across the country, however, the decline in unemployment and in the prevalence of high-poverty neighborhoods that occurred over the 1990s was temporary, and has since reversed. New data, updated to the latter half of the 2000s, indicate that concentrated poverty has returned to Detroit and has been exacerbated by the housing crisis and the national economic downturn. There is minimal talk of economic revitalization in Detroit—instead, the mayor has accepted the reality of a smaller Detroit, announcing a plan to constrict city services to the parts of the city where residents still live and to reduce or discontinue all but the most basic services in the neighborhoods that have mostly emptied out.

Considering the recent history of Detroit and its surroundings, what can be said about the sample of white and black families from the PSID that originated in or around Detroit a generation ago? A first observation is that the sample of first-generation white families was scattered around the outskirts of the city, whereas the sample of African American families was concentrated in the center of the city, the parts of the maps in figure 3.4 that have been almost entirely black for the past four decades and where poverty is most intensely concentrated. Considering the fact that white families were already bordering the Detroit suburbs back in the 1970s, it is perhaps not surprising that the white families in the sample were much more likely than the black families to leave the city, consistent with the trend of white flight from central cities that occurred throughout the nation. Middle-class and working-class African American families have moved outward to the periphery of the city over time, leading to further concentrations of poverty in the center of the city.

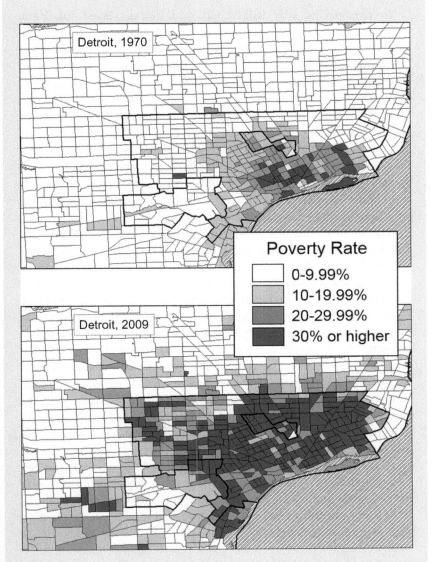

Figure 3.4. Neighborhood poverty in census tracts surrounding Detroit in 1970 (top) and 2005–9 (bottom). Sources: Data from 1970 are based on the 1970 Census; data from 2005–9 are from the American Community Survey.

In considering why whites left and blacks stayed (or, more accurately, why fewer blacks left), it is crucial to understand the racial climate in Detroit over the past half century.[79] Racial conflict was more intense and more violent in Detroit than in almost any other city in the country. It is a city where federal troops have been called in twice, once in 1943 and again in 1967, to control the violence from race riots.[80] It is a city where, in 1963 alone, there were sixty-five reported incidents of white neighbors attacking the homes of black newcomers in their neighborhood.[81] It is a city where a developer built a six-foot wall surrounding his property so that the area would be designated as racially homogeneous, which meant white home buyers would be able to obtain a federally backed loan and could be assured that no African Americans could encroach upon the neighborhood.[82]

This history must be considered in order to place the more recent history of demographic change in context. When Coleman Young was elected in 1973, blacks composed a majority of the city's residents. The demands of the city's African American community could no longer be dealt with through violence, oppression, and political control. Crime was rising sharply in the city, and a Supreme Court decision in the same year mandated busing within the city to integrate public schools.[83] In this racial battleground, whites retreated to the suburbs and never came back. They were able to do so because of federally backed home mortgages, and they prospered because of the concurrent shift of employment opportunity into Detroit's suburbs. Over the next several decades, Detroit faced a formidable set of challenges with a declining tax base, declining aid from the federal government, and a declining population. In considering the fortunes of a city like Detroit, it is crucial to move beyond the question of who left the city and who did not—instead, we must consider why some groups were able to move and others were less able, why the destination suburbs of Detroit were able to fare well over time, and why the city left behind declined so precipitously.

The Growing Link between the Prison and the Ghetto

In the late 1960s the nation started on a decades-long process that has led to the current period of "mass imprisonment." [84] The scale of imprisonment that currently exists in the United States is unprecedented, and its impact has been targeted primarily on young black men. Sociologists Becky Pettit and Bruce Western estimate that black men born in the late 1960s had about a 20 percent chance of spending time in state or federal prison by their early thirties.[85] Among black men with only a high school education, three out of ten were in prison by their mid-thirties, and among high school dropouts the figure rises to six out of ten.[86] Imprisonment has become so common among black men, particularly those with less than a college education, that there is now good reason to conceptualize prison as one of the major transitions in the life cycle, alongside other traditional steps such as entrance into the workforce or into parenthood.[87] Black men are now more likely to have served time in prison than to have a four-year college degree or to have served in the military.[88]

The movement toward mass imprisonment evolved from a rhetorical reaction to the racial unrest of the civil rights period into a series of legislative actions that made it progressively easier to respond to economic dislocation and urban unrest by removing young black men from the streets and locking them up. Hints at the growing movement toward a more punitive social policy could be found in the law-and-order rhetoric of Barry Goldwater in the 1964 presidential campaign, which linked the civil rights protests of the early 1960s with broader issues surrounding safety and disorder. But this rhetoric was accompanied by policy in the decades to come. Accompanying the nationwide "War on Drugs" and the proliferation of "tough on crime" political rhetoric was the emergence of sentencing commissions, the enactment of mandatory minimum sentences, and the scaling back or elimination of parole across the states. By 2000, twenty-four states had limited or abolished parole, forty had truth-in-sentencing laws, and twenty-four had "three strikes" laws, which imposed extreme penalties on repeat offenders.[89]

These changes have led to the emergence of the prison as a central institution in the black community. Loic Wacquant argues that the prison now serves a function previously served by the institutions of slavery, Jim Crow, and the ghetto, as a primary means to control the African American population, to maintain racial segregation and racial domination in the context of widespread economic dislocation in urban areas.[90]

The growth of incarceration and the emergence of the prison as a central institution in African Americans' lives have had complex impacts on African American communities. In considering the diverse set of ways that rising incarceration might affect a community, it is a mistake to ignore the possibility that the rise in incarceration has reduced violent crime in black neighborhoods.[91] Since the 1990s, violent crime has dropped rapidly in America's cities, and even the most conservative estimates suggest that at least 10–15 percent of the drop in crime is attributable to the "incapacitation" effect associated with incarcerating growing numbers of potential offend-ers.[92] Without downplaying the negative effects of aggressive policing that targets poor and minority communities,[93] we should not underestimate the importance of the drop in violent crime to America's urban neighborhoods. Violence undermines community organization and cohesion, and it "gets into the minds" of children to affect every aspect of their daily lives, from their willingness to leave the home to the way they interact with peers to the way that they behave and perform in the classroom.[94]

Even allowing for the possibility that rising incarceration has contrib-uted to the decline in violent crime, however, there are several reasons to believe that any short-term positive effects arising from incapacitation are simply preludes to disastrous long-term consequences for black commu-nities. As more and more young people are arrested and imprisoned over time, the marginal "offender" is more likely to be nonviolent, lacking any history of criminal offending. When young men go to prison they are not only separated from their families; they are separated from the opportunity to obtain education, experience, or skills that are useful in the labor force. When they return, the obstacles they face as they attempt to reenter society are daunting. Returning prisoners often face overwhelming child support obligations that accumulate during their time in prison, they often struggle to find housing and are ineligible for any public assistance, they commonly face chronic health problems and struggle with substance abuse, and their criminal records make them virtually unemployable.[95] As Bruce Western writes: "Men tangled in the criminal justice system become permanent la-bor market outsiders, finding only temporary or unreliable jobs that offer little economic stability".[96] There is now a great deal of evidence demon-strating that a criminal record drastically reduces the chances of securing employment, a finding that is not surprising considering survey research showing that employers in the low-wage labor market are more willing to hire welfare recipients, dropouts, and individuals with minimal experience than they are to hire an applicant with a criminal record.[97] Without the real-istic prospect of stable employment, it is extremely unlikely that these men can support a family, and the pathologies of everyday life in America's pris-ons make it difficult to reengage in the social life of a community. The result is a segment of the community that is detached from the legal labor market and detached from the family unit.

This is the direct effect of incarceration as felt by individuals. Equally troubling is the broader effect of the incarceration boom as felt by all black men. There is growing evidence that the deepening link between the prison and the black community has "marked" an entire segment of the black population with the stigma of criminality, including those with no criminal record.[98] For instance, economist Harry Holzer surveyed employers in the mid-1990s and found that despite their unwillingness to hire applicants with criminal records, few employers actually conduct criminal background checks.[99] Instead, employers may look for "signs" of a criminal record, such as a gap in an applicant's work history, when assessing the qualifications of an applicant. The more dangerous possibility is that employers may use the race of an applicant as a proxy for criminal status, with the assumption that a large portion of black applicants are likely to have criminal records.

Sociologist Devah Pager's research has produced chilling evidence of how this new reality plays out in the low-wage labor market.[100] Pager conducted an experimental audit test to see how criminal backgrounds interact with race to affect applicants' success in applying for low-wage jobs. Similar to the audit experiments conducted to test discrimination in the housing market, in Pager's work pairs of white and black applicants with the same qualifications were sent to apply to the same entry-level jobs in Milwaukee. One member of each pair was randomly assigned to report having a criminal record; the other was assigned to report no criminal record. Pager analyzed the proportion of each pair receiving a callback from the employer as the dependent variable marking "success" in the early stages of the process toward employment. She found that a criminal record is a major obstacle to success in the labor market among both whites and blacks, as one would expect. But what is most shocking about Pager's research is the way that race and criminality are linked together. Not only were blacks less likely than whites to have success in applying for a job, but the rate of success for African American applicants *without a criminal record* was lower than the rate of success for white applicants *with a criminal record*.

This finding reveals the way in which race and criminality have become entangled and inseparable in the era of mass imprisonment. It also reveals the way in which the behavior of blacks and whites has differential consequences in American society—whereas past transgressions of whites may be readily dismissed or ignored by employers, similar transgressions are difficult to overcome for African Americans.[101] As the criminal justice system has become increasingly punitive, the shadow of the prison has been extended over an entire segment of the black population, and the prison has extended its reach deep into the black community. There is a simple, yet powerful statistic that reveals just how enmeshed the prison has become in the black community: as of 2000 about 9 percent of African American children had a father in prison or jail.[102] What does it mean for a community when almost one out of every ten of its children has a father who is incarcerated? We are only beginning to know the answer to this question, but a set of recent studies has already demonstrated a strong association between parental incarceration and children's mental health, aggressiveness, and subsequent involvement with the criminal justice system.[103]

Even this focus on the families of the incarcerated overlooks the impact of mass imprisonment as felt by entire communities. Recent studies of prisoners reentering society reveal patterns of reentry into tightly bounded geographic areas that are already beset by high rates of poverty, joblessness, and crime, and that offer few resources for reentrants.[104] The Justice Mapping Center has created a series of maps showing the remarkable concentration of men in jail or prison originating within specific neighborhoods of New York City, revealing sections of Brooklyn where more than one in twenty adult men are incarcerated.[105] These are communities where a substantial portion of the population is detached from the wider society, ineligible for public benefits, unlikely to secure stable employment, and unable to support a family. The presence of such communities provides the strongest support for Loïc Wacquant's argument about the role that the prison has come to play as a mechanism to reinforce racial segregation and to maintain racial inequality in the post civil rights era.[106] As Wacquant argues, the prison has now become an extension of the ghetto, and the ghetto an extension of the prison. Young men raised in the ghetto are increasingly likely to transition into the prison system on their path through young adulthood, with consequences that permanently alter their life course trajectory by disrupting or ending their educational careers, reducing their chances for stable employment, stunting the normal trajectory of wage growth that occurs in young adulthood, and precluding the formation of stable family structures. With large numbers of men unable to survive in the formal economy, entire communities become extensions of the prison system, where illicit forms of economic activity become commonplace.

These communities are the product of the economic transformation that has taken place in urban centers over the past several decades, in which the jobs that supported a growing black working class disappeared over time. They are the result of the erratic federal commitment to America's cities, reflected in major cuts to housing, to economic development, and to the welfare state at the same time that joblessness in urban centers was growing and the need for support becoming more acute. Finally, these communities are the product of the punitive response to widespread economic dislocation, in which increasingly harsh punishment has led to levels of imprisonment that are unmatched in the world and that are targeted toward the by-products of deindustrialization: young, less educated, minority men.[107]

Perhaps more than any other policy, demographic trend, or economic change in the post civil rights era, the explosion in incarceration rates from the 1970s onward has the potential to create lasting damage to black communities that may extend on to the next generation.

NO LONGER BLACK AND WHITE: THE CASE OF PHILADELPHIA

Until recently, the history of Philadelphia could be told in terms of black and white. In 1980 whites composed 57 percent of the city's population, and African Americans composed 38 percent—all other ethnic groups together accounted for the remaining 5 percent of the city population. Philadelphia's politics have long been dominated by race—and according to a persuasive argument from urban historian Guian McKee, the city's history of racial conflict has played a central role in structuring the fortunes of Philadelphia over time.[108]

Deindustrialization affected Philadelphia in the same way as it did many other northeastern and midwestern cities. However, the flow of jobs outside the city was mitigated by the fact that Philadelphia contained a more diverse mix of small-scale industries that allowed it to adapt to changing economic conditions more easily.[109] Further, through the 1960s the city government and private nonprofits took an active role in attempting to retain industrial firms within the city through planning and land use policy, including programs to provide financing for small and mid-size firms to remain within the city, the establishment of "industrial land banks" within the city, and the creation of community-owned manufacturing enterprises that provided jobs and experience to city residents.[110] While these various programs represented novel approaches to dealing with urban deindustrialization, the programs never coordinated their efforts and were always split along racial lines.

These efforts were overwhelmed by the politics of race, which came to dominate social policy in Philadelphia. After serving as police chief and overseeing one of the most draconian police departments in the country, Frank Rizzo was elected mayor in 1971 and again in 1975. Rizzo's successful candidacy was based on his appeal to poor and working-class whites who were concerned about rising crime, economic insecurity, and minority infiltration of their racially homogeneous neighborhoods. Rizzo's policy agenda during his two terms as mayor featured the distribution of patronage to his white working-class constituency, the provision of generous contracts to municipal employees, and the reversal of affirmative-action mandates affecting hiring in the Philadelphia Police Department.[111] To fund his initiatives, the mayor raised city taxes and ran up unprecedented municipal deficits.[112] Yet poor black neighborhoods were considered to be beyond repair by the Rizzo administration and were ignored in the distribution of patronage and infrastructural projects.

In a period of social change and industrial decline, the Rizzo administration represented the implementation of a politics of racial conflict, inward-looking governance, and myopic fiscal policy. Having alienated blacks with its strong-armed policing and businessmen with its tax hikes, the administration could only garner support through increasing pay for its own employees and through top-down, demagogic appeals to its white working-class constituency. The politics of racial demagoguery were visible in many cities across the country over the 1960s and 1970s, but in few other cities did the resulting social policies exert such long-term damage to the city as in Philadelphia.

The consequences of this social policy were felt most acutely in the city's minority neighborhoods. Elijah Anderson's ethnographic research in Philadelphia provides some of the most vivid description of life in the city's poorest, most racially segregated neighborhoods in the 1980s and early 1990s. The communities that Anderson studies were the object of disinvestment and abandonment, resulting in concentrated poverty, joblessness, dysfunctional institutions, and deep-seated mistrust between residents and the police. Anderson describes the way that the threat of violence had come to structure the daily interactions of residents in Philadelphia's poorest neighborhoods, requiring children to adapt to a "code of the street" in order to survive in public spaces and in the schools.[113]

Since the 1980s the trajectory of change in Philadelphia has shifted in major ways. After the two terms of the Rizzo administration, Philadelphia has seen the election of a succession of Democratic mayoral administrations backed by loose alliances of the business elite and African Americans.[114] After years of inward-looking social policy, a great deal of attention since 1980 has been focused on redevelopment of the downtown and the port in an attempt to make Philadelphia a regional and international hub of commerce. Philadelphia has transformed

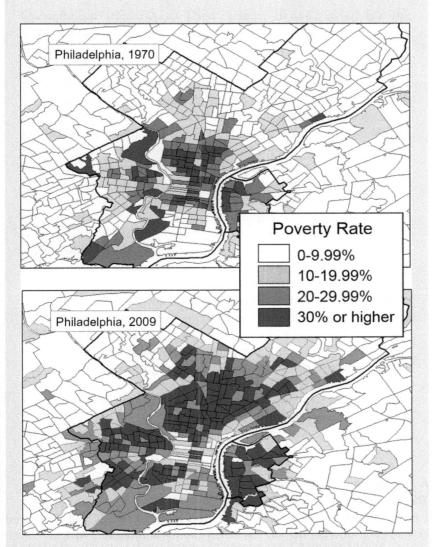

Figure 3.5. Neighborhood poverty in census tracts surrounding Philadelphia in 1970 (top) and 2005–9 (bottom). Sources: Data from 1970 are based on the 1970 Census; data from 2005–9 are from the American Community Survey.

into a global city, and its economy and fiscal situation have improved dramatically over time. Journalist Buzz Bissinger documents much of this revival in his account of Mayor Ed Rendell's administration in the 1990s, a period when Philadelphia's economy transformed.[115]

In the midst of Bissinger's glowing portrait of Rendell, the author tells a less optimistic story about how the dramatic changes occurring in the city never trickled down to affect the lives of its poor residents and their communities. Virtually all of the African American families in the PSID sample from Philadelphia originated in neighborhoods in the south part of the city, on either side of Interstate 76. When the city's economy gained steam in the 1990s, the level of concentrated poverty in these neighborhoods barely changed, and they remain among the poorest communities in the city. As a whole, Philadelphia continues to be a city with extremely high levels of segregation, poverty, and joblessness. Among the country's fifty largest cities, Philadelphia now has the sixth highest poverty rate and the third lowest rate of labor force participation.[116]

The one thing that has changed in these neighborhoods, however, is their racial and ethnic composition.[117] A few decades ago, Philadelphia was a black and white city, but now 12 percent of Philadelphia's population is Hispanic and 7 percent is Asian American. The city's white population continues to drop, meaning its neighborhoods are becoming more diverse over time. To this point, however, neither Philadelphia's new economy nor its new diversity has altered the fortunes of its low-income communities.

A Respite from Urban Disinvestment: The Federal Effort to Confront Urban Poverty

I have highlighted four inter-related processes and trends that have been crucial to reinforcing the walls of urban ghettos and limiting African Americans' prospects for upward mobility out of the ghetto. In doing so, I have focused primarily on the period leading up to the 1960s, when urban renewal was at its peak, and the period from the mid-1970s onward, when the most substantial economic shifts and disinvestments in urban communities occurred. Left out of this discussion is the decade of the 1960s, a period characterized by urban unrest, but also by a series of civil rights advances, by rapid economic advances among African Americans, and by several ambitious programs that fell under the umbrella of the Johnson Administration's War on Poverty. It was during the 1960s when urban schools were forced to desegregate, leading to more equitable educational environments and long-term economic benefits for African Americans.[118] It was during the 1960s when the black middle class grew rapidly, when affirmative action policies allowed African Americans to enter into occupations that were previously restricted, and when an influx of federal resources was shifted to the nation's cities.

The urban initiatives that emerged in this period were diverse, and combined a wide range of philosophies about the causes and solutions to urban poverty. But one set of programs stands out as representative of a unique approach to investing in communities that emerged during this period. The most prominent initiatives that represent this new approach—the Community Action Program and Model Cities—differed from each other in subtle ways, but they shared a strategy for community revitalization that emphasized building from the ground up—that is, providing resources directly to community groups, community leaders, and community residents and allowing them to take a lead role in planning and implementing programs targeted toward their own unique needs.

There are two ways in which the programs implemented during the 1960s might be thought of as challenges to some of the central arguments outlined throughout this chapter. First, the mere existence of several substantial efforts to combat urban poverty during this period might be seen as running counter to the narrative of federal disinvestment in urban areas that has dominated this chapter. Second, while much of the chapter (and the book as a whole) argues that federal disinvestment in urban areas can explain much of the transmission of neighborhood inequality to the children of the civil rights era, one could make the counterargument that, even when attempts were made to invest in the nation's communities, these efforts had minimal impact.

Both of these arguments have some merit. The level of federal spending going to cities rose dramatically over the 1960s and into the 1970s, yet conditions in the nation's urban areas deteriorated over much of this period. Further, the "community action" approach to urban poverty that emerged during this period has come to be viewed by many as an idealistic and misguided failure that ultimately set back the effort to fight urban poverty at the federal level.[119] There are several examples of programs that failed to have much of an impact on urban communities and thus support this perspective.

To understand what went wrong, I argue that it is essential to take into account the historical context in which these programs were implemented—and the manner in which they were abandoned, only years later. As a starting point, it is useful to consider how federal aid to cities was spent over the 1960s and 1970s. As Helen Ladd describes in a detailed study of city finances from the 1960s through the 1980s, much of the growth in federal aid to cities was used to address the rising costs associated with the expansion of the public sector workforce, and to compensate for the declining tax base and the growth in public services in cities experiencing declining overall population and the outmigration of businesses and the middle class.[120] Federal funding was largely a response to the major demographic shifts in the composition of city populations, which had overwhelmed city governments.

Next, one must consider the full history of the "community action" programs implemented during the 1960s, the wavering political commitment to them, and the erratic resources devoted to them. The history of these programs leads to the unmistakable conclusion that the federal investment in programs to confront urban poverty was temporary, and it was half-hearted. It was an effort that was overcome by the new demographic pressures facing America's cities as well as by the forces working to reinforce urban inequality.

The emergence of the "community action" strategy, and the broader federal commitment to the nation's urban neighborhoods, have roots in the Economic Opportunity Act of 1964.[121] This legislation established the Community Action Program, or CAP, the first federal program to incorporate the idea that the federal government should not simply provide resources for urban neighborhoods but also should provide a mechanism for community groups to play a direct role in planning, in allocating resources, and in implementing local projects designed to serve the community. In introducing the legislation President Johnson claimed it would "give every American community the opportunity to develop a comprehensive plan to fight its own poverty—and help them to carry out their plans."[122] Calling for "maximum feasible participation of residents of the areas and members of the groups served," CAP was intended to alter the power structure within America's cities, to make institutions and elected officials more responsive to the communities they serve, and to empower local organizations and residents.[123]

The types of programs that were funded through CAP were extremely diverse. Some were demonstration projects that were devised in Washington, the most notable and successful example being Head Start. Others were local ideas that were planned and implemented by community groups, often without any involvement of local government. From a political perspective, some of the grants included among this group incited controversy, a notable example being grants to train community organizers and to collaborate with local organizations that were working for radical changes in the power structure—such as one grant used in Syracuse to train organizers in the confrontational methods of Saul Alinsky's organizations in Chicago.[124] As these controversial grants gained publicity and city politicians became increasingly upset about the initiatives being supported by CAP, the program began to generate substantial negative publicity and was essentially defunded only a few years into its existence.

The idea of community-based investments did not disappear, however. On the heels of the political turmoil surrounding CAP came the Model Cities Program, another ambitious idea designed to provide concentrated resources to selected communities around the nation, encouraging coordination of planning across communities and across the cities in which they were located, and providing an opportunity for home-grown innovation at the local level.[125] Model Cities was built on the ideal of community empowerment that was central to the Community Action Program, but it was designed to correct for mistakes made in CAP by requiring community members and groups to work with local officials and local government to plan and then implement new, comprehensive programs. Similar to CAP, however, the program was weakened early in its existence. Model Cities was designed to concentrate substantial resources in a small number of selected cities, in an attempt to provide concrete examples demonstrating how the program could transform communities.[126] The distribution of funds to only a small number of cities proved to be too difficult politically, however, and the number of target cities grew to almost two hundred. What began as an effort to direct overwhelming resources to a concentrated area became a program that dispersed funds thinly over a wide range of communities.

Like the Community Action Program before it, Model Cities was focused as much on the process of community mobilization as it was on the programs that were actually implemented. Much of the evaluation of the program was centered on the planning process—which groups took part, how power was distributed, and so forth. Despite documentation of substantial "turbulence" among the various groups asked to work together to develop proposals and implement plans for the new resources,[127] Model Cities received several favorable assessments from organizations and agencies that evaluated the early stages of the program.[128] At the local level, it was much less politically controversial than CAP had been.

The program's biggest obstacle came with the election in 1968 of Richard Nixon, who arrived in office with desires to scale back or eliminate many of

Johnson's programs composing the War on Poverty. The program continued through the first Nixon administration, but no longer. Funds for Model Cities and other urban programs were frozen after Nixon's reelection, at which point the president declared the "urban crisis" to be over. With the decline in urban riots and the nation's continuing entanglement in Vietnam, there was no longer the same urgency surrounding issues of urban poverty as there had been in the late 1960s.[129]

Both CAP and Model Cities are often described as idealistic and misguided efforts that failed to revitalize the ghetto, and there is an element of truth in these characterizations. The idea that community empowerment could turn around ghetto communities, absent any broader changes in the distribution of resources and labor market opportunities, is clearly unrealistic. The idea that community-based efforts to stimulate the local economy could bring substantial jobs to the ghetto was also unrealistic. Politically, the decision to fund programs that directly challenged and antagonized city governments, the major advocates for federal investments in urban areas, was a miscalculation. And from a practical standpoint, the decision to spread thin resources over a wide swath of communities across the nation was misguided.

Seen from a different perspective, however, these critiques do not tell the complete story. In the last decade or so, several scholars have revisited this period of policy history and presented a range of counterarguments to the view that these programs should be remembered purely as policy failures.[130] The first relates to expectations about what a community-based program might reasonably expect to accomplish on its own. While it is certainly true that proponents had high hopes for the impact that community-based programs might have, even advocates acknowledged that these programs were never meant to be implemented without broader changes in the policy landscape targeting jobs, education, health care, and income support.[131] It is even more unrealistic to think that these programs could have had transformative effects on urban communities in the short period during which CAP and Model Cities were running. CAP was abandoned after only a couple of very active years, and Model Cities was abandoned well before any of the programs that communities had planned were allowed to mature.[132]

Despite the short life span of the two programs, several scholars argue that CAP and Model Cities may have had a much more lasting impact than previously considered. Head Start is undoubtedly the best example of a program that was implemented as a demonstration project through CAP and quickly expanded to a national scope. But there were other major success stories as well. Senator Robert Kennedy's efforts to establish funding for community development corporations through a "special impact" amendment in the Economic Opportunity Act resulted in the founding of a set of organizations that have worked to build affordable housing and promote economic development in disadvantaged neighborhoods for more than four decades.[133] These organizations have served as models that set the stage for the proliferation of community development corporations in the years since the passage of the original legislation.

Some assessments of the Model Cities program acknowledge that specific initiatives implemented through this program had minimal impact on conditions within communities, but they argue that the program was effective in bolstering community organization and altering the local power structure. From this perspective, Model Cities made local governments more responsive to residents and community groups, improved the capacity for residents to organize around issues that were central to their communities, and established a foundation for the central role to be played in the decades to come by institutions and community leaders devoted to community development.[134]

The impact of these community-based institutions is difficult to quantify. In some areas like economic development, there is minimal evidence that grassroots efforts to bring jobs to communities have been effective.[135] A much stronger case can be made that community development organizations have played major roles in providing affordable housing and other community resources and amenities that have helped to transform poor communities.[136]

Even acknowledging these possible long-term impacts, however, it is clear that the War on Poverty fell far short of its goals. In the time since Nixon abruptly ended the era of "community action," there have been a series of initiatives and grant programs specifically designed to revitalize urban communities, but the political and financial commitment to these initiatives has continued to be erratic. Funds for housing and urban communities were consolidated into community development block grants through the Housing and Community Development Act of 1974, and the Carter administration bolstered this funding through its Urban Development Action Grant program.[137] But just as the challenges facing urban communities grew in the 1980s, the Reagan administration gutted federal programs targeting urban poverty, famously declaring of Johnson's War on Poverty that "poverty had won."[138] The first Bush administration proposed the idea of Enterprise Communities before dropping the idea from the administration platform in the face of political pressure during his reelection campaign. The Clinton administration went forward with an expansion of the Bush era policy, under the title of Enterprise Communities/Empowerment Zones. Like previous efforts to attract businesses to poor communities, however, this initiative was weakly implemented, and the evidence is mixed on whether it had any substantive impacts on local employment.[139]

This review of social policy is not intended to be a comprehensive discussion of the wide range of policies and programs designed to invest in urban communities and to reduce racial inequality in America's cities. The broad point, however, is that the various sets of policies enacted to confront poverty and racial inequality in America's neighborhoods—policies like the Community Reinvestment Act, Empowerment Zones/Enterprise Communities, and strengthened enforcement of fair housing—represent piecemeal efforts that do not compare in scale or impact to the collection of policies, demographic trends, and economic changes that have served to preserve the racial order in residential America.

In the absence of a robust and consistent national urban policy, the fortunes of urban residents and urban communities over the last several decades have been driven, in large part, by the shifting economic and demographic pressures that have affected the nation's cities. For much of the period between 1970 and the end of the 1980s, cities were faced with a set of formidable challenges, including population loss, the movement of firms outside of central cities, growth of the poverty population, a declining tax base, and newly emerging problems like the AIDS epidemic and the appearance of crack cocaine. The deterioration of urban neighborhoods during this period is not entirely surprising.

Alternatively, the 1990s saw a revitalization of many urban areas around the country. Urban economies began to bounce back during this decade, and urban poverty declined with tight labor markets, the widespread transition of welfare recipients into the labor market, and progressive policies like the earned income tax credit. Investments made in community development groups began to pay off, as neighborhoods that were once written off began to transform into viable communities.[140] At the same time, immigration into cities led to new growth in urban populations and helped fuel the revitalization of some of the most distressed neighborhoods, crime began to drop, home ownership increased, and property values in urban neighborhoods began to rise.

As a consequence of these changes, the problem of urban poverty diminished over the 1990s. After two decades in which poverty became increasingly concentrated in urban neighborhoods, the number of high-poverty neighborhoods declined sharply over this decade.[141] Children's "spells" of exposure to severe neighborhood poverty also became shorter, due largely to declines in the level of poverty surrounding them.[142] In short, many of the issues that I focus on throughout the book became much less severe during the 1990s.

The problem is that the 1990s was a short-term departure from a long-term trajectory of change in the nation's cities. We now know that the sharp reduction in concentrated poverty that occurred in the 1990s has reversed in the years since, as the number of extreme-poverty neighborhoods has grown in cities across the nation.[143] The tight labor markets that were present in urban areas through much of the 1990s are a distant memory, and joblessness is widespread, particularly among African Americans. The rise in home prices and home ownership were products of a speculative bubble, and the resulting foreclosure crisis is most pronounced in the nation's most racially segregated urban areas.[144]

Considering the historical trajectory of urban areas over the course of the last several decades, it is not all that surprising that upward mobility out of the ghetto has been so rare among African Americans. The patterns of multigenerational disadvantage presented in chapter 2 are the product of a combination of persistent forces that have reproduced urban inequality, including the failure to enforce civil rights, the consolidation of African Americans within central city neighborhoods, the transformation of urban labor markets, and the devastating federal response to this transformation. It is important to acknowledge the departures from this pattern of urban disinvestment and decline, but it is also crucial to recognize these periods as deviations from long-term trends. The unique set of programs targeting urban poverty in the 1960s was never provided the resources and the political commitment to generate transformative changes. The period of urban revitalization in the 1990s did produce major changes in urban neighborhoods, yet this period was in many ways a temporary respite from the long-term trend toward concentrated poverty. Throughout all of this period, the absence of a strong and consistent urban policy has meant that urban neighborhoods across the nation have been vulnerable to fluctuations in the economy, fluctuations in local fiscal conditions, and fluctuations in the national political mood. As a result, the broad set of demographic forces and economic changes that I have outlined in this chapter, along with the overarching pattern of disinvestment in urban communities, together have overwhelmed the relatively weak, erratic investments that have been made in our nation's urban neighborhoods.

This is why the ghetto has been passed on to the current generation. In the third part of the book I consider strategies to move toward a more "durable" urban policy with the potential to confront the set of forces that have maintained, and indeed reinforced, the walls of the urban ghetto. But before getting there, we must address the second question raised in the introduction to the book: What have been the consequences of life in the ghetto, over multiple generations, for African Americans?

Chapter 4 | **Neighborhoods and the Transmission of Racial Inequality**

In the midst of the 1960s, during a period when historic civil rights legislation was being pushed through Congress, there were many voices arguing that more needed to be done. In a famous speech at Howard University, President Lyndon Johnson stated, "It is not enough just to open the gates of opportunity. All our citizens must have the ability to walk through those gates."[1] In an essay on the evolution of the civil rights movement, Bayard Rustin wrote, "The civil rights movement . . . is now concerned not merely with removing the barriers to full opportunity but with achieving the fact of equality."[2] This sentiment was echoed in other prominent writings of the time, such as the Moynihan Report and the Kerner Commission Report. But the research of the sociologist Otis Dudley Duncan, which was based on data from the early part of the 1960s, led him to a different conclusion.

Duncan was one of the first sociologists to use large-scale surveys to help understand the structure of educational, economic, and occupational stratification in America. In an analysis of black and white economic success as of 1962, Duncan found that the gap in the adult income of blacks and whites in the early 1960s was not explained by factors related to family background, such as parental economic resources, education, or occupations. If it was not the lingering impact of past disadvantages that was driving present-day racial inequality, Duncan reasoned, then it must be something about race itself—or, more specifically, how race is treated in American society. He argued that persistent racial discrimination was responsible for the lingering gaps between the economic status of whites and blacks. Ironically, this led Duncan to a hopeful vision for the future, a vision based on the idea that if discrimination were eliminated then racial inequality would wither away over time. He wrote, "If we could eliminate the inheritance of race, in the sense of the exposure to discrimination experienced by Negroes, the inheritance of poverty in this group would take care of itself."[3]

Much of the data from the late 1960s and the early 1970s supported Duncan's vision, suggesting that expansions of civil rights were in fact leading to high levels of upward mobility among African Americans. But four decades later, a group of recent studies have updated Duncan's work, and what these studies have found is startling. Examining the relationship between race and economic mobility, the new evidence is surprisingly similar to the old evidence that Duncan produced. Most of the recent studies use the same survey that I have drawn on throughout this book, the Panel Study of Income Dynamics (PSID), and have tracked the economic fortunes of children who were raised during or after the civil rights era.[4] Analyzing the economic status of consecutive generations of family members, a consistent finding has emerged from this research: African Americans in the "second generation" of the PSID have much lower family income than whites in the second generation, even after accounting for their parents' income. Put differently, even if we look at black and white children raised in families with similar economic status, we find that the black children have lower—in fact, substantially lower—income as adults.

This picture is quite different from what Duncan imagined forty years ago, and it leads to a challenging question: why has the first generation that should have been able to take advantage of expanded civil rights made virtually no progress toward racial equality in the economic sphere? The central hypothesis guiding this chapter, and the chapter that follows, is that the unique ecological location of African Americans in the most disadvantaged urban neighborhoods, over long periods of time, has played a central role in reproducing racial inequality across multiple dimensions.

The analyses in this part of the book assess this hypothesis by exploring the role that the inherited ghetto has played in perpetuating racial inequality in America. I begin by building on earlier results showing severe racial discrepancies in long-term exposure to disadvantaged neighborhoods and by examining what role the childhood neighborhood environment plays in influencing patterns of economic and social mobility among black and white Americans. In this chapter I assess whether neighborhood poverty during childhood helps to explain the "mobility gap" between black and white Americans; that is, the average difference in adult social and economic status between first- and second-generation whites and blacks *from similar families*.[5] In chapter 5 I go one step further and examine how the neighborhood environment in one generation may linger on to affect children's life chances in the next generation.

In each case, I find a striking pattern: the impact of a child's neighborhood environment is not instantaneous. Rather, the neighborhood environment structures the experiences and opportunities of children in ways that alter their trajectories, with consequences that persist over the individual life course and across generations.

Race and Economic Mobility

The concept of economic opportunity has always been central to American political discourse and American culture. The idea that every American has the chance to make it, to rise up from rags to riches, is fundamental to the American dream. It is the idea that underlies the story of American immigration, the idea that drove much of the push for civil rights. And it is an idea that is consistent with Americans' conception of fairness—as long as there is widespread opportunity for advancement, Americans are generally content with high levels of inequality.[6]

But what do we mean when we talk about economic opportunity? Because the very idea can be interpreted in so many different ways, it is perhaps more useful to consider what we study when we analyze economic opportunity.[7] To assess the degree of economic mobility in a society, the most common approach is to measure a family's economic status in one generation, measure it in the next generation, and compare the two. This simple approach produces an intuitive answer as to how mobile a society is. If parents and their children have very similar economic status in adulthood, on average, it means that the children of the rich tend to stay rich and the children of the poor tend to stay poor. The society can then be characterized as one that has relatively low levels of economic mobility. If the economic status of children is only loosely related to that of their parents, it means that the children of the poor have a chance to become rich and the children of the rich sometimes become poor. The society can then be characterized as more open, with more opportunity for economic mobility.

The recent literature on economic mobility is dominated by this type of analysis, where income or earnings is measured in consecutive generations and the strength of the relationship between the economic status of parents and children is used to characterize the degree of economic mobility in the society. As it turns out, this method is not quite as straightforward as it seems, as there are several complicating factors that make it difficult to capture just how mobile a society is. The most notable factor is the quality of the data source. Early studies of economic and social mobility used data on families' economic status that often did not measure income well, or did not measure it among a representative sample of American families.[8] The conclusions from this early research were quite optimistic—the consensus view based on the early studies was that America is a remarkably mobile society, a meritocracy that differs in fundamental ways from the western European nations characterized by patronage and rigid class structures.[9]

As the years passed, better data sources became available to measure economic mobility, and assessments of the degree of opportunity in America began to look less rosy. In 1992, Gary Solon published a seminal paper in the *American Economic Review* pointing out that if parents' economic status is measured poorly—that is, if there is a nontrivial amount of error in the measurement of individuals' income or earnings—then estimates of intergenerational mobility will be severely biased and will lead to erroneous conclusions about the degree of mobility in a society.[10] Solon used newly available data from the PSID to measure parents' and children's income over several years, which greatly reduced the amount of error in the measures of income in each generation and thus produced much less biased estimates of economic mobility. What he found was surprising—America has much lower levels of economic mobility than previous estimates had suggested, meaning the rich tend to stay rich and the poor tend to stay poor at much higher rates than previously thought. Subsequent research has gone further and shown that even Solon's estimates were likely biased in favor of high mobility.[11] Even more surprising, the best research available indicates that the United States has less economic mobility than other industrial nations with comparable data.[12] The conclusion from this research, which has slowly made its way from the academic journals to the scholarly think tanks and to Washington, is that the ideal of America as the land of equal opportunity is simply not supported by the evidence.

Along with the consensus that mobility is much less prevalent than previously thought is the recognition that it is essential to understand the *processes* by which parents' economic status is passed on to their children. This turn toward process is motivated, first, by the idea that certain mechanisms producing intergenerational similarities in economic status are consistent with Americans' conceptions of fairness and "equal opportunity" (such as parents' attempts to instill a work ethic in their children), while others are less compatible with the conception of a society whose rewards are open to all (such as higher-quality public schooling available to well-off children).[13] In other words, most Americans don't mind the fact that some children have a leg up on their peers because they have particularly devoted parents. But most Americans would find it troublesome if the child's leg up is due to the quality of the public schools he attends relative to his less affluent peers.

A second, related motivation for turning toward the process of mobility is the idea that this process may work differently for different segments of the population. If patterns of mobility differ depending on one's location in the income distribution, or if mobility differs for blacks and whites, then these differences are essential to our understanding of how our society functions and how opportunity is distributed across the population. To provide another example, most Americans would likely be displeased if there was a great deal of opportunity to become rich among upper-income Americans but little opportunity among middle- and lower-income Americans. In the same way, those who believe in equal opportunity would likely object to a system where poor whites have a decent chance of moving up to the middle class but poor blacks have virtually no chance of doing so.

This last point brings us back to the issue of race and economic inequality. Much of the recent research on the persistence of economic status across generations does not consider the possibility that processes of mobility differ by race. The research from economist Tom Hertz is an exception. Hertz demonstrates in his research how estimates of economic mobility for the population as a whole may not apply to any single racial or ethnic group.[14] If one group has higher income than another over consecutive generations, and the strength of the correlation between parents' and children's income is similar for both groups, then the estimate of the intergenerational correlation in income for the population as a whole will be biased upward. This is the scenario that Hertz describes among whites and blacks in America. At every level of parental income, among children from poor and rich families, there is a gap between the adult incomes of blacks and whites. Stated in a more technical manner, the "expected mobility" of blacks (that is, the average difference between first- and second-generation family incomes) is always smaller than the expected mobility of whites.

While Hertz's research has been extremely important in documenting the existence of this racial mobility gap, less attention has been devoted to explaining why this gap exists. The research that has been done has examined a range of family characteristics that might be thought of as explanations for why black children end up with lower income or earnings than whites.[15] Similar to the findings of Duncan more than four decades ago, the major finding from this research is that family background does not explain much of the racial mobility gap. Once again, we are left to consider alternative explanations for why race continues to be so fundamental to understanding economic mobility in America. This chapter explores one such alternative explanation: the neighborhood environments in which children are raised.

The analyses that follow are guided by the hypothesis that the location of African Americans within America's most disadvantaged neighborhoods over long periods of time does not only make upward mobility less likely, but also places blacks at a distinct disadvantage when it comes to protecting gains made in social and economic status in one generation and transmitting these gains to the next generation. Although they haven't been explicitly tested, similar arguments appear frequently in the classic literature on urban poverty. Kenneth Clark described the debilitating weight of despair and anger among youth growing up in the "dark ghetto" of 1960s Harlem, Lee Rainwater described the social and economic isolation of residents in the projects of St. Louis in his book *Behind Ghetto Walls*, and in *Tally's Corner* Elliott Liebow described the hopelessness of the economic circumstances of black men, driven by the lack of opportunities for work that would allow them to support a family and maintain their dignity.[16] The common theme of these and numerous other classic studies of urban poverty is that barriers to economic mobility may be rooted in the unique economic and social milieu of the urban ghetto.

It is an idea that was reinvigorated by William Julius Wilson's research on social isolation in urban ghettos, as well as Mary Pattillo's extension of Wilson's ideas beyond the boundaries of poor urban neighborhoods and into the neighborhoods of middle-class blacks.[17] Pattillo in particular argues that blacks' middle-class status is particularly tenuous because of the unique spatial, economic, and social structure found in many black communities across American cities. Her ethnographic work on black middle-class neighborhoods in Chicago demonstrates how spatial proximity to extremely poor, disadvantaged areas of the city, and the rigid racial segregation of the city as a whole, combine to make it difficult for middle-class blacks to create separation from the problems of the ghetto, including poorly performing schools, gangs, drug markets, and violence.[18]

This ethnographic research is reinforced by numerous studies showing that blacks and whites of similar economic status live in very different residential environments, with blacks living in areas with higher crime rates, lower-quality schools, higher poverty rates, lower property values, and severe racial segregation.[19] Even if African Americans are able to make gains in economic or social status in one generation, they remain in social environments that are disadvantaged across multiple dimensions and that may make it more difficult to transmit advantages to the next generation. The question driving the analysis in this chapter is this: Do the social environments occupied by African Americans help to explain the racial mobility gap?

Research on Childhood Neighborhoods and Adult Economic Outcomes

The more general question to consider first is whether childhood neighborhood environments appear to have an influence on adult economic success;

this is a question that has been examined in numerous studies, many of which draw on data from the PSID. Linda Datcher was the first researcher to consider where families live in studying economic mobility.[20] Using data from the PSID linked to census data at the zip-code level, Datcher found that neighborhood economic and racial composition was almost as important as traditional measures of family background in explaining black/white gaps in economic mobility. This study was the first of several to incorporate measures of neighborhood conditions into models of economic mobility, and most such studies have found at least some association between neighborhood economic status during childhood and the individual's economic status as an adult. However, the association between childhood neighborhood conditions and adult economic outcomes varies widely depending on the specific neighborhood measures used in the analysis and the subpopulations examined. For instance, a study by Mary Corcoran and Terry Adams finds that high neighborhood poverty has a negative association with adult income and wages among white men but not black men; another study by Corcoran and colleagues finds an association between the prevalence of welfare receipt in a child's zip code and that child's adult earnings; and a third study by Thomas Vartanian finds strong effects of residence in extremely disadvantaged neighborhoods on adult economic outcomes.[21]

While one might conclude from this research that there is a relationship between neighborhoods and adult economic success, this conclusion becomes muddled when one considers a second group of studies that use data on siblings in the PSID. The advantage of the sibling studies is that they are able to adjust for everything that is shared by siblings, such as the quality of their parents or their similarities in genetic background, and then to assess whether any differences in the neighborhood environments of the siblings lead to different economic outcomes in adulthood. Among the studies that take this approach, studies by Aaronson and by Vartanian and Buck report significant effects of neighborhood conditions on adult economic outcomes, providing support for the idea that childhood neighborhoods have a causal effect on adult economic success.[22] However, another study by Plotnick and Hoffman analyzes a different sample and finds no evidence for neighborhood effects.[23]

While all of these findings are based on surveys of families followed over time, the most famous study of "neighborhood effects" on economic outcomes comes from a quasi-experiment conducted in Chicago in the 1970s—the Gautreaux Assisted Housing program. Gautreaux was a court-ordered desegregation program in which low-income Chicago residents (most of whom were in Chicago public housing) were provided housing subsidies and other forms of assistance to move out of segregated neighborhoods and into more racially and economically diverse neighborhoods across the metropolitan area.[24] Although the program was not a true experimental design and participants were not randomly selected, the residential destinations of individuals who volunteered for the program were largely determined by their position on a waiting list for housing, making it possible to compare the outcomes of participants who ended up in different types of neighborhoods and different types of communities.

I review the results from Gautreaux in detail in chapter 6; I mention it here because the remarkably positive findings from the program provided perhaps the most influential evidence in support of the idea that the neighborhood may be crucial to understanding economic inequality. Researchers studying Gautreaux focused their attention on families that were placed in apartments throughout the Chicago metropolitan area, including some of the city's most affluent suburbs, and compared these families to others who were placed in apartments located in segregated neighborhoods within the city. What they found was stunning. Not only did parents who were relocated to the suburbs experience substantial benefits arising from economic opportunities that were not available within Chicago's city limits, but the children in these "suburban" families started to show promising signs indicating future success. Children in families that moved to suburban apartments had substantially higher rates of high school completion, college attendance, and labor force participation than their counterparts who were assigned to apartments within Chicago.[25]

The results provided the first convincing quantitative evidence to support the idea that the problem of racial inequality may in fact be explained as a problem of the urban ghetto. As described in more detail in chapter 6, this evidence turned out to be somewhat less convincing than the early studies suggested, although most of the early conclusions from the research continue to be supported even in follow-up studies of Gautreaux families. Ignoring these details, major media outlets picked up on the story of Gautreaux, highlighting the remarkable stories of families whose lives had been transformed by the opportunity to leave Chicago's worst neighborhoods. Mobility out of the ghetto became the popular solution for resolving the problems of urban communities.

Even if we take the early results from Gautreaux at face value, however, the findings indicate only that moving out of the ghetto may improve the life chances of children. There is a broader question that is not addressed in the studies analyzing results from the Gautreaux program, or in other quantitative research on neighborhoods and economic mobility. It is a question that is motivated by the research that has been produced on race and economic mobility in the post civil rights era, which has found that blacks have been substantially more likely than whites to experience downward economic mobility and have lower rates of upward mobility.[26] It is a question that is motivated also by the findings presented in chapter 2 of this book, which shows that African American children raised in the civil rights era have "inherited" the nation's most disadvantaged neighborhoods from their parents.

The question is whether the persistence of racial inequality in America's urban neighborhoods may be a central explanation, perhaps the central explanation, for the persistence of racial inequality in American society—racial inequality in educational attainment, in the labor market, and in the accumulation of wealth. In other words, can the inherited ghetto help to explain why blacks have not achieved equality in the post civil rights era?

Economic Mobility among the Children of the Civil Rights Era

To explore this question I begin by documenting patterns of economic mobility for blacks and whites among the children of the civil rights era—specifically, black and white children born at some point from the middle of the 1950s through the beginning of the 1970s, a group that was raised during or just after the time when civil rights expanded rapidly for African Americans, and a group that might have been expected to benefit most directly from the changes occurring during this era.

Figure 4.1 describes basic patterns of economic mobility among this group of children by comparing their economic status, in adulthood, to the economic status of their parents, a generation earlier. I do so in two ways. The first approach is to assess whether black and white children have made any advancement within the income distribution relative to their parents. In each generation, I rank all families by their level of income and split the full distribution into centiles, or hundredths. If a parent's family income placed the family at the twenty-fifth percentile of the income distribution, for instance, and the child's adult income placed her at the twenty-sixth percentile or higher, the child would be considered upwardly mobile. If the child's income placed her at the twenty-fourth percentile or lower, she would be downwardly mobile. The first columns of figure 4.1 show the results from this approach, and reveal that a slight majority of black children are located at a higher position in the income distribution than their parents were, a generation earlier. Roughly half of white children occupy a higher position in the income distribution than their parents. These figures provide the first positive news from the chapter—if we consider any movement across the

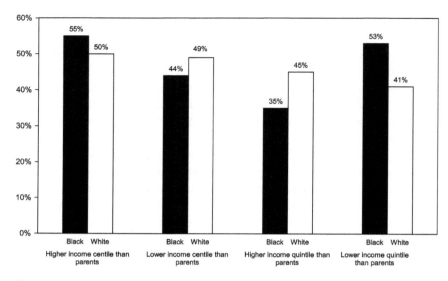

Figure 4.1. Intergenerational upward and downward economic mobility among blacks and whites. *Note:* The first two sets of columns are based on the portion of the sample that begins outside the highest centile and lowest centile, respectively; the second two sets of columns are based only on the portion of the sample that begins outside the highest quintile and lowest quintile, respectively.

income distribution, a slight majority of black children and half of white children of the civil rights era are doing slightly better than their parents. But this is where the good news ends.

The second approach to describing economic mobility is to assess the degree to which black and white children make substantial advances, or declines, in economic status—this analysis focuses only on substantively meaningful movement across the income distribution, rather than considering any change in position to represent economic mobility. To create the figures shown in the second set of columns in figure 4.1, the full distribution of income is broken up into quintiles, or fifths. The figure then shows the proportion of black and white children who advance into a higher quintile of the income distribution than their parents, and the proportion who move downward into a lower quintile of the income distribution. For instance, if a child was raised in a family that was in the poorest quintile, or the bottom 20 percent of the income distribution, and then that child moved up to the second poorest quintile as an adult, or even higher, that child would be characterized as having experienced upward mobility. If a child was raised in a family that was in the richest quintile, or the top 20 percent of the income distribution, and then that child moved downward into the second or third richest quintile, then that child would be characterized as having experienced downward mobility. The reader should note that figures showing upward mobility are calculated among families that begin in the bottom 80 percent of the income distribution, because families beginning in the top fifth of the distribution cannot move upward. Similarly, figures showing downward mobility are calculated among families beginning outside the poorest 20 percent of the income distribution.

When this type of substantive change in the economic position of children is the focus of the analysis, figures on upward and downward mobility reveal a more pessimistic story. About 35 percent of black children advance upward in the income distribution, compared to 45 percent of white children. More than half—53 percent—of black children move *downward* into a lower quintile of the income distribution than their parents, compared to 41 percent of whites.

Consistent with previous research on race and economic mobility, these figures present a startling story of a generation that has not made the progress toward racial equality that one might have anticipated at the peak of the civil rights movement. A majority of black families that begin outside the poorest quintile of the income distribution are not able to transmit this relatively advantaged position to their children; as a result, the children from these families are highly likely to move downward in the income distribution, reversing the American Dream of upward mobility with each passing generation.

Of course, progress toward racial equality is not captured entirely by income. In evaluating the progress African Americans have made relative to their parents, it is important to consider advances in schooling, in the labor market, and in the accumulation of assets. The analysis thus proceeds by moving beyond income and considering educational mobility and occupational mobility—later in the chapter, I consider accumulated wealth as well.

As the first set of columns in figure 4.2 indicate, this generation of African Americans has made more substantial advancement in education than it has in economic status. Roughly 55 percent of African Americans have completed more years of schooling than their parents, compared with 38 percent of whites. This impressive degree of upward educational mobility reflects the very low levels of education among the previous generation of African Americans, where the average amount of schooling was about eleven years. By contrast, whites in each generation average about thirteen

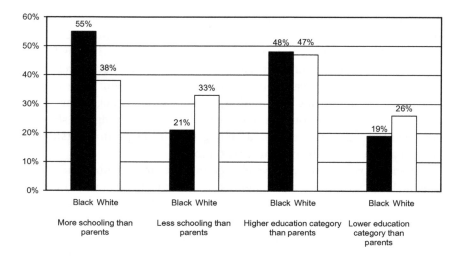

Figure 4.2. Intergenerational upward and downward educational mobility among blacks and whites. *Note:* The first two sets of columns are based on the portion of the sample that begins outside the highest centile and lowest centile, respectively; the second two columns are based only on the portion of the sample that begins outside the highest and lowest educational categories, respectively.

years of schooling, which explains why there has been less upward educational mobility among whites.

To examine more substantively meaningful advancements in schooling, I conducted an additional analysis assessing the degree to which blacks and whites moved into a higher category of educational attainment than their parents. This is done by classifying parents' and children's years of schooling into four categories—the first representing less than a high school diploma, the second representing only a high school diploma, the third representing more than a diploma but less than a four-year college degree, and the fourth representing at least a college degree, which includes any individuals who obtained more advanced schooling. Almost half of black and white children advanced into a higher category of educational attainment using this classification, and only a small fraction of whites and blacks obtained substantially less education than their parents. As we will see in later results shown below, these figures reflect the major advancement in educational attainment made by the children of the civil rights era—and particularly African American children.

As is true with schooling, a majority of African Americans have also made slight advances in the workplace, as shown in the first set of columns from figures 4.3 and 4.4. While one can think about what is a "good" or "bad" job in many different ways, I use a measure of "occupational status" here which reflects the credentials and the rewards provided to members of each occupation.[27] By this measure, high-status occupations are those in which the workers who hold the occupations are generally well educated and earn a high income, and low-status jobs are those which are held by less educated workers and workers that make relatively low income. A complementary measure of labor market success considers how much individuals are working by measuring the average annual hours of work. Together, these figures provide a portrait of the extent to which black and white children have advanced in the workplace relative to their parents.

From the first columns of figures 4.3 and 4.4, we see that more than 60 percent of African Americans have advanced into higher-status occupations than their parents, and 56 percent report working more hours per year than their parents. Among whites, roughly half have moved upward into higher-

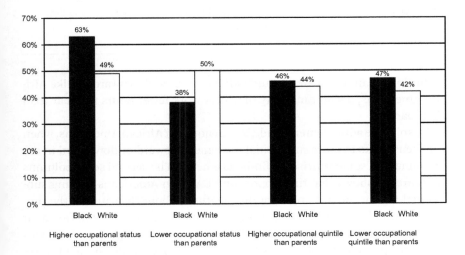

Figure 4.3. Intergenerational upward and downward occupational mobility among blacks and whites. *Note:* The first two sets of columns are based on the portion of the sample that begins outside the highest centile and lowest centile, respectively; the second two sets of columns are based only on the portion of the sample that begins outside the highest quintile and lowest quintile, respectively.

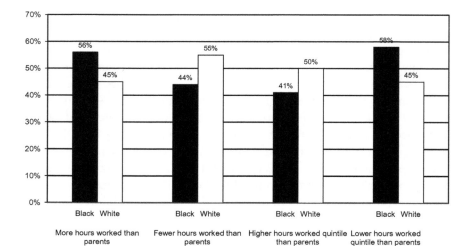

Figure 4.4. Intergenerational upward and downward employment mobility among blacks and whites. *Note:* The first two sets of columns are based on the portion of the sample that begins outside the highest centile and lowest centile, respectively; the second two sets of columns are based only on the portion of the sample that begins outside the highest quintile and lowest quintile, respectively.

status jobs than their parents, and half have moved downward; unlike African Americans, a slight majority of whites work fewer hours per year than their parents.

Despite the advancement made by a majority of African Americans, when the focus shifts to more substantial movement upward or downward in the labor market, some worrisome findings emerge. The second set of columns in figure 4.3 shows that the proportion of African Americans making substantial advancement in occupational status is about the same as the proportion who have experienced substantial downward mobility in the labor market. More troubling, the second set of columns in figure 4.4 indicates that only 41 percent of African Americans have made substantial advancement in annual hours worked, while 58 percent have made substantial declines in hours worked.

In characterizing the progress of African Americans raised in the civil rights era, the story that emerges from this initial set of figures is complex, but several preliminary conclusions can be made. The first conclusion is that there has been widespread, but marginal, advancement in education, income, and labor market success. A majority of African Americans are doing better than their parents across all of these dimensions. A second conclusion is that African Americans have made substantial advancements in education, and only a small percentage have obtained less schooling than their parents. This finding is driven in part by the very low levels of education obtained by the prior generation of African Americans, but it is good news nonetheless. The third conclusion is that relatively advantaged African Americans have experienced extremely high levels of downward economic mobility, and a large majority of African Americans work substantially fewer hours per year than their parents. These results suggest that African Americans are less able to transmit economic success across generations, a pattern that was identified by Duncan in the late 1960s and which remains the case in the current generation.

Neighborhoods and the Black-White Mobility Gap

Whereas the previous analysis describes differences in the degree of upward and downward mobility by race, the analysis that follows attempts to explain, to the extent possible, these racial differences. One way to capture what the economist Tom Hertz refers to as "the racial mobility gap" is to compare the adult outcomes of black and white children who were raised in similar families in order to assess how well these children fare if they come from a similar family environment. In statistical terms, one can evaluate the size of the mobility gap by controlling for childhood family background and then assessing whether there remains any difference between the adult outcomes of black and white children. Figure 4.5 displays the results from such an analysis, focusing first on the racial mobility gap in family income.[28]

In this figure the first column shows the gap between the adult incomes of blacks and whites without considering anything about their childhoods or their family backgrounds. As is plainly visible from this first column, black children have substantially lower family income in adulthood than white children, on average. The size of the column reflects the magnitude of this racial gap—in this case, blacks have family income that is roughly 47 percent lower than whites.

This first column reflects the degree of racial inequality that still exists among the children of the civil rights era. But one could argue that simply comparing the incomes of black children to white children is misleading, because whites were much more likely to be raised in families with relatively high social and economic status—or SES, the acronym used in much of the social science literature. A more appropriate comparison might be to consider the adult incomes of blacks and whites who were raised in families with similar income, whose parents had similar levels of education and

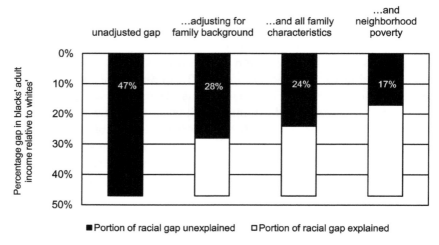

Figure 4.5. Decomposing the gap in adult family income between blacks and whites.

worked in similar types of jobs. This comparison is shown in the second column of figure 4.5. As expected, after adjusting for parental SES there is a much smaller racial gap in family income, indicating that some of the racial inequality that is present in the children of the civil rights era is due to differences in the social and economic statuses of the families in which they were raised. Yet even among blacks and whites raised in families with similar SES, blacks continue to have 28 percent lower family income in adulthood.

Perhaps it is not so much the standard measures of social and economic status that explain black/white gaps, but other aspects of families like the parents' marital status, whether the family receives welfare, or whether the child was raised in a public housing project. The third column in the graph shows the black/white gap after statistically adjusting for these and other dimensions of the family environment. The black/white gap narrows only slightly in this model—adjusting for all of the different dimensions of family life, blacks have about 24 percent lower family income in adulthood than comparable whites.

To summarize these initial results, the first three columns of figure 4.5 indicate that if we were to compare two children, one black and one white, who were raised in the 1970s by families that look extremely similar in every observable way, the black child could expect to have about 24 percent lower annual income as an adult. How do we explain this stark gap in the economic fortunes of the two children? If the core hypothesis of this chapter is correct, it may be that looking purely at characteristics of the children's families is not sufficient for understanding differences in the experiences of black and white children raised in this period. Despite the similarities in their family environments, their neighborhood environments may be entirely different, leading to differences in school quality, in the types of peers and role models surrounding the children, in resources available to them, and in the economic opportunities present as they move into adulthood.

The last column of the figure assesses this possibility by considering neighborhood poverty in addition to the family characteristics already present in the analysis. The results provide support for the idea that neighborhoods are an important piece of an explanation for the black/white mobility gap; but it is only partial support. After considering all dimensions of family life that are possible to capture in the PSID data, neighborhood poverty has a strong association with adult income and explains a substantial portion—more than a quarter—of the remaining black/white gap in mobility. It does not explain the entire gap, however. Black children from similar families and raised in similar neighborhoods still have about 17 percent lower family income than whites in adulthood.

Neighborhood environments clearly do not provide a complete explanation for the black/white gap in economic mobility. Still, the reduction in the size of the black/white income gap from the third to the fourth column suggests that in focusing purely on family background researchers studying race and economic mobility have overlooked a crucial dimension of children's developmental contexts, their neighborhoods. Other than parents' own income, the measure of neighborhood poverty emerges as the single most important explanation for why blacks and white children raised in this period continue to have such disparate economic status as adults.

While neighborhood poverty is an important part of the story of race and economic mobility, it is unclear whether the same findings emerge when we consider racial inequality in educational mobility, occupational mobility, or the accumulation of assets. The remainder of the chapter considers the role that neighborhoods play in helping to explain racial gaps along each of these dimensions, beginning with educational attainment.

Educational Mobility

There is at least suggestive evidence that the neighborhood environment may be an important factor in explaining why the schooling opportunities, the occupational trajectories, and the chance to accumulate wealth among whites and blacks are so different. I have discussed this evidence in regard to the relationship between childhood neighborhoods and adult economic success, but what does the evidence tell us about educational outcomes? Among the numerous observational studies that find an association between neighborhood conditions and educational outcomes,[29] David Harding's study of the effect of neighborhood poverty on high school dropout comes closest to addressing the primary concern of the current study, which is the relationship between childhood neighborhood poverty and later educational attainment. Using data from the PSID and a matching analysis that compares the educational outcomes of children who look extremely similar in every aspect of their lives other than their neighborhood, Harding estimates that living in a high-poverty neighborhood during adolescence doubles the likelihood that a child will drop out of high school relative to living in a low-poverty neighborhood among both blacks and whites.[30] This finding is broadly consistent with the results found in the Gautreaux program, which showed substantial improvements in educational attainment and college attendance among families in Chicago public housing that were relocated to the city's suburbs.[31]

The primary conclusion from this work is that the neighborhood environment may well have an impact on educational attainment, but this literature does not directly assess the extent to which neighborhoods help to explain racial disparities in educational mobility. To begin the analysis, it is first useful to consider how much of a gap there is to explain. The first column in Figure 4.6 provides a sense of the magnitude of the racial disparity in educational attainment, showing that black children get about .74 fewer years of schooling than whites, without considering anything about children's background or neighborhoods. Despite the progress that African Americans have made in the sphere of education, this figure indicates that there is still a substantial amount of racial inequality in educational attainment.

The second column presents a comparison of white and black children raised in families with similar educational background, occupational status, and income. Surprisingly, when I adjust for these aspects of family background, the racial gap in educational attainment is reversed—as the second column in the figure shows, African American children obtain *more* schooling than white children with similar family backgrounds. The reverse racial gap widens when I adjust for additional characteristics of children's families, and it widens further when I adjust for neighborhood poverty during childhood. In the final model, I find that blacks obtain about .55 more years of schooling than whites raised in similar families and in similar neighborhoods.

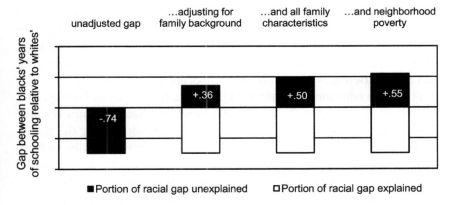

Figure 4.6. Decomposing the gap in educational attainment between blacks and whites.

Although surprising, the reverse racial gap in education has appeared in several studies covering a wide time span. [32] As noted earlier, this finding is partially driven by the very low levels of education obtained by the prior generation of African American adults, and evidence from other research suggests that an additional factor is the differences in schooling among low-SES black and white children. Unlike the other dimensions of social and economic status, then, blacks are actually advantaged in terms of educational attainment relative to whites of similar background. Further, the neighborhood environment does not appear nearly as important to educational mobility as it does to economic mobility.

Employment and Occupational Mobility

Next let us turn to the issue of race and employment, a topic that has occupied a central place in the sociological literature on status attainment and social mobility. [33] The majority of research in this area focuses on describing how patterns of mobility differ for blacks and whites, and how black mobility changed with the expansion of civil rights and economic opportunity in the civil rights period. The literature has not delved deeply into the role that the social environments surrounding blacks and whites play in the process of mobility. There is, however, a strong theoretical connection between race, neighborhoods, and employment networks and opportunities. [34] In addition to the debate on the role that the spatial location of jobs plays in producing high rates of joblessness among central-city blacks, [35] theoretical models of racial and ethnic labor queues suggest that race and ethnicity, and the employment networks of job seekers from different racial/ethnic groups, play an important role in shaping the distribution of employment opportunity within urban labor markets.[36] This research suggests a plausible link between the neighborhood environment, employment networks, and racial differences in employment and occupational mobility.

Similar to educational attainment, however, the empirical findings provide incomplete support for the idea that neighborhood environments help explain racial gaps in occupational mobility. Before describing the role of neighborhoods, again I begin the analysis of occupational mobility by highlighting the raw gap between blacks and whites in occupational status—as shown in the first column of figure 4.7. Without adjusting for family background, black children have about 22 percent lower occupational status, as adults, than whites. After adjusting for the family background of black and white children, however, this gap in occupational status disappears. Comparing black and white children from similar families, I find no difference in occupational status when the children reach adulthood. This finding does not change when I consider neighborhood poverty.

Patterns of occupational mobility thus differ from patterns of economic mobility and from patterns of educational mobility. Unlike the analysis of economic mobility, basic measures of family background fully account for the black/white gap in occupational mobility. Unlike the analysis of educational attainment, there is no evidence for a reverse racial gap in occupational status. But the broader point, when considering the analyses of education and occupation together, is that children's neighborhood

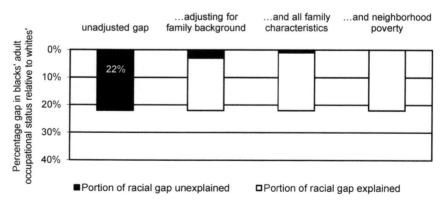

Figure 4.7. Decomposing the gap in adult occupational status between blacks and whites.

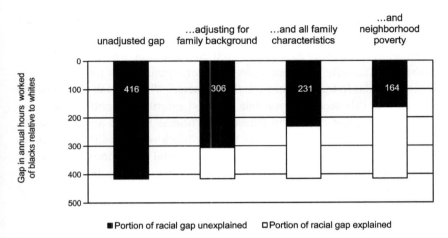

Gap in annual hours worked of blacks relative to whites

0
100   416   306   231   164
200
300
400
500

■ Portion of racial gap unexplained   □ Portion of racial gap explained

Figure 4.8. Decomposing the gap in annual hours worked between blacks and whites.

environments clearly do not play as important a role in explaining the black/ white gaps in education and occupational status as they do in explaining racial gaps in income.

This conclusion does not pertain to the second measure of success in the labor market, annual hours worked. As shown in the first column of figure 4.8, African American children report working more than four hundred fewer annual hours than whites. Considering the average worker spends roughly 1,800 hours per year working, this is an enormous deficit in employment. The gap between blacks' and whites' hours worked declines to about 300 hours after adjusting for parents' education, occupation, and income, and declines further to 231 hours after adjusting for other dimensions of family background. The last column of figure 4.8 shows that adjusting for neighborhood poverty reduces the remaining racial gap in employment by more than a quarter, from 231 hours to 164 hours. Again, neighborhood poverty during childhood does not explain the entire discrepancy between the annual hours worked of whites and blacks, but it emerges as an important part of the explanation.

Wealth

The pattern of results produced to this point suggests that the neighborhood environment may be most relevant to explaining racial inequality in economic status and in employment, and is less important for racial gaps in educational attainment or occupational status. I conclude the analysis by considering an alternative dimension of adult economic status—the accumulation of financial assets. Research on wealth and wealth mobility has grown substantially in recent years as higher quality data on wealth have become available from multiple U.S. data sets.[37] The relationship between race and wealth accumulation has received extensive attention from two major studies, one by Melvin Oliver and Thomas Shapiro and another by Dalton Conley, both of which show that the black/white wealth gap is more severe than virtually all other dimensions of social or economic status and has important consequences for racial inequality more broadly.[38] Oliver and Shapiro suggest that one primary mechanism by which the neighborhood may relate to racial inequality in wealth is through the different rates of appreciation of real estate in primarily white and primarily black communities. Considering the role that real estate plays as a primary component of wealth among Americans, the finding that housing in white neighborhoods tends to appreciate at a faster rate than in black communities could potentially lead to large racial gaps in wealth over long periods of time. While I do not test this specific hypothesis, the analysis provides a more general test of whether the neighborhood plays any role in explaining black/white gaps in the accumulation of assets.

Because the PSID only began asking questions about wealth in 1984, it is not possible to analyze intergenerational wealth mobility in the same way that I have done with the other outcomes in this chapter. However, it is possible to examine adult wealth among black and white children and to decompose the wealth gap in the same way that I have done for income, education, and so forth. The raw racial gap in wealth is clearly evident in the first column of figure 4.9—without adjusting for family background, black children have about 75 percent less wealth than whites as adults. The magnitude of this gap reflects the dramatic racial discrepancies in wealth described by both Oliver and Shapiro and by Conley. The second column in the figure indicates that only a portion of this inequality is explained by considering the family background of black and white children. After adjusting for parents' education, income, and occupation, black children still have 47 percent less wealth than whites. The size of the racial gap in wealth is reduced further if we compare black and white children whose parents are similar across all dimensions that are measured in the PSID survey, such as whether parents received welfare, owned their homes, and so forth. Even after accounting for everything we can measure about children's families, I find that African Americans still have 40 percent less wealth than comparable whites.

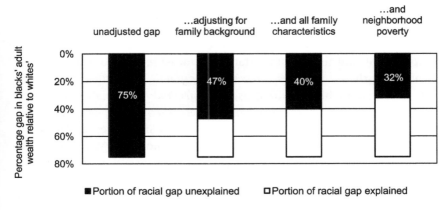

Figure 4.9. Decomposing the gap in adult wealth between blacks and whites.

The last specification assesses whether children's neighborhood environments help to explain the remaining racial gap in wealth. Similar to the analyses of income and hours worked, neighborhood poverty during childhood is a strong predictor of adult wealth and substantially reduces the black/white wealth gap, by about a fifth. Still, comparing black and white children who are raised in similar families and who live in similar neighborhoods, I continue to find that black children have, on average, about 32 percent less wealth than whites. While neighborhood poverty helps account for a substantial portion of the black/white wealth gap, much of this gap remains unexplained.

The Lingering Influence of Childhood Neighborhoods
The empirical results from this chapter suggest, first, that processes of economic, occupational, and educational mobility remain structured to a large extent by race. Across every dimension of social and economic status that I consider, African Americans raised during the civil rights era continue to trail behind whites. To anyone who has paid attention to patterns of inequality in American society, this is not surprising news. What is surprising is the role of different factors that help to explain this persistent racial inequality. Racial gaps in education and occupational status can be explained by pointing backward in time, and analyzing the types of family environments in which children were raised. If one were to compare a black and a white child raised in similar families and in similar neighborhoods, one would find, on

average that the two children end up with roughly equivalent types of jobs as adults, and the black child would end up with more education.

A very different pattern emerges when we consider racial inequality in employment and in economic status, as measured by both income and wealth. For these outcomes, aspects of the *family* environment play little role in explaining black/white gaps, while *neighborhood* conditions explain a substantial portion of the racial gap in each outcome. Adjusting for everything about a family that is measurable in the PSID survey, a black child raised in the 1970s could expect to work 234 fewer hours per year and to have 25 percent lower family income and 40 percent less wealth than a comparable white child upon reaching adulthood. But this is before considering the residential environments in which the two children were raised. When we make comparisons among children raised by similar families and in similar neighborhoods, the racial gaps in hours worked and income is reduced by more than a quarter, and the racial gap in wealth is reduced by about a fifth.

Neighborhood Disadvantage and Downward Mobility

Differences in the neighborhood environments of whites and blacks do not explain the entire racial gap in employment or economic mobility. But the role of the neighborhood is powerful, and it becomes even more powerful when one focuses on the *direction* of economic mobility—that is, the likelihood that a child moves upward or downward in the income or asset distribution.

As part of a broad initiative focusing on patterns of economic mobility in the United States, a recent study published by the Pew Charitable Trusts was among the first to document in detail the extraordinary racial gaps in the degree of downward mobility across generations. According to this report, almost half of black children whose parents were middle class fall downward to the bottom of the income distribution as adults, compared to only 16 percent of white children.[39] Having established the presence of this gap in downward mobility, officials at Pew asked me to carry out a study to investigate what role the neighborhood environment might play in explaining it.

What I found was somewhat surprising. While neighborhood poverty is often thought of as a barrier to upward mobility among blacks, I found only qualified support for this idea in the data. Neighborhood poverty during childhood was associated with less upward mobility, but it did not help to explain the differential rates of upward mobility among whites and blacks. Instead, the neighborhood environment emerged as a powerful explanation for why blacks are less likely than whites to maintain an advantaged position in the income distribution and to transmit this position across generations. The clearest finding to emerge in the analysis suggested that racial differences in children's neighborhood environments are an important part of the explanation for why blacks have experienced so much more downward economic mobility than whites, and this is especially true among children raised in middle-income and relatively affluent families.[40]

While less intuitive, the role of neighborhood conditions in explaining black/white gaps in downward mobility is consistent with the idea that the social environments surrounding African Americans may make it difficult for families to preserve their advantaged position in the income distribution and to transmit these advantages to their children. When white families advance in economic status, they are able to translate this economic advantage into spatial advantage by buying into communities that provide quality schools and healthy environments for children. An extensive research literature demonstrates that African Americans are not able to translate economic resources into spatial advantage to the same degree.[41] One consequence of this pattern is that middle-class status is tenuous for blacks, and downward mobility is more common as a result.

This observation is captured most vividly in Mary Pattillo's research within middle-class, predominantly black neighborhoods of Chicago. Pattillo describes a vibrant black community in which the majority of families in the community are working, where institutions such as the church are active parts of the community, where the community is organized and residents are actively engaged, where severe poverty is less prevalent and less concentrated than in the desolate Chicago neighborhoods described in William Julius Wilson's classic *The Truly Disadvantaged*.[42] Yet even in this community, Pattillo relays stories of youth who were, in her words, "jailed or killed along the way. The son of a police detective in jail for murder. The grandson of a teacher shot while visiting his girlfriend's house. The daughter of a park supervisor living with a drug dealer who would later be killed at a fast-food restaurant. These events were jarring, and all-too-frequent, discontinuities in the daily routine of Groveland residents."[43] Pattillo goes on to analyze the way that middle-class African Americans were caught between two worlds, one dominated by the ideals of education and advancement up the income ladder, the other dominated by the presence of gang activity, poorly functioning schools, and violence. This is the reality of middle-class status for many African American families, and it is a reality that is entirely different from that experienced by most middle-class whites in America.

It is a reality that is directly related to the unique residential environments of whites and blacks, and one that may have profound implications for understanding why there has been so little progress toward racial equality, at least in economic terms, since the civil rights era. Even if a white and a black child are raised by parents who have similar jobs, similar levels of education, and similar aspirations for their children, the rigid segregation of urban neighborhoods means that the black child will be raised in a residential environment with higher poverty, fewer resources, poorer schools, and more violence than that of the white child. These differences have an important impact on children's opportunities as they move toward adulthood. While the black child may receive the same amount of schooling as the white child, it is likely that he will attend schools of lower quality than his white counterpart because of the area in which he lives. While the black child's parents may have the same amount of income and the same education as the parents of the white child, neighborhood inequality means that the black child is likely to be surrounded by peers who have been raised by parents with less education and fewer resources to devote to their children, less cultural capital and social connections to draw upon. While the white child is likely to be surrounded by peers who aspire to go to college, the black child is more likely to be surrounded by peers who fear going to prison.[44]

In other words, even if the family environments of black and white children raised in the 1970s were similar, their residential environments were likely to be very different. This is the lingering influence of neighborhood inequality, and the findings in this chapter suggest that this lingering influence has been a primary mechanism for the reproduction of racial economic inequality in the post civil rights era.

This chapter thus represents an initial step toward the goal of understanding the long-term consequences of the inherited ghetto. The next chapter goes a step further and considers the impact of neighborhoods from one generation to the next.

Chapter 5 | **The Cross-Generational Legacy of Urban Disadvantage**

We have seen the impact that children's neighborhoods have on their economic trajectories as they move into adulthood. But there is no reason to think that this impact is limited to the individual who is raised in a poor neighborhood. One of the basic, yet crucial insights of sociologists who study the reproduction of inequality is that human lives are linked together in various complex ways, but most notably through the family unit. This idea of "linked lives"[1] means that the advantages or disadvantages accumulated over a lifetime—the human and cultural capital acquired, the physical and mental health status of an individual, the resources that an individual obtains and works to protect—all of these accumulated hardships and assets are not felt solely by the individual in adulthood, but instead are transmitted, at least in part, to the next generation. The products of accumulated advantages are used to secure the same advantages for children: to impart the same cultural capital, to purchase housing in areas that are safe and healthy and that offer quality learning environments and well-functioning institutions. The hardships accumulated over a lifetime may be passed on to children via the physical and mental health of parents or the diminished resources available for the purchase of a quality and safe home, neighborhood, and school environment.

It is in this sense that the disadvantages faced during childhood in one generation may linger on to affect the life chances of the next generation—that is, to form a legacy of disadvantage. How, specifically, might such intergenerational pathways of influence emerge? As we saw in the previous chapter, there is strong evidence that childhood neighborhoods affect adult outcomes, a finding that is supported in an enormous literature from sociology, economics, epidemiology, and other disciplines. While this literature is not perfect, if one accepts the idea that children's neighborhoods affect *any* dimension of adult social or economic status, health, or family life that is important for child rearing then there is the potential for cross-generational impacts to be present. For example, if the childhood neighborhood influences adult mental health, and if mental health is an important aspect of effective parenting, then there is the potential for an indirect pathway of influence linking one's childhood neighborhood to one's mental health as an adult to one's offspring's development. The number of potential pathways such as this one is almost limitless. If we think about all of the pathways collectively, then we begin to see the ways that neighborhood inequality may extend across generations, meaning disadvantages experienced in one generation may linger on to affect the life chances of the next generation.

This idea reinforces the core argument of the book, which is that to understand neighborhood inequality we must think in terms of generations, not single points in time or even single periods in an individual's life. It is not only that a child's neighborhood environment might affect her adult economic status, but that disadvantage (or advantage) experienced by a child is often a continuation of disadvantage experienced by her parents, and it is often disadvantage that is then passed on to her own children. To understand neighborhood inequality we have to consider the accumulation of disadvantage and advantage over generations.

The introductory chapters of the book described in detail the persistence of neighborhood inequality across generations—I now examine the consequences of cumulative, multigenerational disadvantage. While I have analyzed already the effects of spending childhood in disadvantaged environments, the central argument of this chapter is that there is something very different about neighborhood disadvantage that is experienced continuously over time and that is passed on from parents to children, across generations.

One way to investigate this claim is to examine the raw differences in the developmental outcomes of children from families that have lived in poor neighborhoods for consecutive generations, compared to those from families that have lived in poor neighborhoods for a single generation and those from families that have never lived in poor neighborhoods. The time frame of the PSID, which began in 1968, allows for an analysis of children from families that have been observed for two generations. A special supplement to the PSID, consisting of a set of questions asked of children, allows for a particularly interesting look at how children's developmental outcomes differ depending on the family's history of neighborhood environments.[2]

Consider first the comparisons in figure 5.1, which displays the average scores on two tests of cognitive skills, a reading/language test and an applied problems test, among children from four different groups of families. The tests, which are among the most widely used assessments of children's intelligence, are scaled to have a mean of about 100 in the population, meaning children who score above 100 are above average for their age group and

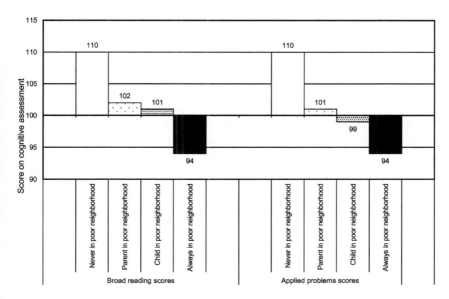

Figure 5.1. Raw average scores on tests of broad reading skills and applied problems skills, by neighborhood poverty status over two generations.

those below 100 are below average. Like a common IQ test, these tests are scaled to have a standard deviation of 15 points, which means that about 70 percent of the population scores within 15 points of the mean, somewhere between a score of 85 and 115, and 95 percent of the population scores within two standard deviations of the mean—that is, between a score of 70 and 130.

On the far left of figure 5.1 are scores on the "broad reading" test among children from families that never live in poor neighborhoods over the two generations in which we are able to observe them. These children have an average score of 110, meaning they are 10 points above the population average. Moving to the right, the graph then shows the average scores among children who have a parent that was raised in a high-poverty neighborhood—but the child him/herself was not raised in a poor neighborhood. These children have an average score of 102, about 8 points lower than the first group. This tells us that children raised by parents from poor neighborhoods score lower than those raised by parents who were not from poor neighborhoods, despite the fact that the children did not grow up in a poor environment. The third group consists of children who were themselves raised in poor neighborhoods, but whose parents were not raised in poor neighborhoods. These children have similar scores as the second group—they score 101, on average. From the scores of these two groups of children, it is difficult to know which is more important for children's cognitive development: the child's own environment or his parent's childhood environment. If one were to look only at these scores and guess, the conclusion would be that a parent's childhood neighborhood and the child's own neighborhood are equally important. By itself, this is an interesting observation, when one considers that virtually the entire literature estimating the impact of neighborhoods has focused exclusively on the child's environment.

More intriguing is the last group in the figure, the group comprising children from families that have lived in poor neighborhoods for *consecutive* generations. These are children who have spent their own childhoods in poor neighborhoods and who also have a parent who was raised in a poor neighborhood. As is clearly visible from the graph, these children score markedly lower than their peers in any of the three other groups, with an average score of 94 on the broad reading test. If we compare them to the group of children from families that never lived in poor neighborhoods, they score 16 points lower, a cognitive deficit that is comparable to missing somewhere between four and eight years of schooling. But an equally striking result emerges if we instead compare this group to children who also were exposed to neighborhood poverty in their own childhoods but whose parents were *not* raised in poor neighborhoods. If it is only the child's environment that matters, we might expect to see roughly equivalent test scores among children raised in equivalent environments. Instead, we see that the effects of neighborhood poverty may be amplified if it is experienced over generations—children exposed to neighborhood poverty over multiple generations score substantially lower than any other group, even children who were raised in similarly poor neighborhoods but whose parents were not raised in poverty. This finding provides the initial, suggestive evidence indicating that the consequences of life in poor neighborhoods may not be captured fully in a single generation.

Interestingly, the patterns present in figure 5.1 are not uniform as we look at other dimensions of children's lives. In some domains, it is the child's own neighborhood that appears to be most salient; in others it is the parent's neighborhood; and in others it is the combination of the environments in which the family members have lived across successive generations.

Consider the area of health, another important dimension of successful child development. Unlike the patterns present for cognitive ability, the parent's childhood neighborhood appears to matter little for her child's health.

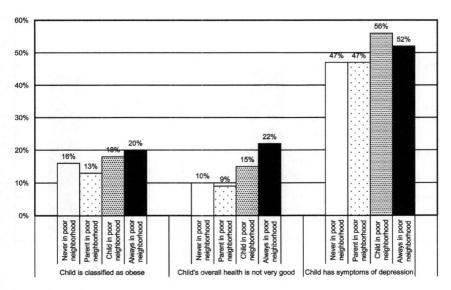

Figure 5.2. Children's obesity, overall poor health, and depression symptoms, by neighborhood poverty status over two generations.

Figure 5.2 presents the evidence, displaying rates of obesity, parent-reported poor health, and symptoms of depression among children in families who have lived in each type of neighborhood. While rates of obesity do not vary sharply by neighborhood poverty, children from families that have lived in poor neighborhoods over consecutive generations are the most likely to be obese. This group is also the most likely to report relatively poor overall health. However, children who have spent childhood in poor neighborhoods, but whose parents did not, are the most likely to report symptoms of depression. For all of the health measures, the general pattern is that the child's own environment and the cumulative experience of neighborhood poverty over consecutive generations are most strongly associated with physical or mental health problems.

The same patterns are present when children are asked about anxiety toward the future, as shown in figure 5.3. Children who are raised in poor neighborhoods, whether or not their parent was raised in a similarly poor neighborhood, are most worried about getting a good job when they reach adulthood and are most discouraged about their future. The immediate environment surrounding children seems more important than any lingering influence of the parent's childhood environment.

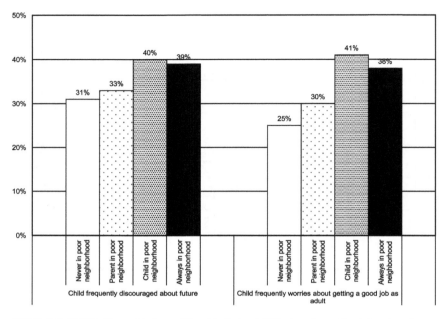

Figure 5.3. Children's anxiety toward the future, by neighborhood poverty status over two generations.

This is not true when we examine children's and parents' thoughts about how far the child will go in school. Here it is the parent's childhood neighborhood that seems to have the strongest relationship with aspirations and expectations about the child's educational attainment, as shown in figure 5.4. For instance, if we examine parents' expectations about whether their child will graduate from a four-year college, as shown in the second set of columns in the figure, we see that about half of parents who were raised in poor neighborhoods do not expect their child to earn a college degree, compared to just 33 percent of parents who are raising their children in poor neighborhoods but did not grow up in a poor neighborhood themselves. In this case, the experience of being raised in poverty seems to have lasting influence on the parent's conception of the possibilities for her child's education.

The influence of the parent's childhood neighborhood extends to the child's own expectations and aspirations about his or her educational future. Children who do not live in poor neighborhoods but are raised by parents who grew up in poor neighborhoods are most likely to neither aspire nor expect to graduate from a four-year college. More than half of children in this group say that they do not want or expect to earn a college degree, perhaps indicating that the child's own mindset is influenced more by the expectations of parents than by what he sees in his own environment.

These descriptive figures do not offer a perfectly clear picture of whether it is the parent's childhood environment or the child's own environment that matters more. They do suggest that in focusing exclusively on the child's neighborhood we may be missing something important about the lingering or cumulative influence of the residential environments that family members have experienced over time. What children see around them appears to be most salient in how much they worry about their own future, but it is the parent's childhood environment, experienced a generation earlier, that seems most important in influencing the child's aspirations and expectations about her own education. What is common to virtually all of the figures I have shown is that the cumulative experience of life in neighborhood poverty, over multiple generations, appears to be a very different experience than exposure to neighborhood poverty at a single point in time, or in a single generation. More than a fifth of children from families that have lived in poor neighborhoods over consecutive generations are obese or have

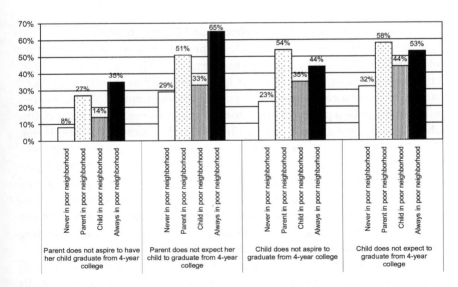

Figure 5.4. Aspirations and expectations for graduating college, by neighborhood poverty status over two generations.

poor health, more than a third are discouraged about their future or worry about getting a job, and more than half have no expectations about getting a college degree. These figures provide initial evidence suggesting that the cumulative experience of life in poor neighborhoods may matter most for many of the most important indicators of successful child development.

But there are other ways to interpret the findings. It could be that something about the families that find themselves in the nation's poorest neighborhoods for long periods of time leads to their children scoring lower on cognitive assessments or being less ambitious or less healthy than their peers. In other words, it could be that characteristics of the families themselves explain the patterns in these figures, rather than anything about the neighborhoods in which these families have lived.

The remainder of the chapter attempts to address this possibility, and it does so by utilizing new methods that are designed to isolate the cumulative impact of life in neighborhood poverty over multiple generations, as distinct from the impact of any family characteristics that might lead to worse child outcomes regardless of where a family has lived. Rather than examining a whole range of outcomes at once, I focus on a single outcome that developmentalists consider crucial for children's successful trajectories, and the outcome with which I began the chapter: cognitive skills.

The Connection between Neighborhoods and Cognitive Skills

Why focus on the child's cognitive development, as opposed to some other measure of the child's skills, opportunities, or life chances? For one thing, children's cognitive ability, whether it is interpreted as intelligence, IQ, or simply performance on tests of cognitive achievement, is almost universally shown to be a powerful predictor of future success. While most claims about intelligence and cognitive ability are hotly debated, this one is not. Cognitive skills are not the only predictor of future educational, economic, or social outcomes, but there is extensive evidence linking children's performance on cognitive assessments to a wide range of developmental and adult outcomes, including educational attainment, adult economic status, and health.[3] If the neighborhood environment influences the development of early cognitive skills, this relationship may be a key to understanding inequality across a number of domains.

Of course, a more basic assumption that needs to be justified is that cognitive skills are malleable; that is, that the development of cognitive skills is affected by the type of home, school, or neighborhood environment that surrounds us. While there is little doubt that cognitive ability has a genetic component, there is also widespread agreement that development is sensitive to children's social environments.[4] Children's cognitive skills have been shown to be associated with parents' education, alcohol use, mental health, social and economic status, and parenting practices and various aspects of the home environment.[5] These same characteristics of parents may affect the schooling experiences of children, which also influence children's cognitive development.[6]

For the true skeptics, those who believe that cognitive skills are purely a function of an inherent, fixed, genetic intelligence, we can point to experimental evidence that is very difficult to dispute. One such piece of evidence comes from a study of children who were given up by their birth families and were living in Romanian orphanages early in life. The institutions from which the study's sample was selected were notorious for their dull and regimented environments, which offered little stimulation or individual attention to children.[7] Although Romanian orphanages are a somewhat extreme context within which to study cognitive development, the severity of the institutional environment in which the children were being raised makes the evidence particularly powerful, as it reveals just how detrimental it is to be raised in a setting that offers little stimulation and minimal attention.

To carry out the experiment, researchers from Harvard's Medical School received permission from the Romanian government to follow a sample of infants in the orphanages and to randomly assign a group of these orphans to be placed with foster families who were screened by the researchers. The researchers then followed the sample over time and administered cognitive assessments to the children in the sample at age five.

The results from the study provide powerful evidence in support of the idea that the developing child requires a nurturing, enriching environment in order to experience cognitive growth. Children who were randomly assigned to foster parents scored substantially higher than those who remained in the orphanage, with the most pronounced differences found among children who had been fostered at the earliest ages. Further, the scores among children who remained in the orphanages throughout the study indicated borderline mental retardation, a shocking finding revealing the full extent to which the institutional environment in which the children were raised was stunting their cognitive development. While Romanian orphanages of the early 1990s may represent the most extreme form of environmental deprivation, the findings from the experiment are not limited to orphans in Bucharest. There are numerous intervention studies in the United States that are conducted in less severe settings, but that support the central findings from the Bucharest Study. These studies demonstrate very clearly that providing enriched and nurturing environments for children is crucial to their cognitive development.[8]

Still, most of this research assesses the effects of a change in the home or school environment on cognitive development—what do we know about the effects of the neighborhood environment in particular? In the abstract, there are several ways in which children's residential environments may influence their cognitive development, including the presence or absence of environmental toxins such as lead in the home, the soil, or the air, the degree and character of interpersonal verbal interactions within disadvantaged or violent neighborhoods, the quality of the schooling environment (which is in part determined by one's neighborhood), and the quality of parent/child interactions within the home, which may be affected by the surrounding environment.[9] These are all plausible links between neighborhood inequality and cognitive outcomes. Despite these theoretical connections, the research assessing the relationship between neighborhoods and children's cognitive development has produced conflicting results.

One set of studies is based on data from the Moving to Opportunity (MTO) social experiment, in which low-income families in public housing were randomly offered vouchers that allowed them to move to low-poverty neighborhoods. One analysis pooled data from all five cities in the MTO experiment and found that moving to low-poverty neighborhoods had null effects on cognitive test scores, with the exception of a positive effect on the reading scores of African Americans.[10] However, subsequent re-analysis of the same data suggests a more complicated story. In the two cities where families lived in the most severely disadvantaged neighborhoods, Chicago and Baltimore, the impact of moving to a new, lower-poverty neighborhood was substantial.[11] The strong impact found in the Chicago site of MTO is consistent with another recent study of families who were offered housing vouchers through a lottery system within Chicago's public housing waiting list,[12] reinforcing the possibility that moving to a new neighborhood may have large impacts on children's cognitive test scores if it occurs in cities like Chicago, which feature some of the poorest, most violent and racially segregated neighborhoods in the nation. This evidence is examined in more depth in chapter 6.

There is a broader issue to consider when evaluating and attempting to synthesize the results from studies of families that move from one neighborhood to another, however. In these studies, experimental or not, the very design of the study and the experimental "treatment" under study do not provide any information about the impact of long-term, or multigenerational, exposure to disadvantaged environments. In assessing the effect of a point-in-time move to a new neighborhood, for instance, the Moving to Opportunity experiment does not consider the possibility that the neighborhoods experienced at earlier points in time have a lingering influence on family members. For instance, it is highly likely that caregivers in families residing in public housing have lived in similarly poor neighborhoods throughout their entire lives. Growing up in an impoverished community is likely to have influenced the quality of a mother's school experience, which may have influenced the options available to her in the labor market, which may have affected her income, which may have affected the quality of the home environment in which she raises her own child, which ultimately may have affected the cognitive development of the child. In assessing the impact of a move to a new environment, we must make the implicit assumption that an abrupt change in environment has the potential to overturn, or at least disrupt, this lifetime of disadvantages that have accumulated over time. If we think in terms of generations, then the limits of residential mobility experiments in revealing how the neighborhood may alter the life chances of individuals and families become clearer.

Whereas the goal of research from residential mobility experiments is to identify the impact of a point-in-time change in the environment, the goal of this chapter is to identify the impact of living in the nation's most disadvantaged neighborhoods over two generations of a family. This is a challenging task.

The most common way to assess the relationship between neighborhood characteristics and children's cognitive ability is to use observational data collected from sample surveys, but this approach presents several additional complications that make it difficult to identify the cumulative impact of the neighborhood environment. The studies that are based on survey data typically show statistically significant associations between neighborhood socioeconomic composition and cognitive test scores, after controlling for various measures of family socioeconomic status and demographic characteristics.[13] However, the strength of the relationship often is found to vary by age and to be substantively weak, leading some to question the importance of neighborhoods for children's cognitive development.

But the key problem with many of these studies, from the perspective of this book, is that they preclude the possibility of multigenerational effects by controlling for aspects of a child's family background that may be influenced by a parent's own neighborhood during childhood. For instance, a researcher may examine the association between a child's neighborhood characteristics and her cognitive ability while controlling for the family's income, marital status, and health. This approach is problematic, because it ignores the possibility that parents' childhood neighborhoods affect these aspects of their adult lives. For instance, if a parent's childhood neighborhood influences her adult income—and, as we saw in the previous chapter, there is good evidence suggesting this to be the case—then controlling for family income will "block" the indirect relationship between the parent's childhood neighborhood and her child's cognitive ability, a generation later. In other words, this approach would reveal only the portion of the impact of the parent's childhood neighborhood that does not run through her own income as an adult, leading to an underestimate of the total impact of the parent's childhood neighborhood.

To attempt to identify the cumulative impact of neighborhoods on children's cognitive development is thus a methodological problem as well as a theoretical problem. The methodological problem is one that arises in any scenario in which important factors like family income are potentially influenced by experiences at an earlier time point—or in an earlier generation. Instead of traditional regression models, recent research I have conducted with sociologist Felix Elwert draws on newly developed methods from biostatistics that were designed to generate unbiased effects in exactly this type of situation.[14]

Although the methods are complicated, they are designed to facilitate a relatively simple set of results that are easy to interpret. To understand the set of results that I will present below, first imagine an experiment—in truth, it is an experiment that would be difficult or impossible to carry out, which is why it's necessary to use statistical methods instead of experimental methods to try to produce the same results. In this experiment, which we'll imagine began in the 1970s, a group of black and white families with children are selected from across the country. Each of these families flips a coin. Those who flip "heads" are assigned to live and raise their children in poor neighborhoods—which I will define as neighborhoods with at least a 20 percent poverty rate. Those who flip "tails" are assigned to live and raise their children in nonpoor neighborhoods, meaning neighborhoods with less than 20 percent poverty. This is the first part of our imagined experiment.

Now fast forward in time twenty-five or so years later, to the mid-1990s, when the second round of the experiment takes place. The children of our original families are now grown and are raising their own children. Once again, we ask each of these families, whom we have followed over time, to flip a coin. And again, those who flip "heads" are assigned to live and raise their children in poor neighborhoods, and those who flip "tails" are assigned to live and raise their children in nonpoor neighborhoods. After continuing to follow the families for several years following the second coin flip, we then travel to the homes of these families and ask their children, the second generation of the experiment, to complete two assessments of cognitive skills. Having tracked the families for several decades, over two generations, we are now ready to examine the results of the experiment.

How do the children in families that have always lived in nonpoor neighborhoods score on these tests of cognitive skills? Do their scores differ from children whose parents were raised in poor neighborhoods, but who themselves were not? What about the children from families that, by virtue of two coin flips, have lived in poor neighborhoods continuously for two generations?

The methods that we utilize are designed to reproduce this exact experiment and to allow us to estimate the answers to all of these questions.[15] The main results from the analysis are shown in figure 5.5. This figure is identical to the first figure of the chapter, figure 5.1, except that instead of presenting "raw" average scores for the four groups of children, figure 5.5 presents "adjusted" scores for all four groups. These adjusted scores are designed to reflect the score that the children in each group would achieve if we had conducted the experiment described above. That is, if children were randomly assigned to live in poor neighborhoods or nonpoor neighborhoods over consecutive generations, how would these different groups score on tests of cognitive skill?

First considering children's scores on tests of reading and language ability (the left side of the figure), the first column shows that children from families that never live in poor neighborhoods over the two generations score about six points higher than the national average, with an average score of 106. If the family lived in a poor neighborhood in the first generation but not the second, children scored about 101 on average, five points lower than the first group. Children from families that lived in poor neighborhoods in the second generation, but not the first, scored about the same as those that only lived in poor neighborhoods in the first generation. The average score for this third group is 102. Lastly, we have children from families that lived in poor neighborhoods in both generations. These children scored substantially lower than any of the other groups, with average scores of about 97, nine points below the group of children from families that never lived in poor neighborhoods. This is evidence for an enormous cognitive deficit, and it is a deficit that is due entirely to living in neighborhood poverty over consecutive generations.

The pattern of results for the second test of applied problems is somewhat different—results are shown on the right side of figure 5.5. With this

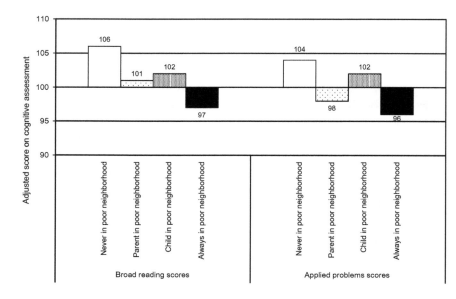

Figure 5.5. Statistically adjusted scores on tests of broad reading skills and applied problems skills, by neighborhood poverty status over two generations.

test, the impact of neighborhood poverty is even more pronounced and has a substantial, lasting influence on children's cognitive skill. Children from families that never lived in poor neighborhoods again score the highest, with average scores of 104. But the second group, children from families that lived in poor neighborhoods only in the first generation, scores substantially lower. The average score for this group of children is 98, six points lower than the first group. These children also scored much lower than children from families that only lived in poor neighborhoods in the second generation of the experiment, who score 102 on average. And finally, children in families that live in poor neighborhoods over consecutive generations have an average score of 96, lower than any of the other groups.

Considering the overall patterns present in figure 5.5, two results stand out. First, while research examining how neighborhoods affect children's outcomes has focused exclusively on the child's own environment, there is very strong evidence suggesting that the parent's childhood neighborhood, experienced a generation earlier, is at least as important to the development of cognitive skills—and in the case of the applied problems assessment, the evidence suggests the parent's environment during childhood may be more important than the child's own environment. Second, the multigenerational impact of neighborhood poverty is substantial. Living in poor neighborhoods over two consecutive generations reduces children's cognitive skills by roughly eight or nine points on the standard IQ scale, or slightly more than one half of a standard deviation.

To provide some perspective on the magnitude of this estimated effect, it may help to consider some estimated effects of other factors that are thought to be related to intelligence or cognitive ability. For example, in 2007 a study was published showing that firstborn children had higher IQs than their second-born siblings.[16] The study received an enormous amount of attention in the press and scrutiny in the academic world, as it purported to show strong evidence that firstborn children were smarter than their siblings. With all of this attention, the magnitude of the estimated difference between firstborn children and their siblings was about three points on the same scale that I am using for the current analysis. The cumulative impact of neighborhood poverty is about three times as large as the "firstborn" effect.

Another, perhaps more relevant example is the effect that schooling has on children's cognitive ability. After considering the literature on this subject, Christopher Winship and Sanders Korenman concluded that a year of schooling improves children's cognitive ability by somewhere between two and four points.[17] This means that the effect of being raised in a family that lives in a poor neighborhood over two consecutive generations is roughly equivalent to missing two to four years of schooling.

The Legacy of Disadvantage

The magnitude of the effects of multigenerational neighborhood poverty is striking. But just as important as the size of the effects is their meaning. If nothing else, this analysis demonstrates that the full impact of neighborhood inequality cannot be captured by looking at a single point in a child's life or even at a single generation in a family's history. In chapter 2, I showed that the large majority of African American families living in today's most disadvantaged residential areas are the same families that occupied the most disadvantaged neighborhoods in the 1970s, raising the possibility that we may be missing something important if we fail to consider the history of families' environments, or if we fail to think about neighborhood disadvantage as a multigenerational process. This chapter shows just how important that history can be.

Thinking about neighborhood environments in this way complicates the way we study and assess the impact of neighborhoods on individuals.

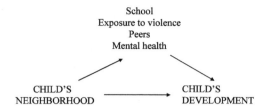

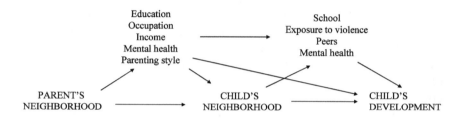

Figure 5.6. Moving from a single-generation model to a multigenerational model of neighborhood effects.

Instead of considering a relatively straightforward set of mechanisms by which a child's neighborhood might influence her developmental trajectory, a multigenerational perspective forces one to consider a more complicated and expansive set of pathways by which families' neighborhood environments may have a lingering influence that extends across generations.

This new, multigenerational conceptual model of neighborhood effects is represented in figure 5.6. The top panel of the figure shows a "standard," single-generation, model of how neighborhoods affect child development. Under this model, a child's neighborhood is linked with a given developmental outcome measure (such as cognitive skills) through, for instance, the child's peers, the quality of the school setting, or exposure to violence or environmental toxins. The extension to this model that I propose is shown in the second panel of the figure. In this multigenerational model, a child's neighborhood environment, in Generation One, is linked with a range of outcomes as she approaches adulthood, including her cognitive development, her educational attainment, her mental health, her occupational trajectory, her economic success, and even her potential romantic partners. These impacts of the childhood neighborhood environment do not disappear when the child enters adulthood, but linger on and affect various aspects of her adult life, including the family and neighborhood environment in which she raises her own children, her parenting style, and the resources she is able to devote to her children. In this way, the effect of the child's environment in Generation One persists over time, and affects the development of the child in Generation Two. From this perspective, disadvantages experienced by the child in Generation Two can be viewed as a legacy of disadvantage experienced in Generation One, with the potential for cumulative disadvantages to emerge over time.

The evidence presented in this chapter suggests that this type of multigenerational perspective is crucial to understanding the relationship between neighborhood environments and cognitive ability, one of the most important predictors of children's future educational and economic success. But the results from this chapter do more than contribute to our understanding about how neighborhoods may influence the development of cognitive skills. The findings also offer a new perspective that may influence how we interpret results from other studies that have been produced in this literature.

Consider, for instance, the experimental and quasi-experimental evidence available from residential mobility programs, including the Gautreaux program in Chicago, the Moving to Opportunity experiment, and other similar programs.[18] In all such programs, participants (typically low-income families living in public housing) are provided the chance to move to less disadvantaged environments, frequently in the same city or within the metropolitan area. Research using data from such programs takes advantage of the fact that the residential destinations of participating families are determined, at least in part, by factors outside of their own choosing. Because there is some random variation in the destinations of participating families, these studies provide more convincing evidence on the causal effect of a change in the neighborhood environment arising from a residential move.

By design, however, these studies do not capture the cumulative effects of a family's neighborhood environments experienced over time. The exclusive focus on a family's current neighborhood environment overlooks the possibility that the impact of neighborhood environments extends across generations. A change in a family's neighborhood may bring about an abrupt and radical change in the social environment surrounding children, but for many families—particularly African American families—this change is a short-term departure from a familial history of life in disadvantaged environments. The shift in context may improve the opportunities available to adults and children, the child's peers and school environment, and the parent's mental health, but it cannot undo the lingering influence of the parent's childhood environment. In short, a temporary change of scenery is unlikely to disrupt the effects of a family history of disadvantage.

This assessment should not be taken as a critique of the residential mobility literature, but as a lens with which to interpret the results from this strand of research. Evaluations of residential mobility programs provide powerful evidence for policy makers interested in designing programs to move families into areas that may be less violent than the worst public housing projects, areas that may offer better schools and safer streets. But these programs tell us little about the cumulative disadvantages facing a family living in America's poorest neighborhoods over long periods of time, unless the residential move creates a lasting change in the neighborhood environment that persists over multiple generations. Most of the more prominent programs, such as the Moving to Opportunity project, did not produce this type of change in families' environments. For example, the initial drops in neighborhood poverty among families in MTO's experimental group have faded quickly, due to moves back to high-poverty neighborhoods and rising poverty in the destination neighborhoods of experimental group families.[19] If the most powerful effects of neighborhoods stem from exposure in prior generations, as the evidence presented here indicates, it is perhaps not surprising that research from mobility programs has generated inconsistent and relatively small impacts.

Next, consider the extensive literature on neighborhood effects based on observational survey data. The most common analytic approach in this literature involves estimating neighborhood effects while controlling for a set of family background measures. A common claim made in reviews of these studies is that the family environment is more important for child development than the neighborhood environment.[20] A multigenerational framework suggests that such a conclusion is misleading. Aspects of family background that are linked with child developmental outcomes, such as parental income or education, are likely to be influenced by neighborhood conditions in the prior generation. In this sense, individuals and families *embody* neighborhood histories, and these histories can have consequences that extend across generations.

It is in this sense that I refer to a "legacy" of disadvantage. When we think about the reproduction of inequality, in income, education, occupations, wealth, or cognitive ability, it is not sufficient to focus on a single point in an individual's life or even on a single generation of a family. Instead, we must understand the history of disadvantages experienced over generations of family members. When one thinks about the past four decades in American urban history, what stands out most visibly are the persistent racial divides that are present in our nation's workplaces, its schools, and its neighborhoods. It is more difficult to follow the experiences of individual families that occupy these workplaces, schools, and neighborhoods. But if we focus on these families over long periods of time, we come to a different view of racial inequality. We come to see that it is the same families that have suffered the consequences of inequality for multiple generations. We come to see the cumulative impact of disadvantage, and it is severe.

I believe this perspective is essential to understanding American inequality. But where does this perspective leave us? How do we move forward, when the inequalities of the past continue to be felt in the present? It is to these questions that I turn in the final two chapters of the book. Despite the overwhelming challenges that emerge when we begin to think about inequality from a multigenerational perspective, the forthcoming chapters provide hopeful evidence to suggest that ending the cycle of intergenerational disadvantage is possible. The investments required to do so present the true challenge.

Chapter 6 | **Confronting the Inherited Ghetto**
An Empirical Perspective

In late August 2005, the nation was given a startling reminder of the problem of urban poverty. Hurricane Katrina hit New Orleans on the twenty-ninth of August, and while the storm itself was vicious, it wasn't until the winds had subsided and the sun beat down on the city that the true devastation began to come to light. When the levees protecting the city were breached, neighborhoods throughout the city were flooded, including some of the poorest and most segregated sections of New Orleans. Residents, stranded in their homes as water crept higher and higher, searched for ways to escape the rising water and reach higher ground. Those who were able to reach higher ground found themselves stranded once again, this time by an emergency response that took days to reach the city. While the plight of those who never made it out of their homes was not visible to the American public, the plight of those who survived to experience the aftermath of the storm was broadcast to the nation. The indelible images from news coverage in the aftermath of the storm showed stranded families throughout the neighborhoods of New Orleans, desperate hordes of people at the Superdome and the Convention Center, and the wreckage and debris that the storm left behind in the poorest sections of the city. Virtually all of the faces captured by the news cameras were black, and the visible state of desperation among the stranded victims of the storm suggested deep poverty.

In retrospect, one might wonder whether the media coverage of New Orleans's poor black population was, in part, a product of sensationalistic journalism. The evidence that has since been compiled suggests it was not. Sociologist John Logan analyzed where the damage from the storm was most severe, and found that the neighborhoods that sustained the most structural damage were, in fact, the city's poorest, most racially segregated neighborhoods.[1] The human toll from Katrina reinforced this finding. African Americans died in numbers that far surpassed their presence in the population, and the neighborhoods where death was most concentrated were overwhelmingly black.[2] But perhaps more important than the empirical observations about the victims of Katrina were the images of those stranded in New Orleans, which proved most salient to the American public. The scenes from New Orleans, which resembled the footage that Americans are used to seeing from war-torn or developing countries, stunned the American public and pushed the issue of ghetto poverty back into the political realm. Liberals focused their anger on the Bush administration's response, but even conservatives described the disaster as a breach of the social contract between the government and its citizens.[3]

As time passed and the images of the storm faded from the daily news and the public's consciousness, the problem of concentrated poverty remained and became one of the most prominent issues among Democratic candidates in the run-up to the 2008 primaries. John Edwards launched his presidential campaign from the backyard of a home that had been severely damaged by Katrina, and he presented a plan to subsidize one million vouchers that would allow families to move out of the nation's poorest neighborhoods. Candidate Barack Obama presented an alternative plan that would combine increased aid for community development with targeted, intensive investments in a small number of severely disadvantaged communities across the nation—his Promise Neighborhoods proposal. Academics and policy wonks took sides on the issue, some throwing their weight behind the residential mobility approach of Edwards, others backing the investment approach of Obama.[4]

And while these proposals were described as bold solutions and unveiled with grandiose rhetoric, unmentioned in the speeches and the policy briefs was the fact that the ideas put forth in 2008, and the debates surrounding them, were essentially the same ideas and debates that have resurfaced over and over again among scholars, activists, and policy makers with interests in addressing the problem of urban poverty. It is a discussion that is as old as America's ghettos themselves, and one that centers around a long-standing debate that pits against each other two views on urban poverty. One perspective focuses on discrimination in the housing market as the primary barrier to residential mobility and argues that when families are free to live where they choose, they will find opportunities. Mobility out of the ghetto is seen as the solution to urban poverty, from this perspective. The alternative perspective focuses on policies and trends that have led to the concentration of poverty, the deterioration of public schools, and the rise in violence in the most distressed urban neighborhoods, and argues that if these policies were reversed, and a sustained commitment to these neighborhoods was made, then residents of such neighborhoods could create their own opportunities. Investments in ghetto communities are seen as the solution to urban poverty, from this perspective.

They are sometimes presented as distinct, conflicting approaches to the problem of urban poverty—but at other times they are presented as complementary approaches, as exemplified in a passage from a speech delivered by Martin Luther King Jr. just months before his assassination and before the passage of the 1968 Fair Housing Act. In King's words: "We must constantly work toward the goal of a truly integrated society, while at the same time we enrich the ghetto. We must seek to enrich the ghetto immediately in the sense of improving housing conditions, improving the schools, . . . improving the economic conditions. At the same time we must be working to open the housing market so that there will be one housing market only. We must work on two levels. We should gradually move to disperse the ghetto, and immediately move to improve conditions within the ghetto."[5]

King's comments echo the conclusions published months earlier in the report of the Kerner Commission, which President Johnson established with the charge to uncover the causes of the riots that had swept through the nation's cities in the summer of 1967. In one of the most basic, yet poignant, conclusions made in the report, the members of the commission argued for a national commitment to urban ghettos that focused on "combining ghetto 'enrichment' with policies which will encourage Negro movement out of central city areas."[6]

More than a few years have passed since King's hopeful words and the Kerner Commission's ambitious proposals, but the two overarching approaches to urban poverty described in 1968 are not all that different from the approaches that have been put forth by dozens of urban scholars, policy makers, and politicians in the years that have since passed.[7] The tension between the two philosophies for ghetto policy has grown in the meantime, with momentum swinging from the "mobility" approach to the "investment" approach and back again, over and over.[8] This history of discourse on urban poverty is informative because it serves as a reminder that the problems of the urban ghetto and the debates on how to confront these problems are not new. They are debates that have taken place, and that have remained unresolved, for decades.

There are numerous reasons why the debates have never been resolved entirely, but one important reason is that the evidence base for each strategy has remained limited, incomplete, and often unconvincing. This chapter represents an attempt to synthesize that evidence and to generate new evidence that might fill in important gaps in the literature and inform this debate as it moves forward. In doing so I delve into the decades-long arguments about the correct approach to confront concentrated poverty, but I attempt to do so without dwelling on the ideological underpinnings of each strategy or the political constituencies that have lined up on one side or the other. Instead, I take an empirical approach and focus on the evidence that has been produced.[9] What do we know about the impact of residential mobility programs that move families out of the ghetto? What do we know about the impact of investments designed to transform neighborhoods from within? In each case, the evidence available is neither complete nor perfect, but it is informative nonetheless.

In particular, policy makers can turn to the results from multiple experimental and quasi-experimental residential mobility programs to inform potential proposals adopting the mobility approach.[10] I begin the chapter by reviewing the evidence from such programs that have been implemented since the 1970s.[11] While the results from these programs can be interpreted in multiple ways, a tentative conclusion from the evidence available suggests that a residential mobility approach is most likely to succeed if it is focused on families in the most severely disadvantaged, violent neighborhoods across the country, and if it provides families with a substantial and sustained change in environment. As we have seen, the majority of families living in today's poorest urban neighborhoods have resided in similar environments over multiple generations; it is unrealistic to think that the disadvantages faced by these families will be wiped away with a move that results in a marginal, temporary reduction in neighborhood poverty. There is at least some evidence, however, that more dramatic changes in the neighborhood environment may have lasting beneficial effects.

There is no equivalent evidence with which to evaluate the assumption that is implicit in the second approach: that a sustained effort to reduce concentrated poverty by investing in neighborhoods, rather than moving residents out, will have a positive impact on the residents of disadvantaged neighborhoods.[12] This is not to say that this approach has not been attempted. There are numerous examples of initiatives that have been conducted at various points in time to assess whether intensive investments can transform communities. In addition to the examples described previously from the 1960s, such as Model Cities and the Community Action Program, there are many well-known community-based efforts that have attracted a great deal of attention, including the Dudley Street Neighborhood Initiative in Boston and the Harlem Children's Zone in New York City. Other examples are initiatives undertaken in a particular neighborhood or set of neighborhoods that are sponsored by a core institution or foundation, such as the

West Philadelphia Initiatives sponsored by the University of Pennsylvania, the MacArthur Foundation's New Communities Program in Chicago, and the Annie E. Casey Foundation's Making Connections Initiative in various sites around the country.

An excellent review of these types of community change initiatives was recently put together by researchers at the Aspen Institute's Roundtable for Community Change.[13] The overarching conclusions from this review are mixed: while many programs could point to positive developments in the targeted communities, the impacts of the programs were typically limited to the community residents that were the direct recipients of resources made available through the initiatives. The idea that neighborhood-based initiatives might have transformative effects that spread throughout a community did not materialize in most settings. At the same time, few of the programs were designed in a way that allowed for rigorous empirical evaluation. In most cases, there is no convincing "control" community to provide a point of comparison with the communities that receive intensive interventions (the Jobs-Plus program is an important exception that is discussed in more detail in the concluding chapter). Residential mobility out of the targeted neighborhoods presents another complication to evaluating the effectiveness of these initiatives, because many residents who might benefit from the programs were highly likely to move in and out of the community during the period of the intervention.[14] Lastly, the most convincing conclusions about community-based initiatives are derived from evidence examining the effect of actual participation in programs being conducted within the community, rather than from evidence on changes in the lives of the larger set of individuals or families living within a targeted community. For instance, a rigorous evaluation of the Harlem Children's Zone did not focus primary attention on whether the area composing the Zone had changed the lives of residents, but instead focused on the impact of attending one of the "Promise Academy" charter schools.[15]

In sum, the evidence available from the range of community-based initiatives is useful for understanding how community change initiatives are implemented, how the targeted communities change over time, and how participants in programs or recipients of resources are affected by the presence of the initiatives. The evidence is less useful for understanding how changes in a child's environment, such as a decline in poverty, may affect that child's life chances—this is a central question in the debate over how to confront concentrated poverty, yet it is a question that has received little attention in the empirical literature.

The second part of this chapter thus produces original evidence on the impact of neighborhood change occurring around children living in disadvantaged neighborhoods. While several previous studies have examined the relationship between childhood neighborhood characteristics and adult economic and social outcomes, many of these studies are unconvincing because of serious methodological problems. I develop a new method that is designed to confront these problems directly, and one that provides evidence on an issue that is central to the current policy debate: what is the long-term impact of neighborhood change—specifically, the deconcentration of poverty and segregation—on children's economic trajectories?

Residential Mobility out of the Ghetto

The idea of residential mobility as a way to confront the problems of the urban ghetto began to garner attention largely because of some surprisingly positive research findings emerging out of Chicago, from the famous Gautreaux Assisted Housing Program. The program was named after Dorothy Gautreaux, who initiated one of the original lawsuits filed against the Chicago Housing Authority (CHA) in the late 1960s. The lawsuit charged that the CHA's site selection and tenant placement procedures served to reinforce and exacerbate racial segregation in the city. As part of the settlement, the CHA was required to use resources through the Section 8 program to offer public housing residents opportunities to live in private apartments throughout the metropolitan area that they otherwise would not be able to afford. Some families were placed in new apartments within Chicago's city limits, but others were placed in apartments within largely white, affluent suburbs, providing a dramatic change of scenery for poor black families living in one of the most segregated cities in the nation.[16]

One of the key aspects of the program that emerged from the Gautreaux lawsuit is that the apartments to which families were assigned were not chosen by the families themselves, but were selected by the organization administering the program. Families that volunteered for the opportunity to move were placed on a waiting list and were assigned to an apartment once their name moved to the top. According to the original researchers studying the program, this feature of Gautreaux meant that families' residential destinations were largely outside their own control. In other words, these researchers argued that Gautreaux could be thought of as a type of natural experiment, one in which families were assigned to very different environments on the basis of their spot on the waiting list and then followed over time to see how they fared in these new environments. If the economic outcomes of families assigned to different environments were found to differ, according to these researchers, these differences could be attributed to the environment itself, as opposed to any characteristics of families that might lead them into a given type of environment under normal circumstances. While families were technically allowed to decline an apartment offered to them, researchers pointed to the fact that virtually all families accepted their initial offer to support the idea that families' residential destinations were essentially determined by their position on the waiting list, not by their own characteristics.[17]

Resting on the assumption that Gautreaux could be thought of as an experimental assessment of how residential environments matter, James Rosenbaum and several colleagues studied a group of families that had moved as part of the Gautreaux program, tracking parents' fortunes in the labor force and tracking their children's progress in school and in the labor market.

What they found was quite remarkable. Rosenbaum and his colleagues found that families placed in Chicago's suburbs experienced substantial economic benefits when compared with families placed within the city limits. Parents in the suburbs found jobs at higher rates than their city counterparts, earned more, and were less likely to be on welfare. Children did report problems adjusting to their new school environments, but ultimately they had higher rates of high school completion, college attendance, and labor force participation in early adulthood than their counterparts in the city.[18] Only 5 percent of children in families assigned to the suburbs dropped out of school, compared to 20 percent of children in families assigned to apartments within Chicago. More than half attended college, and 27 percent attended a four-year college. Only 21 percent of children who remained in Chicago attended any college, and 4 percent attended a four-year college.

The findings were widely publicized and made their way into the popular press— *Newsweek* covered results from one study of families in Gautreaux, and *60 Minutes* ran a segment interviewing children who were thriving in their suburban neighborhoods. Unsurprisingly, mobility came to be seen by many as the solution to the ghetto and all of its social problems.

Since the original research on Gautreaux, a more complicated story has emerged. As it turns out, the original research that showed such tremendous results was based on a very select sample of families participating in the program that were tracked down by researchers, rather than all families that were placed into an apartment via Gautreaux. This is problematic, because it forces one to wonder whether the families that became unreachable had problems or challenges that might explain why they could no longer be found. Further, whereas the original research assumed that families' residential destinations were determined purely on the basis of their positions on the waiting list, subsequent research on the sample of families that took part in Gautreaux suggests that this assumption is not entirely accurate. Families' own preferences appear to have played at least some role in determining where they were placed, undermining the idea that Gautreaux should be thought of in the same way as an experiment.[19]

The combination of these problems with the Gautreaux research suggests that the original claims surrounding the program may have been overstated. However, subsequent researchers have re-analyzed data from all of the families that moved as part of the Gautreaux program, and even after attempting to adjust for any differences between families that moved to different residential environments, they have continued to find that families placed in low-poverty neighborhoods or less-segregated neighborhoods fared much better than families placed in high-poverty or highly segregated neighborhoods.[20] Despite the flaws inherent in the design of the Gautreaux program, these studies continue to indicate that mobility out of Chicago's ghetto seems to have been beneficial—perhaps extremely beneficial—for poor families.

Roughly three decades following the initial lawsuit against the Chicago Housing Authority, another, even more prominent mobility program was implemented, called Moving to Opportunity (MTO). Carried out in five cities (Baltimore, Boston, Chicago, Los Angeles, and New York) and fueled largely by the public attention given to Gautreaux's early results, MTO was implemented as a true social experiment where families in public housing that volunteered for the program were randomly assigned into a "control" group that received no vouchers and remained in their current housing or into an "experimental" group that received vouchers that allowed them to move into any neighborhood across the city as long as its poverty rate was below 10 percent.[21]

Beyond the general idea of allowing public housing residents to exit the ghetto, Gautreaux and MTO differed on several fronts. Unlike Gautreaux, the racial composition of the neighborhood was not a factor in the design of MTO, and families in the experimental group could select their own apartments as long as the destination neighborhood had a sufficiently low poverty rate. As a result, the destinations of MTO families looked entirely different from the destinations of Gautreaux families. Very few families offered vouchers in MTO made dramatic moves that crossed the boundaries of the cities in which they started, and most moved to neighborhoods that were quite similar to their origin neighborhoods, with the exception of the poverty rate.[22] The economic environment in which MTO was implemented was also very different from the environment in the 1970s, when many of the families in Gautreaux moved. The most notable difference was that urban labor markets were booming in the mid-1990s, unemployment was low, and jobs were growing more quickly in the cities than in the suburbs.[23] Welfare reform also was passed and implemented in the mid-1990s, which imposed time limits and mandatory work requirements on families receiving welfare and pushed large segments of the public housing population into the workforce. The expansion of the earned income tax credit during the same period bolstered the returns to work, combining with the tight labor market to provide a strong set of incentives for low-skilled workers to enter the labor force. Lastly, the Department of Housing and Urban Development was in the midst of tearing down many of the most notorious public housing projects around the country through the HOPE VI program. As a result, even if eligible families in MTO cities were randomized to the control group, some of them ended up moving when their housing complexes were torn down through HOPE VI.[24]

Considering the differences between the types of moves made in Gautreaux and MTO, and the differences in the economic and policy context in which these moves were made, it may not be altogether surprising that they produced quite different results. As an example, some of the strongest results from Gautreaux were found in analyses of parents' economic success in suburban neighborhoods. Analyses of MTO did not show any improvements in parents' labor market participation or income.[25] But a closer look at the data suggests a reason why this might be the case. During the mid-1990s, when urban labor markets were booming, there were substantial increases in labor market activity for all poor families. Families in the "control" group of MTO—that is, those who received no vouchers—roughly doubled their rate of employment over the years during which the evaluation took place. Families in the experimental group—those who received vouchers—also doubled their employment rate over the same period, meaning there was no "effect" of the program on employment simply because everyone was doing well in the labor market, no matter where they lived.

This example makes clear how important it is to consider the contexts in which Gautreaux and MTO were implemented when comparing results from the two programs. However, there are some discrepancies in results that are more difficult to explain. For instance, families that moved to Chicago's suburbs through the Gautreaux program seemed to have fared better across virtually all dimensions of the family's lives that researchers studied; by contrast, several years after Moving to Opportunity started, researchers analyzing results from the five MTO cities found only a few substantive differences in outcomes between families offered a voucher and those not offered a voucher. One important finding was that parents in the treatment group reported feeling much safer in their new neighborhoods and showed marked improvements in measures of mental health and slight improvement in levels of obesity.[26] Other than these outcomes, however, the program has had minimal impact on parents. As for children, the most comprehensive assessment of results from MTO shows that the effects of residential mobility on several children's outcomes appear to vary by gender, with girls showing positive effects across several developmental outcomes and boys showing null or negative effects. For instance, girls in families that moved to low-poverty neighborhoods appear to do better in school, feel safer, and take part in fewer risky behaviors when compared to girls in families that did not move. Boys that move to low-poverty neighborhoods, on the other hand, are *more* likely to commit property crimes in the years after moving and show elevated rates of other risky behaviors. The experiment has not been running long enough to assess whether the trajectories of children will change as they move into adulthood, but the conclusion from results produced to this point suggest that the experiment has failed to produce the anticipated benefits for all groups that were present in Gautreaux.

On the basis of these somewhat disappointing results, enthusiasm for the "mobility" approach to neighborhood poverty has faded abruptly. Media coverage of Moving to Opportunity largely ignored the few positive findings from the experiment, focusing instead on broad assessments of the overall mixed results and concluding that the experiment was a failure.[27] An article written in *The Atlantic Monthly* in 2008 added fuel to the fire, claiming that voucher programs that had formed the basis of the federal effort to "deconcentrate" poverty had simply spread crime and violence across a wider swath of many smaller cities across the United States.[28] The tacit message of the article was that it was not the environment in which people lived that was causing violence, but the types of people living in that environment. The enthusiasm for moving families out of the ghetto that was so prevalent in the 1980s was dampened further, replaced by a growing cynicism about the very idea that neighborhoods actually matter at all for the life chances of children.

But just as the early results from Gautreaux may have overstated the positive impacts of mobility out of the ghetto, the growing sentiment that neighborhoods are unimportant in the lives of youth is based on empirical claims that are greatly exaggerated. For one thing, the types of moves that were made among families in the Moving to Opportunity experiment were entirely different from the types of moves made by families in the Gautreaux program. Families taking part in Gautreaux did not simply move to neighborhoods with a different racial and economic composition; they moved into new social worlds that were outside of the severely unequal residential landscape of Chicago. A recent follow-up of Gautreaux families shows that the changes in neighborhood environments arising from the program were not temporary departures from the ghetto, but long-term escapes—fifteen years after the original Gautreaux families moved, researchers have found that most of them continue to live in neighborhoods that are much less poor and much less segregated than their origin neighborhoods in Chicago.[29]

By contrast, families offered a voucher in the MTO program moved to neighborhoods with lower poverty rates, but they experienced minimal change in the racial composition of the neighborhood and the quality of the school system, virtually all of them remained nearby their origin neighborhoods, and a large number of them returned to higher poverty neighborhoods within a few years. Considering the figures presented earlier in this book showing that many families living in the nation's poorest neighborhoods have occupied similar neighborhoods for multiple generations, the moves made in MTO might be best characterized as short-term departures from a family history in the ghetto. Seen in this way, perhaps it is not so surprising that the changes generated by MTO do not seem to have altered the life chances of children in a major way.

But even this conclusion may be too abrupt. Moving to Opportunity has typically been studied as a single experiment implemented in five cities across the United States; when one examines the data in more detail, a very different picture emerges.

In 2009 I was invited to join a team of researchers who came together to investigate why there seemed to be so much conflicting evidence on whether residential mobility programs that move families out of the ghetto generate positive impacts on children.[30] We reviewed evidence from studies that have already been published, and we re-analyzed data from several mobility experiments and one major observational study. With each study, we focused our attention on the impact of moving out of high-poverty neighborhoods on children's academic and cognitive test scores, the one outcome measure that was available in all of the data sets. What we uncovered was a set of results that did not align with either the recent, pessimistic view that moving out of the ghetto has no impact on children or the earlier, optimistic view that escaping the ghetto is sufficient for changing the lives of youth. Instead, we uncovered a set of results that require a more nuanced, complex interpretation.

A summary of the basic findings from this effort is shown in figure 6.1. The figure displays results from five data sets, all of which were used to examine

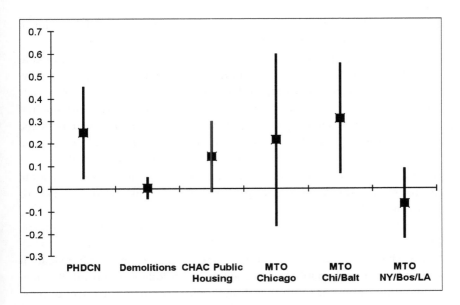

Figure 6.1. Estimated effects of moving out of high-poverty neighborhoods on children's reading/language skills, based on four independent studies. *Note:* The *X*-axis lists the name of each study: Project on Human Development in Chicago Neighborhoods (PHDCN; Sampson, Sharkey, and Raudenbush, 2008); Chicago public-housing demolition study (Jacob, 2004); Chicago CHAC voucher study for families living in public housing at baseline (Ludwig et al., 2010); and results from the Moving to Opportunity (MTO) study for different cities (Sanbonmatsu et al., 2006). The *Y*-axis shows the estimated effect of changing neighborhoods on children's verbal test scores in each of the studies, expressed as an effect size (share of a standard deviation in the test score distribution, so that an effect size of .2 means children living in less distressed areas have average scores about one-fifth of a standard deviation higher than children living in more distressed areas).

the effect of moving from a high-poverty neighborhood to a low-poverty neighborhood on children's performance on tests of reading/language skills. Because there is a great deal of information shown in this single figure, it is worth spending a couple paragraphs to describe its features in some detail. On the *y* (vertical) axis of the figure is a scale representing the degree of improvement or decline in reading scores attributable to moving out of high-poverty neighborhoods. The effects of mobility on reading scores are measured in terms of "standard deviations," which allow us to make comparisons of results using a common metric. Any estimate that lies above o indicates a positive effect of moving out of high-poverty neighborhoods, meaning test scores improved, and any estimate that falls below 0 indicates a negative effect, meaning test scores declined.

On the x (horizontal) axis are all of the studies that were reviewed or analyzed. The point above each study indicates the estimated impact of moving to a low-poverty neighborhood based on the results available from that particular study—these points represent the "best guess" as to how much of an impact there was in the given study. Because these are estimated effects, there is uncertainty built into each estimate—therefore, each point has a bar around it which indicates the range of the "confidence interval" around the estimate, which is included as an acknowledgment that there is some imprecision involved in estimating the effect of moving out of poverty with relatively small samples.

The first estimate to consider is on the far left of the figure, from the Project on Human Development in Chicago Neighborhoods (PHDCN). This is the one estimate that did not come from an experiment; instead, it comes from a study published in 2008 in which Robert Sampson, Stephen Raudenbush, and I used statistical methods to estimate the effect of moving out of highly disadvantaged neighborhoods in Chicago among African Americans.[31] We limited our sample to African Americans for a few reasons, the most notable being that this was the only group in Chicago exposed to severely disadvantaged communities in substantial numbers. We found that moving out of disadvantaged neighborhoods within Chicago leads to substantial improvements in black children's verbal ability. The effect size was roughly 0.25 standard deviations, a positive and substantively large effect. To provide a point of reference, our estimate suggests moving out of a highly disadvantaged neighborhood is roughly equivalent to obtaining between one and two additional years of schooling.

When this study from the PHDCN was first published in 2008, the results seemed to be inconsistent with the findings that had been published from the Moving to Opportunity study, which showed no overall effect on test scores of moving out of high-poverty neighborhoods across the five cities.[32] The results from the PHDCN were also different from those obtained in a separate study conducted by economist Brian Jacob, who analyzed test score results among children living in public housing complexes in Chicago that were demolished, and whose families had to relocate to new neighborhoods when their buildings were torn down.[33] Jacob found that families in demolished projects made moves into neighborhoods with lower poverty, which is not surprising considering they were coming from some of the most dilapidated public housing complexes in Chicago. As the second point in figure 6.1 shows ("Demolitions"), these moves to lower-poverty neighborhoods did not produce any gains in children's test scores.

Still, moving to a new neighborhood because your home is destroyed is likely to be very different from moving to a new neighborhood after volunteering for a housing voucher program. A more appropriate comparison might be another experimental study of Chicago families that volunteered to move to lower-poverty neighborhoods. The results of such an experiment are shown in the third study in figure 6.1, labeled "CHAC Public Housing" and based on a study conducted by economist Jens Ludwig and several colleagues.[34] This experiment came about when the private firm administering the city's housing voucher program opened the waiting list for the first time in more than a decade and randomized the overflowing number of applicants for housing vouchers to positions on the waiting list. The families that received vouchers made moves that led to declines in neighborhood poverty very similar to those made through the MTO program. Similar to the results from the PHDCN, these moves also led to substantial improvements in reading test scores. As shown in figure 6.1, moving to lower-poverty neighborhoods in this experiment led to improvements in reading test scores of just under 0.2 standard deviations.

Why would results from these two studies based on data from Chicago—the PHDCN study and the CHAC study—differ so substantially from quite similar research based on the Moving to Opportunity experiment? One possibility is that MTO was conducted in five cities, not just Chicago; perhaps there is something about Chicago that makes moving out of high-poverty neighborhoods particularly beneficial for youth. One test of this idea is to examine only the Chicago sample from the Moving to Opportunity experiment. Results from this test are shown in the fourth column in figure 6.1, labeled "MTO-Chicago." Interestingly, the sample from Chicago showed substantial positive effects of moving out of poor neighborhoods. A quick comparison of the estimate from MTO Chicago with that from the PHDCN reveals remarkable convergence—in each case, the estimated effect is between one-fifth and one quarter of a standard deviation.

This finding, which is very different from what had been published with the Moving to Opportunity data, reflects a more general observation about the MTO experiment—in reality, this was truly five different experiments being conducted in surprisingly different settings. For instance, while the Chicago and Baltimore samples were predominantly black, the samples from New York, Boston, and Los Angeles were much more ethnically diverse, with greater representation of Latinos. Families in the Chicago and Baltimore sites were also living in much more severely disadvantaged neighborhoods at the outset of the experiment, with stark racial segregation, extreme poverty, and high levels of crime. Families in the three other sites were also living in poor communities, but the degree of crime and concentrated disadvantage did not approach what was found in Chicago and Baltimore.

Considering how distinct Chicago and Baltimore are from the three other MTO sites, the researchers involved with the project decided to analyze data from these two cities alone. The second-to-last estimate from figure 6.1, labeled "MTO-Chicago and Baltimore," reveals that the estimated effect of moving out of high-poverty neighborhoods in these two cities is even larger than in Chicago alone. Equally interesting, there is no effect at all when the data from the three other cities, Boston, Los Angeles, and New York, are analyzed separately. In these cities, moving out of poor neighborhoods doesn't seem to lead to any improvements in children's reading scores.

Returning to the debate on how to confront the problems associated with concentrated poverty, where does this evidence leave us? One initial conclusion is that neither the "old" view of residential mobility as the solution to the problem of the urban ghetto nor the "new" view that residential mobility is useless is entirely accurate. The evidence available suggests that programs that offer families the opportunity to move out of the ghetto can positively affect different aspects of families' lives *under certain circumstances*.[35] Understanding what those circumstances are will require more data and more experiments, but the research that I have reviewed provides some clues.[36]

A first clue is that the children who showed the biggest improvements in cognitive skills were those who moved out of the most severely disadvantaged environments. Out of the five cities in which Moving to Opportunity was conducted, Baltimore and Chicago featured neighborhoods that had a level of concentrated poverty and racial segregation on a different scale than in Boston, New York, and Los Angeles, the other MTO sites. The families that were offered housing vouchers in Baltimore and Chicago moved out of some of the most disadvantaged neighborhoods in the nation, and their children's cognitive skills improved substantially as a result.

The families in these two cities also experienced the largest declines in exposure to violent crime in their communities, a second clue as to what might explain the differential effects of mobility across the various studies. There is now a large research literature documenting the impact of community violence on various aspects of child development, including the development of cognitive skills.[37] The stress and trauma that arise from children's experiences with violence, whether the child is a victim or a witness, have been shown to sharply reduce children's ability to concentrate or focus, to disrupt sleep, and to induce anxiety.[38] All of these responses to violence in a child's environment may impede his ability to learn, to focus in school, and to concentrate during assessments of cognitive skills. In this sense, the finding that families in the Baltimore and Chicago sites experienced the largest changes in community levels of violent crime may be crucial to understanding why the children in these families experienced such improvements in their performance on tests of cognitive skills.

One final clue as to what types of moves might produce important change in a family's life comes from the earliest study of residential mobility, the Gautreaux program. While research from Gautreaux has been justifiably critiqued because of the flaws of the design, even acknowledging these imperfections it is hard to dismiss the substantial changes that the program seemed to induce in the lives of families that moved to Chicago's suburbs. Two features of Gautreaux made it a truly unique program: first, families moved outside of Chicago's city limits and they moved to affluent and integrated suburbs throughout the metropolitan area; and second, families that made such dramatic moves remained in their new communities for long periods of time.[39] It could be the combination of these two features that led to such dramatic changes in the lives of participating families. Thus, one plausible interpretation of the results from Gautreaux is that a *substantial* and *sustained* change in the neighborhood environment is necessary if residential mobility programs are to have a substantial impact on families in disadvantaged areas. Whether this type of change is possible on a large scale is questionable—I address this issue in more detail in the concluding chapter.

The evidence that I have reviewed to this point pertains to only one of the two primary approaches to confronting the ghetto: residential mobility. Whereas providing families the opportunity to move out of the ghetto is a fairly straightforward idea, the alternative of investing in disadvantaged neighborhoods to create change from within is more amorphous. Further, while scholars have generated a substantial amount of evidence to guide decisions about what types of mobility programs are likely to foster positive results, there is not a similar body of evidence to evaluate when we consider the likely effects of neighborhood change on the life chances of residents.[40] In fact, the very idea that improvements in the neighborhood environment would improve the lives of residents is contested by some.

As a beginning point in thinking about the idea of neighborhood change, then, it may be useful to reconsider the more general question of why neighborhoods matter in the first place. A crude summary of the past few decades of theory and research suggests various possible ways in which neighborhoods may affect residents, including the quality and stability of key institutions within a community (e.g., city governments, churches, and schools), the presence or lack of resources for parents and children (e.g., parks and city services), the availability and quality of economic opportunities (e.g., industry and public employment), the characteristics of adult and youth social networks and role models within the community (e.g., employment networks, welfare recipients, and youth gangs), the degree and character of social organization within the community (e.g., neighbors' capacity and willingness to maintain social controls), and the spatial clustering of various social phenomena (e.g., physical disorder, air pollution, toxic soil, and violence). As is apparent from this laundry list, there is no shortage of arguments for how the social and physical environments surrounding children and families might affect their life chances.

However, understanding how characteristics of neighborhoods affect children and families may not be adequate to understanding how a *change* in the neighborhood may affect children and families. For example, an improvement in the economic status of residents in a poor neighborhood may lead to more political influence and perhaps more resources for schools, but this type of change may not improve the level of trust and cohesion within a community if class or racial tensions arise. It is also possible that original residents may not benefit from "improvements" in their neighborhood. Rents may rise, forcing families to leave the improving neighborhood, or the police may crack down on the day-to-day activities of original residents in public spaces within gentrifying neighborhoods.

These uncertainties about the impact of neighborhood change are revealed most clearly in research on gentrification, as in the work of Lance Freeman, a scholar of urban planning who has studied two gentrifying neighborhoods in majority-black sections of Harlem and Brooklyn.[41] Freeman's research within these communities shows how an influx of relatively well-educated, higher-income residents, many but not all of whom were white, seemed to have very different impacts on original residents depending on the specific aspect of change under study. Many original residents did not have much social contact with newer residents, resented the changes in social norms within the neighborhood, and often did not see well-educated newcomers as role models, particularly if they were of a different race. By contrast, residents recognized the improvement in city services, retail stores and amenities, and in some cases resources for local institutions such as the public schools within the neighborhood, all of which emerged at least in part due to the changing demographics in the neighborhood and the political influence and social capital of the newcomers.

From Freeman's study and other ethnographic accounts of neighborhood change, such as Mary Pattillo's research in Chicago,[42] we are not led to a simple hypothesis about the likely impact that neighborhood change has on the original residents of a neighborhood. There is ample reason to think that when concentrated disadvantage becomes less severe, everyone in the neighborhood benefits. Alternatively, it could be that original residents do not share in the benefits that come with a neighborhood "on the rise." Indeed, the question of whether a positive change in the neighborhood environment actually has a positive impact on original residents is an open one, and it has never been studied in a systematic manner. While the ethnographic research that has been produced on the topic is extremely well-suited to examine the complex process of neighborhood transformation and the mechanisms mediating its influence, the difficulty of following people over long periods of time and the relatively small sample sizes in many such studies make it difficult to examine the long-term trajectories of original residents living in changing neighborhoods.

The remainder of the chapter represents an effort to begin to fill in some of the gaps in this research, and to do so by drawing on data from the Panel Study of Income Dynamics to provide a long-term perspective on a basic question that is essential for thinking about how to confront concentrated poverty: what impact does neighborhood change have on the life chances of children?

Estimating the Effect of Neighborhood Change

One basic problem in studying the effect of neighborhood change is that change does not occur in a random manner—some neighborhoods are more likely than others to deteriorate or to improve quickly, and some individuals are likely better equipped to predict how a neighborhood will change in the future. One might imagine, for instance, that some parents have more foresight than others in considering how their neighborhood is likely to change in the future. This means that simply comparing individuals who live in changing neighborhoods to others who live in stable neighborhoods would produce biased results—any impacts of the change in the neighborhoods might truly be a product of the parent's eye toward the future. If the goal of the analysis is to understand the impact of the change in the neighborhood, as opposed to the impact of the parent's foresight, then an alternative approach is necessary. This section describes the intuition behind the approach I've developed to estimate the impact of neighborhood change, and the details of the method can be found in the online appendix to the book.[43]

The central insight underlying the method is a simple one: although families living in neighborhoods across the United States have a choice about where they would like to live, they often have little control over how their neighborhood environment will change once they are there. In other words, if we begin with families that live in the same types of neighborhoods, it is reasonable to think of change occurring around the family as something akin to a random event. More specifically, the method begins by creating matched pairs of children in families that look extremely similar, but which undergo different trajectories in the years following the matching. One of the children from the pair lives in a neighborhood that improves over time; the other lives in a neighborhood that does not improve or that deteriorates over the same period.

To give an example, imagine two twelve-year-old African American children—I'll call them Ray and Kevin—each living in poor neighborhoods somewhere in the midwest in 1980 (the year in which we begin to follow the matched pairs). Ray's neighborhood looks remarkably similar to Kevin's neighborhood; they live in areas that are mainly black, with high poverty rates, a large number of families on welfare, and widespread joblessness. Their neighborhoods also changed in the same ways over the prior decade, the 1970s. In each neighborhood, some of the white families moved out and were replaced by more African American families, making the neighborhoods even more segregated. Many of the neighbors lost their jobs over the decade, and poverty became more prevalent.

Ray and Kevin are the types of children that would be matched together in the analysis, because their families have selected neighborhoods that are virtually identical and that have shown identical patterns of change over the 1970s, the decade prior to the matching. Neither Ray's parents nor Kevin's parents would have been likely to notice any difference in the direction their neighborhoods were moving that might have given them a hint about what the neighborhoods would look like in the future.

Now let's fast forward to the 1980s, where the two neighborhoods begin to change in very different ways. Ray's neighborhood sees an influx of Latino immigrants, making it slightly less racially segregated. The economic environment improves as well, as a new market develops, new jobs appear, and many of the neighbors go back to work. Crime drops, there are more resources for the schools, and many of the neighbors leave the welfare system. In short, the degree of concentrated disadvantage declines in Ray's neighborhood.

Kevin's neighborhood does not experience the same changes. There are no new immigrants moving in, and some of the remaining white families move out, making the neighborhood even more racially segregated. With declines in population, some of the local retail stores close, a manufacturing plant shuts down, and even more of the neighbors become jobless.

Whereas Ray's neighborhood and Kevin's neighborhood looked identical in 1980, they look very different in 1990. But how have Ray's and Kevin's own lives changed over this period? Based on common theories of neighborhood effects, we might think that Ray would be doing much better than Kevin in 1990 because of the changes occurring around him. Or perhaps not—perhaps all of the new jobs in the neighborhood went to the newcomers, and Ray experienced none of the benefits of the changes taking place there.

The central goal of this analysis is to examine how these different neighborhood trajectories alter the economic trajectories of children like Ray and Kevin as they move into adulthood. To pursue this goal I follow matched pairs of youth into adulthood and compare their economic outcomes after their neighborhoods have diverged. In doing so I ask whether the types of changes that occurred in Ray's neighborhood lead to more economic opportunities for him and other children within his neighborhood relative to matched counterparts like Kevin, whose neighborhood did not improve. If this is so, we would expect to find that Ray is more stably employed in adulthood, perhaps earning more than Kevin, with a better-paying job. Or, alternatively, the changes in Ray's neighborhood may make no difference to his own trajectory. If this were true, we would expect to find no differences in adult economic outcomes when compared to Kevin. These are the types of comparisons that the matching procedure makes possible.

I estimate the impact of this type of change by again drawing on data from the PSID. For this analysis I select a sample of children who were between the ages of five and fifteen in 1980, and who are then followed into adulthood. Whereas in previous chapters I categorized neighborhoods by the rate of poverty, in this analysis I use a more comprehensive measure of neighborhood disadvantage, which considers poverty, racial segregation, welfare receipt, unemployment, and other characteristics of the children's neighborhoods. These various characteristics are incorporated into a scale of *concentrated disadvantage*.[44] The analysis differs from earlier chapters in another way; here I focus on African Americans exclusively, the group that is likely to benefit most from any policy targeted to confront concentrated poverty, and the only group commonly exposed to severe neighborhood disadvantage in urban settings.[45]

The Impact of Neighborhood Change

As a first step it is useful to examine the types of change occurring in neighborhoods where concentrated disadvantage declined over the last few decades. Figures 6.2a through 6.2c display several basic demographic and economic characteristics of neighborhoods that experienced the sharpest declines in concentrated disadvantage from 1970 to 1980 (fig. 6.2a), from 1980 to 1990 (fig. 6.2b), and from 1990 to 2000 (fig. 6.2c), respectively.[46] The accompanying table 6.1 shows where these neighborhoods were located, displaying the twenty metropolitan areas with the largest number of neighborhoods that experienced sharp declines in concentrated disadvantage. For a point of reference, the table also shows their rank in terms of the total number of neighborhoods in the metropolitan area.

If one considers the patterns of decadal changes collectively, a relatively consistent and somewhat surprising pattern emerges. In each decade, neighborhoods that saw the biggest declines in concentrated disadvantage experienced substantial improvement in economic circumstances, as one

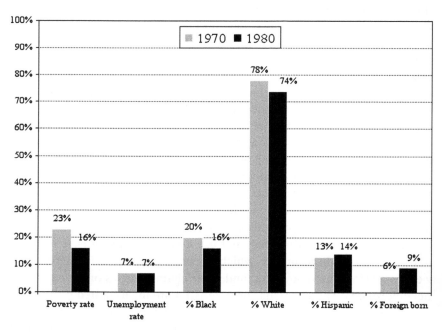

Figure 6.2a. Characteristics of the 10 percent of U.S. neighborhoods where concentrated disadvantage declined the most from 1970 to 1980.

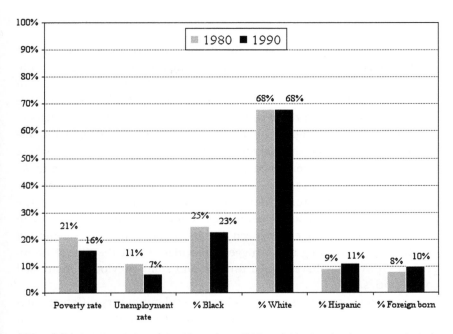

Figure 6.2b. Characteristics of the 10 percent of U.S. neighborhoods where concentrated disadvantage declined the most from 1980 to 1990.

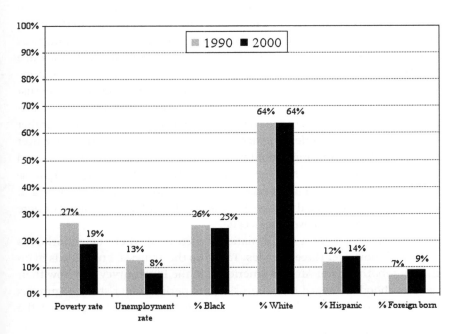

Figure 6.2c. Characteristics of the 10 percent of U.S. neighborhoods where concentrated disadvantage declined the most from 1990 to 2000.

would expect. The figures show sizable drops in poverty in each decade and similar drops in unemployment in each decade except the 1970s, when unemployment did not change. Changes in the racial/ethnic composition of these neighborhoods are somewhat more surprising. While the percentage of African Americans in these neighborhoods declined slightly in each decade, these were not neighborhoods where whites were moving in and displacing blacks. In fact, the percentage of whites in neighborhoods where disadvantage declined remained stable in the 1970s and the 1990s and *declined* in the 1980s. The groups moving into such neighborhoods were Latinos and immigrants from different nations of origin. In each decade, the percentage of Latinos and the percentage of foreign-born residents rose in the neighborhoods that experienced the sharpest declines in concentrated disadvantage, providing some suggestive evidence that the tide of immigration growth may have helped turn around some previously distressed communities.[47]

As table 6.1 shows, these changes have played out in very different parts of the country over the past few decades. In the 1970s, metropolitan areas in the south—including cities like Houston, Memphis, and New Orleans—and metro areas on the west coast—including cities like San Francisco, Fresno, and Seattle—had a disproportionate number of neighborhoods where disadvantage was declining rapidly. Metropolitan areas containing rust-belt cities like Chicago, Philadelphia, Detroit, and Cleveland had few such neighborhoods relative to the size of these cities. This changed in the 1980s, when the location of neighborhoods where disadvantage was declining was more spread out across the country. Whereas some west coast cities like San Diego and Sacramento continued to have larger numbers of "improving" neighborhoods than one would expect based on population, the rust belt cities began to see some neighborhoods with declining levels of disadvantage during this decade. These cities then saw growth in the number of neighborhoods experiencing declines in concentrated disadvantage over the 1990s. The Detroit metropolitan area, which was not even represented on this list in 1970–1980, had the largest number of "improving" neighborhoods in the 1990s, and other metro areas like those containing Cleveland and Milwaukee also had disproportionate numbers of neighborhoods where disadvantage declined over the decade.

These figures paint a broad, national picture of where neighborhoods improved most over three decades. To set up the analysis, I now focus in on the neighborhoods of African Americans in the PSID survey and how their neighborhoods changed over the 1980s, the period under study. Figure 6.3 examines how the neighborhoods of African Americans changed over the

Table 6.1. *Metropolitan areas with the largest number of census tracts experiencing substantial declines in concentrated disadvantage from one decade to the next*

1970–1980

Rank in number of neighborhoods where disadvantage declined	Rank in total number of neighborhoods	Metro area
1	2	Los Angeles-Riverside-Orange County, CA
2	7	San Francisco-Oakland-San Jose, CA
3	1	New York-Northern New Jersey-Long Island, NY-NJ-CT-PA
4	12	Seattle-Tacoma-Bremerton, WA
5	11	Houston-Galveston-Brazoria, TX
6	9	Dallas-Fort Worth, TX
7	17	Phoenix-Mesa, AZ
8	5	Washington-Baltimore, DC-MD-VA-WV
9	56	Fresno, CA
10	25	Sacramento-Yolo, CA
11	16	San Diego, CA
12	26	New Orleans, LA
13	29	Orlando, FL
14	43	Memphis, TN-AR-MS
15	8	Boston-Worcester-Lawrence, MA-NH-ME-CT
16	3	Chicago-Gary-Kenosha, IL-IN-WI
17	22	Portland-Salem, OR-WA
18	39	West Palm Beach-Boca Raton, FL
19	48	Tulsa, OK
20	4	Philadelphia-Wilmington-Atlantic City, PA-NJ-DE-MD

1980–1990

Rank in number of neighborhoods where disadvantage declined	Rank in total number of neighborhoods	Metro area
1	1	New York-Northern New Jersey-Long Island, NY-NJ-CT-PA
2	5	Philadelphia-Wilmington-Atlantic City, PA-NJ-DE-MD
3	2	Los Angeles-Riverside-Orange County, CA
4	7	San Francisco-Oakland-San Jose, CA
5	4	Washington-Baltimore, DC-MD-VA-WV
6	6	Detroit-Ann Arbor-Flint, MI
7	3	Chicago-Gary-Kenosha, IL-IN-WI
8	8	Boston-Worcester-Lawrence, MA-NH-ME-CT
9	19	San Diego, CA
10	25	Sacramento-Yolo, CA
11	12	Seattle-Tacoma-Bremerton, WA
12	28	Norfolk-Virginia Beach-Newport News, VA-NC

(Continued)

Table 6.1. (Continued)

13	38	Memphis, TN-AR-MS
14	52	Honolulu, HI
15	30	Orlando, FL
16	23	Cincinnati-Hamilton, OH-KY-IN
17	11	Cleveland-Akron, OH
18	33	Buffalo-Niagara Falls, NY
19	19	Atlanta, GA
20	35	Charlotte-Gastonia-Rock Hill, NC-SC

1990–2000		
Rank in number of neighborhoods where disadvantage declined	Rank in total number of neighborhoods	Metro area
1	6	Detroit-Ann Arbor-Flint, MI
2	1	New York-Northern New Jersey-Long Island, NY-NJ-CT-P
3	3	Chicago-Gary-Kenosha, IL-IN-WI
4	7	San Francisco-Oakland-San Jose, CA
5	2	Los Angeles-Riverside-Orange County, CA
6	11	Cleveland-Akron, OH
7	8	Boston-Worcester-Lawrence, MA-NH-ME-CT
8	10	Houston-Galveston-Brazoria, TX
9	14	Pittsburgh, PA
10	9	Dallas-Fort Worth, TX
11	25	New Orleans, LA
12	5	Philadelphia-Wilmington-Atlantic City, PA-NJ-DE-MD
13	4	Washington-Baltimore, DC-MD-VA-WV
14	17	Denver-Boulder-Greeley, CO
15	15	Phoenix-Mesa, AZ
16	43	Austin-San Marcos, TX
17	13	Minneapolis-St. Paul, MN-WI
18	23	Cincinnati-Hamilton, OH-KY-IN
19	33	San Antonio, TX
20	24	Milwaukee-Racine, WI

decade, focusing on the neighborhoods that experienced any decline in the degree of concentrated disadvantage. As is visible in the figure, these neighborhoods were extremely poor and racially segregated in 1980 but became slightly more ethnically diverse and saw improvements in economic status over the decade. In 1980 the average poverty rate in these neighborhoods was 28 percent, and only 51 percent of adult residents were employed. The neighborhoods were racially segregated, on average 69 percent black, 28 percent white, and only 4 percent Hispanic/Latino. Over the course of the 1980s,

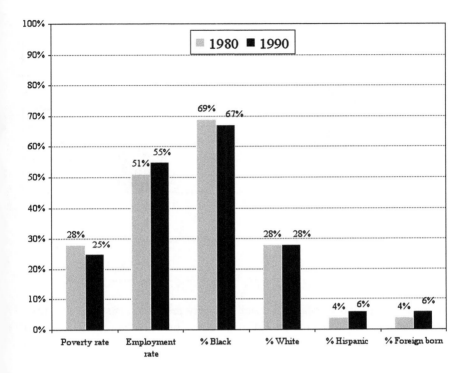

Figure 6.3. Characteristics of African American sample members' neighborhoods where concentrated disadvantage declined from 1980 to 1990.

the neighborhoods that became less disadvantaged did not experience complete transformation, but they did become more diverse, both ethnically and economically. On average, the poverty rate in these neighborhoods dropped to 25 percent, and the rate of employment rose to 55 percent. The average percentage of black residents dropped slightly to 67 percent, the percentage of white residents did not change, while the percentage of Latino residents and foreign-born residents rose to 6 percent. Similar to the national picture over the past several decades, the neighborhoods that experienced declines in concentrated disadvantage over this decade were not neighborhoods that attracted an influx of whites, but were instead neighborhoods that saw an increase in ethnic heterogeneity due to growing numbers of Latinos, many of them immigrants.

This pattern is very different from the common conception of "gentrification," which often connotes a racial turnover where new white entrants

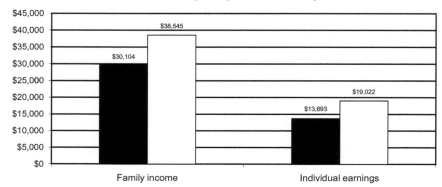

Figure 6.4. Effects of a decline in concentrated disadvantage on adult economic outcomes among African Americans.

to a neighborhood displace original minority residents. Instead, the most common pattern of neighborhood "improvement" for African Americans in the 1980s entailed improvement in the economic status of residents combined with ethnic diversification in the form of a rise in Latino and foreign-born newcomers.

How do these patterns of change affect the economic trajectories of African American youth as they move into adulthood? Figure 6.4 provides the first piece of an answer to this question. The figure shows the average earnings and income in adulthood for pairs of African Americans matched during their youth. For each outcome, the columns shaded black represent the average economic status for youth in neighborhoods that experienced no change over the 1980s, while the white columns represent the average economic status for youth in neighborhoods that improved over the 1980s. Specifically, the latter column shows the average outcomes for youth in neighborhoods where the degree of concentrated disadvantage declined by one standard deviation over the 1980s, which is roughly the average amount of change over all neighborhoods that experienced any decline in disadvantage.

As is visible in the figure, there is strong evidence that when neighborhood disadvantage declines, the economic fortunes of black youth improve, and improve rather substantially. Whereas the average black child in a neighborhood that does not change earns about $13,700 per year in early adulthood, the average child in a neighborhood where the degree of racial segregation and poverty decline earns about $19,000 per year. The child in a stable neighborhood has average family income of roughly $30,000, compared to $38,500 for the child whose neighborhood improves over the decade. This large effect on family income may indicate that living in an improving neighborhood influences the quality of marriage partners available to individuals, in addition to improving individuals' own economic opportunities.

To test this and other possible mechanisms, I examined a number of outcomes in addition to adult economic status, including educational attainment, marriage, welfare receipt, and wealth. Interestingly, while improvements in the neighborhood had positive impacts on all of these outcomes, none of the effects were as strong as those found for earnings and income, and none were statistically significant. For instance, a decline in neighborhood disadvantage led to only a marginal increase in educational attainment of about a quarter of a year of schooling and had no impact at all on the likelihood that children would get married in early adulthood. Instead, all of the positive results relate to individuals' experiences in the labor market, including slight improvements in the number of hours worked annually, in wages, and in wealth. These findings suggest that the most important benefits of living in an improving neighborhood appear to lie in the labor market experiences of residents, as opposed to their schooling experiences or family life.

To put these results in perspective, it may be helpful to return to the fictitious pair of young men that I described earlier, Ray and Kevin. In 1980, the two lived in virtually identical neighborhoods that had changed in virtually identical ways over the 1970s. But at that point, their neighborhoods diverged. Ray's neighborhood became more diverse, both ethnically and economically. Kevin's neighborhood remained segregated and poor. The results presented in this chapter suggest that these changes would likely have profound implications for the individual trajectories of the two young men. After living in their neighborhoods and experiencing the changes in each of them over the 1990s, Ray and Kevin would each be twenty-two years old and would likely be starting their careers in the labor force. My results suggest that they each could be expected to have equal levels of education and would be equally likely to get married. However, the results shown in figure 6.4 suggest that the two young men are on the verge of very different economic trajectories. As they move further into adulthood, Ray can expect to earn $5,000 more per year than Kevin, and to have an annual income that is more than $8,000 higher.

These differences in the economic trajectories of Ray and Kevin are not attributable to characteristics of the children themselves or to character-istics of their families. They are attributable exclusively to changes in the neighborhood environments surrounding the youth. This is a startling finding when one considers the research literature examining patterns of economic mobility. Whereas most research on the mechanisms by which economic and social status are transmitted from parents to children fo-cuses on factors within the home, the workplace, or the individual, this re-search provides support to bolster the findings in chapter 4, suggesting that neighborhoods, communities, and metropolitan areas may also be central to processes of economic mobility. In other words, there is strong evidence that the fortunes of people and places are closely linked.

This observation is important not simply from an academic perspec-tive; it also suggests that interventions designed to alter the neighborhood environments of families in the most disadvantaged communities could have substantial impacts on the economic trajectories of residents, possibly disrupting the cycle of intergenerational inequality that I have described throughout the book. Further, the pattern of improvement observed in the neighborhoods of African Americans and described in this analysis is very different from common conceptions of gentrification, which typically con-note a racial transition from minority to white. The neighborhoods of Afri-can Americans that experienced the most dramatic declines in concentrated disadvantage were *not* neighborhoods that saw an influx of white residents. Instead, they were neighborhoods in which poverty, and associated charac-teristics like welfare receipt and unemployment, became less severe. They were neighborhoods that became more ethnically diverse, due in large part to growing numbers of Latinos and immigrants.

These patterns suggest that reducing the concentration of disadvantage does not necessarily mean taking steps to attract whites to segregated neigh-borhoods. The most common form of neighborhood advancement over the last several decades has not entailed a transition from black to white, but rather a transition from racial and economic segregation to ethnic and eco-nomic diversity, fueled largely by immigration. As the evidence presented in this chapter suggests, this type of neighborhood transformation holds promise as a means to foster economic mobility among African Americans and provides a very hopeful vision of the possibilities of change for families in America's most disadvantaged communities.

But this vision is somewhat incomplete. The main problem with the foregoing analysis of neighborhood change is that it does not reveal much about what types of interventions are likely to bring about a decline in the degree of concentrated disadvantage within a neighborhood. This is the inevitable drawback of conducting an analysis that pools data from across the country and analyzing neighborhood change arising from a wide assortment of local factors. While there is strong evidence that improvements in the neighborhood environment lead to substantial economic benefits later in life, the preceding analysis provides no guidance on how to generate such improvements.

The concluding chapter turns to the literature on this topic, in another search for hints as to what types of interventions are the most likely to bring about sustained change in urban communities across the nation. The evidence is not entirely conclusive, but there are models of programs that provide resources and services to communities that have been shown to be effective—or in some cases, that at least hold the promise of being effective. The primary point of the current analysis is more abstract. If policy makers and community leaders are able to develop and implement interventions and investments that transform a community, there is strong evidence indicating that this transformation would have profoundly beneficial impacts on the youth living within the targeted neighborhoods.

Chapter 7 | **Toward a Durable Urban Policy Agenda**

Most of the evidence presented throughout the book leads to a sobering conclusion: despite the optimism of the period, the generation of African American children raised during the civil rights era has made virtually no advancement out of the nation's poorest neighborhoods. While previous research has documented the persistent poverty and segregation that continue to characterize urban ghettos, this study has uncovered an additional empirical observation that adds a layer of complexity to the study of concentrated urban poverty and racial inequality. The families that occupied the ghettos of the 1970s are, in large part, the same families that occupy today's ghettos. Neighborhood advantages and disadvantages have been passed down to the current generation, and the consequences for racial inequality have been severe.

These findings bring us back to the opening chapter of the book, where I argued for an expanded view of inequality in America, one that looks beyond the individual and beyond the family to understand patterns of racial inequality and economic mobility. The analyses presented provide strong support for this expanded perspective—but even after one considers the influence of neighborhoods and cities, there are residual gaps between blacks and whites on many dimensions of child development and adult economic success. These results lead to the unmistakable conclusion that there is more to explain. The persistence of racial inequality is not explained, in full, by lingering disadvantages that are passed down from parents to children, nor is it fully explained by the fortunes of neighborhoods and cities over time. There is "new" inequality that is driven by a wide array of sources, some of which are only indirectly related to "places," some of which have no relation at all. Support for affirmative action and desegregation policies has declined over time, reversing some of the reductions in racial inequality brought about by these policies.[1] The rate of unionization in America has dropped steadily, eroding the economic security of the working and middle classes.[2] The emergence of global cities that serve as hubs for international finance and other forms of commerce have led to a restructuring of urban resources and urban space in a growing number of cities across the nation and the world.[3] All racial and ethnic groups have seen a decline in the proportion of families headed by two parents, but the prevalence of single-parent households continues to be highest among African Americans.[4] Cultural responses to racial and ethnic identity and inequality are powerfully linked to behavior in the school and work settings, and they play a complex role in reproducing inequality.[5]

The point in noting all of these factors, many of which have received little or no attention in the text, is that coming to a full explanation of racial inequality in America is exceedingly complex and is well beyond the scope of any single study. The central point of this study is that in moving toward a more complete understanding of why racial inequality has been so persistent we cannot limit our attention to characteristics of individuals and families, to policies targeting individual poverty, or to macro-level forces leading to growing income inequality. We must also consider places. We must consider the various sets of forces that affect neighborhoods and cities and the ways that the trajectories of people and places are connected over time.

In doing so, I find that the environments surrounding African American and white families have played a central role in the reproduction of racial inequality. The extraordinary amount of downward mobility among African Americans who were raised during the civil rights era is difficult to explain without considering the neighborhoods in which these children were raised. The continuing racial disparities in cognitive skills and academic achievement that have received so much attention among scholars and the media make more sense when we consider the cumulative disadvantages experienced by blacks over generations. The findings in this book make clear that neighborhood poverty experienced in one generation lives on in families to affect the life chances of the next generation, creating a cross-generational legacy of disadvantage. These findings provide an idea of the scope of the problems that face us when we attempt to confront the challenges of the urban ghetto. They are challenges that are not limited to the current generation, but that have roots in lifetimes and generations of disadvantage. This is the overwhelming, even deflating, conclusion from much of the analysis I have presented.

Alternatively, the encouraging evidence I have presented shows that when families are able to move out of the most violent, poorest, racially segregated neighborhoods in the nation, their children's academic and cognitive test scores rise sharply. Similarly, when the degree of concentrated disadvantage surrounding a family declines, children's economic fortunes improve substantially as they approach adulthood. Despite the challenges inherent in confronting the problem of the inherited ghetto, this evidence provides hope that shifts in the nation's approach to its most disadvantaged communities can have tangible impacts and may begin to alleviate the persistent, multigenerational problem of racial inequality. This chapter draws on the evidence produced and described throughout the book, along with the proposals of leading urban scholars, and puts forth a set of ideas about what such a shift of approach might look like.

The central argument underlying all of the ideas I will review is that to confront the problem of multigenerational disadvantage requires investments, policies, and programs that have the potential to have a lasting impact on families and that have the potential to be sustained over time. The disadvantages faced by families in the nation's poorest neighborhoods are disadvantages that have been experienced across generations, meaning point-in-time investments in the lives of families living in the most disadvantaged neighborhoods are unlikely to have long-term beneficial impacts. Similarly, the federal government's erratic commitment to the viability of the nation's cities means that any short-term or underfunded investments in urban neighborhoods are unlikely to generate enduring change in these communities. For these reasons, the key goals of any urban agenda should not end with proposals for effective programs that may generate positive impacts; instead, an urban agenda should focus on promising programs and policies that have the capacity to withstand fluctuations in the economy and in the nation's political commitment to its cities and neighborhoods, as well as the potential to generate sustained effects that persist over generations of families. In other words, I argue for a "durable" urban policy.

There are two components of durable urban policy. The first component is the potential of the given policy to generate enduring changes in the lives of targeted families. Programs that provide sustained support, resources, opportunities, or enriched environments for families over time meet this criterion, as do programs that are designed to reach multiple generations of a family. Programs that provide point-in-time resources or services to a family, or short-term opportunities that are likely to fade away, would not fit this criterion.[6] Much of the chapter focuses on this dimension of durable urban policy, with a particular focus on programs that have the potential to have cross-generational impacts.

The second component of durable urban policy is the capacity for a given program or policy to generate change that persists over time. This component relates both to policies and to politics. There are some policies that carry with them the potential to create long-term or even permanent changes in urban settings—an example might be the establishment of a regional coalition to coordinate transportation policy or to expand economic opportunities for residents living across a metropolitan area; another example might be the demolition of public housing projects as part of a broader shift in the goals and strategies of public housing within a city. The sequence of changes induced by such policies is never fixed or determined ahead of time, but the policy may still be thought of as "durable" if it has the potential to generate long-term shifts in approach or permanent changes to a community. Political considerations are central to this second dimension of durable urban policy. Issues related to coalition building and the framing of policies to appeal to wide segments of the population are important for the design of policies that have the potential to generate broad support and thus to be sustained when political winds shift or when budgets tighten. These issues are crucial to urban policy, as there are numerous examples of programs that have been implemented with great promise only to be diluted in the political process and dismantled before they have the chance to work. I focus less attention on the political strategies that can be used to design durable urban policies, simply because this is not my area of expertise and others have written extensively on the subject.[7] Despite this lack of attention, generating the political will to sustain investments over time is crucial to the type of durable urban policy that I advocate. Before describing the types of policies that fit (and do not fit) the criteria of durable urban policy, however, I begin with a more general discussion of debates surrounding the relevance and the merits of "place-based" policy.

The Case for Urban Policy *and* Place-based Policy

In making the case for place-based policies, it is important to reiterate a point that has been made repeatedly by urban scholars over time. It is very clear that policies that target resources toward specific places, if implemented on their own, are unlikely to have broad impacts that will reduce racial inequality.[8] The fortunes of urban neighborhoods are driven in large part by forces that lie outside the neighborhood,[9] and there are numerous examples of place-based interventions that have been overwhelmed by broader economic, political, and demographic forces. What is most essential to the fate of the nation's urban neighborhoods is a federal commitment to economic equality along with a federal commitment to the nation's cities and metropolitan regions. The central goals of this "metropolitan" focus have been outlined in detail by other authors, and thus I will summarize them without repeating the details of the arguments.[10]

As described most comprehensively in the work of Bruce Katz, the fate of urban communities depends in large part on investments made in the development of human capital and health, in transportation policy, in criminal justice and policing, in research and development, in regional cooperation and governance, and in immigration policy.[11] Urban neighborhoods will deteriorate if the nation's cities are not competitive in global markets, if they are not producing jobs that offer living wages and affordable housing, if they are not attracting immigrants, if they do not offer high-quality schools, if they do not offer healthy and environmentally sustainable settings, if they are not safe, if they do not have efficient public transportation, and if they are competing instead of cooperating with suburbs. Any place-based program implemented without a broader commitment to making cities livable, welcoming to different groups, competitive, efficient, clean, and prosperous is doomed for failure.

There is a flip side to this point, however, and one that is rarely mentioned among scholars advocating a metropolitan-focused policy agenda. Broad-based urban policy agendas focusing on competitiveness and prosperity for metropolitan regions as a whole are not sufficient for confronting the problems of the urban ghetto. The experience of cities such as Atlanta provides an example as to why this is the case. While the Atlanta metropolitan area is seen by many as a story of successful adaptation to a service sector economy, the laissez-faire approach to economic growth taken in Atlanta has resulted in severe inequality within the region. Predominantly black communities within the city limits have been the losers in this process, experiencing growing poverty even during a time of rapid economic expansion in the metro area as a whole.[12]

Further evidence for this point can be found in figures on economic growth and unemployment from the 1990s forward. In the 1990s the nation experienced a sustained period of economic growth, urban labor markets were tight, and a large number of nonwhite women were drawn into the labor force because of welfare reform, expansion of the earned income tax credit, and the strong labor market. Despite the growth of employment in the nation's central cities, the fortunes of African American men in the labor market did not improve.[13] As economist Harry Holzer commented in an article for the *New York Times*, "If you look at the numbers, the 1990's was a bad decade for young black men, even though it had the best labor market in 30 years."[14] While jobs were growing in the nation's cities, black men were not in a position to take advantage of this growth because of the shockingly high number of such men with criminal records, because of their low levels of human capital, and because of the types of service sector jobs that were growing most quickly.

The lack of progress for black men, even in the strongest labor market of the past several decades, underscores the point that economic growth alone is not enough to counterbalance the array of forces that have acted to limit economic mobility among specific segments of the urban population. The research of Rebecca Blank has shown that high rates of economic growth are no longer linked with reductions in poverty among minority populations to the same degree as in the past.[15] Further, low-skilled minorities are consistently shown to be the "last hired" in times of economic growth and the "first fired" during periods of slowdown.[16] The consequences of this pattern are now becoming visible, as the rate of unemployment for nonwhite populations has skyrocketed during the current downturn. As of May 2010, the unemployment rate for blacks was 15.5 percent, almost double the rate for whites[17]—and this figure does not include those out of the labor force or incarcerated.

Just as the benefits of economic prosperity are not distributed evenly across urban populations and urban neighborhoods, the costs of economic downturn have disproportionate impacts on poor, racially segregated communities. In 1990 Douglas Massey published an important article in the *American Journal of Sociology* in which he conducted a simulation that examined what happens to racially segregated communities when the poverty rate of African Americans increases.[18] In the absence of racial segregation, Massey demonstrated that a rise in the black poverty rate has only minimal effects on the overall concentration of poverty. In the presence of severe racial segregation, similar to what would have been found in a city like Chicago in the 1970s, the consequences of a rise in black poverty are very different. Within a highly segregated urban landscape, a rise in the black poverty rate leads to an enormous increase in the level of concentrated poverty. Put differently, when poverty increases in a particular racial group and the majority of that group lives within a spatially distinct area of the city, then the consequences of the rise in poverty will be concentrated within a small number of communities that are characterized by racial and class segregation.

While this is a somewhat intuitive observation, the simulation conducted by Massey reveals in a very clear way why overall changes in the economic status of urban populations can have very different consequences for different communities within the city. One implication of this result is that in periods of economic downturn the impact of a rise in joblessness or poverty is likely to be concentrated within a small number of communities, with the potential to generate a range of social problems that are associated with concentrated poverty, including increased crime, depopulation, homelessness, declining resources for families, and overall deterioration of an area.

The presence of "concentration effects" means that policy makers cannot simply rely on broad-based urban policy in order to avoid the set of social problems, and the associated costs, that are unique to the ghetto.[19]

In addition to an overarching urban agenda focused on broad-based prosperity, then, I argue for a set of supplementary policies that are designed specifically to target areas of concentrated disadvantage.[20] In doing so, I enter into a long-standing debate about the relative merits of mobility strategies versus place-based strategies in confronting concentrated poverty. This debate rose to prominence once again with the competing proposals from the Edwards and Obama campaigns in 2008, with Edwards recommending vouchers and Obama proposing resources for communities. Political campaigns aside, the reality is that any comprehensive policy strategy must combine elements from each approach, and there is substantial overlap in policies that might be considered "mobility" approaches with those that might be classified as "investment" approaches. The ideas I describe below include multiple policies that have traditionally been considered mobility strategies as well as several that have been considered place-based investment strategies, and much of what I propose synthesizes the ideas of scholars who have been writing on these issues for a long time.

The approach I put forth differs in emphasis, however, from some of the prominent calls for bold plans to confront concentrated poverty. In particular, I propose a shift away from the long-standing conviction of some urban scholars and advocates that moving families out of the ghetto, en masse, should be a primary dimension of our efforts to confront concentrated poverty. I believe that the evidence available suggests this approach is not only unrealistic but would likely have harmful consequences for many eligible families and would have unanticipated distributional consequences for urban communities. This is not to say that residential mobility is unimportant. In the section that follows I describe a set of strategies designed to enhance freedom of residential mobility, continue the shift away from high-rise public housing projects, and push forward limited, targeted mobility programs—but to do so in a way that generates enduring changes to families' environments and sustainable shifts in policy.

Toward a "Durable" Mobility Policy

On the basis of the early evidence from the Gautreaux program, the idea that vouchers could be the solution to the problems of the urban ghetto took hold among several prominent urban scholars, advocates, and politicians. But after reconsidering the evidence from Gautreaux, Moving to Opportunity, and other mobility programs that were reviewed in chapter 6, this idea needs to be updated and revised. While mobility programs can have substantial positive impacts on families, these effects have been found only in very specific settings, in specific types of programs, and for a limited number of outcomes of interest.

Evidence from Gautreaux indicates that moves that bring about a substantial and sustained change in a family's residential environment may lead to equally substantial changes in the family's life. Evidence from Moving to Opportunity indicates that moves out of high-poverty neighborhoods can lead to improvements in caregivers' peace of mind and health, and new evidence suggests that when families living in cities with the poorest, most segregated, most violent communities are given the chance to move into less distressed environments, the children in those families may benefit substantially.[21] But there is little evidence that mobility out of a wider range of poor neighborhoods produces similar benefits.

In addition to the mixed evidence on the impact of residential mobility, my hesitation in relying on mobility as a primary approach to confronting concentrated disadvantage stems from other interrelated concerns. The first is that it is unclear how these programs would work if taken to scale—that is, if they became the basis for a more expansive program that offers vouchers to large numbers of public housing residents or to the larger population living within areas of concentrated poverty. We must keep in mind that the prominent mobility programs that have been implemented, like MTO and Gautreaux, affect only a tiny fraction of families living in urban ghettos, but proposals to build on these programs envision large expansions. For instance, John Edwards's proposal during the presidential campaign of 2008 called for an additional million housing vouchers for low-income families.[22] Alexander Polikoff, the lead counsel in the court case that established the Gautreaux Assisted Housing Program, has proposed a "national Gautreaux Program" available exclusively to "black families in urban ghettos" across the nation.[23] Yale law professor Owen Fiss proposes a program to offer subsidies to allow every resident of poor, racially segregated neighborhoods to move to economically and racially diverse neighborhoods across the metropolitan area.[24] Fiss estimates that six million families would be eligible.

How might such an expansion affect the families and communities targeted? A first consideration is the distributional consequences of shifting large segments of an urban population across neighborhoods within a city or a metropolitan area. The urban economist George Galster is one of the few scholars to consider how large-scale mobility might alter the residential landscape of entire cities, and the conclusions from his work in this area have important implications for understanding the likely impacts of proposals like those of Edwards and Fiss.[25] Central to Galster's analysis is the idea that it is crucial to consider how patterns of mobility will affect both the neighborhoods that families leave and the neighborhoods that they enter. Under one scenario that Galster envisions, large numbers of low-income families might be compelled to leave high-poverty neighborhoods and disperse across the metropolitan area into a range of neighborhoods of extremely low poverty.[26] While the destination neighborhoods in this scenario would have slightly higher poverty rates, the poverty rate in these neighborhoods may be small enough at baseline that the community continues to have relatively minimal levels of concentrated poverty. This is the ideal scenario for a residential mobility program, as it would bring about a decline in concentrated poverty in the sending neighborhood and minimal, widely diffused increases in poverty in receiving neighborhoods that are unlikely to have a major impact on these communities.

There are several alternative scenarios, however, that have very different implications for the concentration of poverty in sending and receiving neighborhoods. In one such alternative scenario, large numbers of low-income families exit high-poverty neighborhoods and move into a small number of lower-poverty neighborhoods that are on the verge of becoming poorer. In this case, the sending neighborhood would have lower poverty but the poverty rate in the receiving neighborhoods would climb higher, so that these neighborhoods would now be high-poverty themselves.

This is a simplified version of some of the scenarios that Galster describes in a set of simulations. Still, this scenario looks quite plausible, even realistic, when one considers the patterns of movement that have occurred in the MTO experiment. Robert Sampson analyzed data from MTO's experimental group in Chicago and found that families moved largely within the city, and they moved in large numbers to a small number of destination neighborhoods.[27] The flows of families in MTO followed a remarkably structured pattern, in which families moved to communities that had low poverty but where the neighborhood was changing, on its way to becoming more poor. Only a few hundred families moved in each MTO city, making it unlikely that any communities "tipped" to become high-poverty areas as a result of the experiment. But if a similar program were implemented on a broader scale, it is highly likely that the program would produce new neighborhoods of concentrated poverty across the city, thus shifting the location of concentrated poverty instead of reducing it.

Beyond the distributional impacts of broad-based mobility programs, there are serious political concerns that would likely arise with such a proposal. One of the most unique aspects of the Gautreaux program was that families living in public housing within Chicago were assigned to apartments throughout the metro area, including many predominantly white suburbs outside of the city limits. But no more than a few families were assigned to each area, meaning there was no threat of a change in the demographics of the community. In all likelihood, the limited scope of the program explains why it met with little political resistance.

The Moving to Opportunity program worked differently, as families were free to choose any neighborhood with the requirement that they pick one with a poverty rate of less than 10 percent. Across the five cities where MTO was implemented, a total of roughly 4,500 families participated in the program—but only a few hundred actually moved to low-poverty neighborhoods in each city.[28] Even though MTO was implemented on a scale small enough so that it affected only a small fraction of the public housing population, the program generated intense opposition in one of the five cities—Baltimore—among residents of working-class, largely white communities who feared it was part of a broader plan to gradually shift the city's poorest residents into their neighborhoods. The opposition exposed explicit racial and class tensions, and its impact was enormous. After a series of tense community meetings and an organized campaign to halt MTO, Democratic senator Barbara Mikulski, who had originally supported the program, called for it to end. Although the initial phase of the MTO program continued, the plans for a second phase of MTO in Baltimore were called off.[29]

Of course, social policy ideas should not be discarded because of resistance that is based, at least in part, on thinly veiled racism and preferences for segregated communities. At the same time, attempts to engineer the types of "ideal" communities that policy analysts or academics envision by moving large numbers of residents across a city will never end well. The episode in Baltimore might serve as caution for those who advocate a more expansive residential mobility program that would seek to disperse the ghetto population across a metropolitan area. As political scientist Jennifer Hochschild wrote in response to Owen Fiss's proposal to offer vouchers to the entire ghetto population, "Absent a revolution in most Americans' preferences with regard to the race and class of their neighbors, Fiss's proposal is politically hopeless."[30]

On the basis of the evidence available on the likely impact of large-scale residential mobility, and given the political realities of urban America, it is time to discard the idea that moving large numbers of families out of the ghetto can be a primary solution to concentrated poverty. This does not mean that enhanced options for residential mobility should not be a priority for urban policy, however. There are two sets of findings from this book that are relevant for thinking about what types of mobility policies might be particularly effective in disrupting the cycle of multigenerational neighborhood disadvantage. The first set comes from chapter 6, where I review evidence suggesting that movement out of the most intensely violent communities or public housing projects in the nation leads to substantial developmental benefits for youth. These results suggest that small-scale residential mobility programs targeting families that are eager to move out of high-poverty, violent neighborhoods across the country have the potential to be effective in improving the mental health of parents and the developmental trajectories of children. If implemented with intensive assistance for families as they search for new homes and with sustained supports for families as they become integrated within their new communities, this type of program is more likely to produce enduring changes in families' environments that represent more than temporary departures from life in the ghetto.

The second set of relevant results comes from chapter 2, where I show that one primary reason why disadvantaged neighborhoods are passed down across generations is that African Americans are highly likely to remain in the same place as they move from childhood to adulthood. While we should be hesitant in assuming this finding is causal, it is nonetheless important to note that when children grow up and move to a new county, they are much more likely to enter into new social worlds that feature ethnically diverse communities with lower concentrations of poverty than those in which they were raised.[31] The beneficial effects arising from geographic migration are broadly consistent with a long line of historical research demonstrating that African Americans have benefited tremendously from long-range geographic mobility. Research on the impact of the Great Migration of African Americans out of the rural south and into the cities of the northeast, midwest, and later the west has argued that this geographic movement accounts for much of the economic progress that blacks have made over the twentieth century.[32] More recently, there is growing evidence suggesting that if individuals from highly disadvantaged communities make moves that lead them across the borders of their home city—and not just from one neighborhood to another—they show sharply reduced levels of involvement in crime and violence.[33] Lastly, evidence from Gautreaux suggests that movement out of Chicago's city limits was the crucial ingredient that enabled caregivers to take advantage of new economic opportunities, that enabled children to go further in school and steer clear of violence and involvement with the criminal justice system, and that allowed families to remain outside of poor neighborhoods for long periods of time.[34]

It is less clear how public policy can be used to induce long-range movement of families across cities or even regions, or whether this is advisable. That said, it is certainly possible for public policy to help facilitate long-range mobility for groups that are seeking out new opportunities in different places, or otherwise seeking to "knife off" from an unhealthy or disadvantaged social environment that surrounds them. For instance, a special fund might be established to provide loans to less-educated or low-income families that allows them to make long-distance moves out of depressed areas,[35] or criminal justice agencies might consider programs that allow returning offenders to start anew in a different city.[36] A special class of housing vouchers might be designed to provide incentives for public housing residents to locate units in the larger metropolitan area.[37]

An alternative approach is to ensure that housing policies do not constrain families from leaving high-poverty or highly violent neighborhoods. With this idea in mind, I would argue that the ongoing effort to replace the high-rise model of public housing with scattered-site, mixed-income housing represents an important shift in the nation's approach to public housing with the potential to lead to permanent transformations of distressed urban neighborhoods. HOPE VI, the federal program designed to demolish high-rise public housing projects and replace them with scattered-site housing, has been criticized widely for forcibly relocating public housing residents, for misleading residents about opportunities to return to newly built developments in their original neighborhoods, and for failing to provide adequate housing and transitional resources for those displaced during the process.[38] The criticisms are warranted. HOPE VI continued a long tradition of housing policy that has largely ignored the needs and desires of residents while dismantling communities.[39] Even the program's strongest advocates acknowledge that not enough was done to ensure that residents had assistance in finding new housing.[40] Still, the underlying goals of HOPE VI are sound, even if the process to implement the program has been seriously flawed. Many of the public housing projects that have been torn down across the country are structures that have served to reinforce segregation and concentrate poverty, and many had deteriorated to a point where they needed to be rebuilt and rethought, or else demolished.[41] This was not an inevitable outcome. As I described in chapter 3, the fate of high-rise public housing projects has been determined by the wavering commitment to these buildings, their residents, and the communities and cities in which they are located.

The Choice Neighborhoods initiative, which is being implemented on a small scale by the Obama administration, represents a more promising approach to replacing high-rise public housing projects and rebuilding communities in the settings where projects have been torn down.[42] The program will select a limited number of communities across the country where public housing complexes were torn down through HOPE VI and will aim to redevelop the communities by providing investments to physical infrastructure, resources for key institutions like the schools, and services for former and new residents.[43] Although the limited scope of Choice Neighborhoods and the limited funding attached to the initiative make one wonder whether the program can lead to meaningful changes in urban neighborhoods, the spirit of the initiative reflects a commitment to urban communities and their residents that has been largely absent from much urban policy. Choice Neighborhoods represent the type of commitment that should have been made to public housing residents and their neighborhoods a long time ago—but at current funding levels it will provide a relatively meager amount of resources to a small number of neighborhoods across the country. Still, it is important to highlight this program because it reflects a shift away from a long-standing pattern of policy toward public housing projects that has involved concentrating the poor within large complexes, abandoning these complexes, and then dispersing residents elsewhere. Considering both its goals and its limitations, Choice Neighborhoods might be thought of as a program that reflects the *ideals* of durable urban policy even if it lacks the resources necessary to realize these ideals on a broad scale.[44]

Finally, any proposal aiming to address issues of segregation and the concentration of poverty must begin with the recognition that freedom of mobility is an essential goal for urban public policy and for social justice, and any form of discrimination in the housing and lending markets must be challenged aggressively. Despite legislation designed to bolster the enforcement mechanisms of the Fair Housing Act and make it easier to prosecute claims of discrimination in the housing market, the actual number of claims that make their way through the system is remarkably small and the evidence available makes clear that housing and lending discrimination remain prevalent in America's cities.[45] Making progress toward ending blatant and even subtler discrimination in the housing and lending markets remains imperative. One of the more promising approaches to reducing discrimination in these markets is to shift from "passive" enforcement, where individual complaints are tried in court, to "active" enforcement, where the federal government conducts systematic audits of landlords and lenders and then prosecutes or fines those who are found to be discriminatory.[46] This shift in approach represents one way to remedy the weak enforcement mechanisms that make it so difficult to confront racial and ethnic discrimination in the housing market. If implemented along with a broader influx of resources for the enforcement of fair housing and fair lending laws, the shift to an active enforcement approach has the potential to live up to the ideals of the fair housing movement.[47]

Along with the continuing transformation of public housing, shifting strategies to reduce discrimination in the housing market and to end predatory and discriminatory lending in the mortgage market should be priorities in a durable urban policy agenda focusing on freedom of residential mobility. Mobility programs that target families in the most violent, disadvantaged neighborhoods across the country and that provide sustained supports to these families also fit into this agenda because they have the potential to generate changes in families' lives that are likely to endure over time. However, a broader program that provides vouchers to large numbers of families, or that targets families in all poor neighborhoods, is unlikely to generate lasting change in families' lives and is highly likely to have unanticipated consequences for communities and cities. Instead of proposals for large-scale mobility programs, I argue for direct and sustained investments in poor urban neighborhoods.[48]

Toward a Policy of Durable Investment in Urban Neighborhoods

Underlying the "durable investment" approach is the idea that living among poor, minority neighbors is harmful not because of any unique character deficiencies of poor families, but because areas composed primarily of poor racial and ethnic minorities have been the object of severe disinvestment and abandonment for most of the past half century. If segregated neighborhoods with concentrated poverty had greater levels of political influence, amenities that are taken for granted in middle-class communities, quality public services and schools, a vibrant economic base, and effective policing, then segregation and the concentration of poverty would decline and would not necessarily be associated with gang activity, crime, and violence, teenage childbearing and high dropout rates, poor community health, joblessness, homelessness, and blight. The social problems that are prevalent in America's ghettos are the product of decades of shortsighted policies, intentional efforts to isolate or exclude minority communities within cities, and major economic and demographic shifts. These problems are not the product of character deficits among the urban poor, and addressing these problems does not mean we must move the poor out.

There is also good reason to believe that if the pattern of disinvestment in urban neighborhoods were mitigated or reversed, some level of economic and racial integration would follow. In her book *Sharing America's Neighbor-*

hoods, Ingrid Gould Ellen makes a convincing case that one primary reason whites avoid neighborhoods with a substantial black presence is the fear that the racial makeup of the neighborhood will bring about a process of deterioration, rising crime, failing schools, and declining property values.[49] What is crucial to note is that it is not solely the race of potential neighbors that is most important, but the *implications* of race in today's urban residential markets. This is not to say that "pure" racial prejudice has disappeared or that race itself is unimportant, but that race becomes meaningful in explaining residential patterns in part because of everything that is tied up with a neighborhood's racial composition.[50]

The association between race and neighborhood deterioration is not inevitable. It is a result of decades of public policies that have served to strengthen and reinforce the walls of the ghetto while systematically disinvesting in black urban communities. The impact of this disinvestment cannot be reversed with anything but a similar commitment, in scale and duration, to America's urban neighborhoods.

What would such a commitment entail? At a general level, it would entail a shift in the approach of urban policy. For the last several decades, much of urban social policy has been dominated by an approach that might be characterized as punitive in nature, with an emphasis on federal retreat from urban social problems and the dismantling and dispersal of poor urban communities.[51] This approach is reflected in the federal abandonment of public housing, in the razing of neighborhoods during urban renewal, and in the progression toward mass imprisonment. Urban policy must shift away from the abandonment and dispersal approach toward an alternative approach that emphasizes investment and integration. By investment, I am referring to a commitment in resources and planning that must be made to urban communities and that must be sustained over time. By integration, I am referring to a more abstract set of strategies designed to create coordination between localities within metropolitan areas, as well as linkages within communities that extend from children to adults to local officials to key institutions in an effort to facilitate social cohesion and generate positive social capital.[52]

The argument for investment in urban communities begins with the recognition that the prosperity of any community is dependent on investment from the state. To cite a common example, suburban prosperity, where it exists, has been facilitated by federal investment in a highway and regional transportation system that allowed firms and workers to relocate outside of the central city. The expansion of home ownership in suburban America was possible because of federally backed mortgages, and homeowners continue to be the recipients of the largest housing policy the federal government operates: the home mortgage interest deduction, which disproportionately benefits middle- and upper-income homeowners and dwarfs any housing policy targeting low-income populations.[53] Prosperity is maintained through local financing of public education and through exclusionary zoning that allows communities to exclude individuals and families that may require more resources or that contribute less to the local tax base. The overarching point is that where suburban communities have fared well, it is because of enormous support from the federal government. It is not unreasonable to suggest that similar investments are necessary to support *all* communities and their residents, including urban communities and minority communities in particular.

The argument for integration begins with the widespread consensus that the U.S. system of extreme local control over land use and regulation, public services, and economic development has resulted in unhealthy fragmentation and competition among central cities and surrounding suburbs/ smaller cities within the nation's metropolitan areas.[54] Integrating metropolitan areas by confronting exclusionary zoning, promoting and expanding fair-share housing plans, and developing coordinated metropolitan-wide plans for transportation, housing, education, and economic development is essential to promoting prosperity across urban areas. There is widespread consensus about the need for equitable development at the regional level.[55] Generating the political coalitions necessary to create regional planning structures and to confront exclusionary zoning is the true challenge.[56] We are guided in this effort by the lessons learned from activists, scholars, and politicians who have been working for equitable development for decades, and who have developed a core set of strategies to generate the types of political coalitions necessary to challenge exclusionary policies and fragmented government in America's metropolitan regions.[57] There are also a number of promising examples of programs and strategies that might be used to break down the barriers between local towns and municipalities that are used to maintain regional inequality and to link regional development with tangible goals for community residents. Manuel Pastor and Margery Turner review a number of these strategies, ranging from federal incentives for inclusionary zoning, to the use of Community Benefit Agreements that require developers to meet standards for the employment of local residents and for living wages in exchange for support for their projects, to the development of more stringent requirements for the Low Income Housing Tax Credit, to the development of community land trusts that allow communities to maintain affordable housing in periods of gentrification.[58] The

Department of Housing and Urban Development's Neighborhood Stabilization Program, which provides funds to local groups to acquire and redevelop land in areas hit hard by the foreclosure crisis, is an excellent example of how the federal government can play a role in fostering more equitable development projects.[59] Unfortunately, this example is quite uncommon, as the federal commitment to breaking down the barriers that allow for regional inequality has been erratic over time.

Within communities, the argument for integration is bolstered by the research of Robert Sampson and others who have demonstrated the ways that internal organization and social cohesion allow communities to develop the types of social capital and informal social controls that facilitate the attainment of common ends.[60] There is minimal concrete evidence on how to support organization, social capital, and institutional strength within communities, but an array of formal and informal approaches have been proposed. As a starting point, public spaces like parks, school buildings, and even sidewalks must be maintained and monitored, so that crime is less of a threat, signs of physical disorder are less prevalent, and public spaces are open to all segments of the community.[61] Policing strategies such as community policing, and linkages between the police and other key institutions in a community, such as the church, can serve to alter the role of the police so that they are seen as partners within a community as opposed to adversaries.[62] The entrance of new immigrants into urban communities, a group that helped to revitalize some of the nation's most distressed neighborhoods over the past few decades, should be welcomed and supported not only to promote vibrant and inclusive neighborhoods within the city, but also as part of an effort to break down rigid and longstanding walls of segregation between African Americans and whites.[63] Local community organizations focusing on housing and physical redevelopment, economic development, asset building, and resident organization must continue to be supported, as these types of organizations provide a stabilizing force in city neighborhoods, even in the most challenging economic and political climates.[64] Finally, one of the most formidable challenges to maintaining cohesive urban communities in the years and decades to come will be dealing with the destabilizing consequences of mass imprisonment. While it is crucial to reverse the trend of mass imprisonment, it is also important to recognize that simply changing sentencing laws or releasing prisoners is not enough. Extensive systems of support must be developed to ensure that formerly incarcerated individuals are integrated into their communities and into the labor market in order to avoid the destabilization of neighborhoods that is likely with large numbers of formerly incarcerated individuals residing within a small number of communities.[65]

The set of ideas in the preceding paragraphs provides a sense of what an urban policy focusing on investment and integration might look like across various policy arenas. The remainder of the chapter describes a set of more concrete ideas and proposals to confront two very specific dimensions of neighborhood disadvantage that have been identified by numerous scholars as crucial to the functioning of urban communities and to the well-being of children and families within these communities based on a long line of research and theory. The programs that I highlight share an additional common feature: their impact has the potential to extend across generations, affecting both parents and children. In each case, the evidence available does not allow for definitive conclusions about the impact that specific interventions will have, but there is enough accumulated knowledge to offer ideas about the form that a policy agenda might take.

We know, first and foremost, that widespread joblessness is debilitating for families and for communities. This point has been made repeatedly by some of the most thoughtful and influential urban scholars over the past century, and it is described most forcefully in William Julius Wilson's book *When Work Disappears*.[66] Wilson argues that in areas where joblessness is rampant, the structure of everyday life and expectations for common norms of behavior are altered. When large numbers of residents are without work, employment no longer provides a coherent structure to the everyday lifestyle of individuals or the community. With the absence of role models who have achieved a stable, middle-class lifestyle through steady employment, this model loses its relevance to youth. A niche is created for illicit or underground markets to emerge, and informal social control of public spaces is weakened. In this sense, the impact of concentrated joblessness alters community life in fundamental ways that go beyond the loss of financial resources.

We know, second, that providing safe and stimulating environments for children, particularly young children, is crucial for their developmental and learning trajectories. Evidence from the field of child development has pointed to the importance of early childhood for several decades, but there is new momentum behind the call for investments early in children's lives.[67] The new momentum is attributable in large part to the research of James Heckman, a Nobel Prize–winning economist, who has made a convincing argument for the efficiency of investing in children's environments early in life, during the period when the brain is actively developing and before a child's trajectory is firmly established.[68] Simply investing in children's settings at a single point in time is not enough, however. A durable policy agenda focusing on children's environments entails investments that reach across generations, targeting both parents and children, and that are sustained over the child's life. With these two overarching points serving as a backdrop, the following discussion describes a dual strategy for confronting the multigenerational cycle of neighborhood disadvantage, with a focus on children's environments and adult employment.

Confronting Joblessness in Disadvantaged Communities

The destructive impact of joblessness is clear, but it is less clear how to chart a course leading toward full and stable employment for the entire labor force, including job seekers in poor and racially segregated communities. General macroeconomic policies designed to facilitate economic growth and full employment are clearly the most important part of any approach, but the evidence suggests they are not enough. In the mid-1990s the economy grew at an unprecedented rate, creating a period of tight labor markets and sustained job growth in central cities. Despite these unprecedented economic conditions, the economic boom provided only a temporary respite from the problem of joblessness in black communities, and particularly from the underemployment of black men. The long-term trend showing rising rates of joblessness for black men paused slightly during the 1990s, but it did not reverse. When the economic boom ended, the long-term trend continued.[69] This was not true for black women, whose employment rose sharply in the mid-1990s due to a combination of tight labor markets, welfare reform, and expansion of the Earned Income Tax Credit. But that period of economic growth is long gone, and we are now in a situation where unemployment of African Americans is almost double that of whites.[70] Policies that facilitate economic growth are clearly important in reducing the problem of joblessness, but when the economic cycle turns downward the same communities are left to bear the brunt of widespread unemployment.[71] If there is a single lesson to be learned from the sustained economic boom of the 1990s, it is that economic growth is not enough to resolve the problem of concentrated joblessness.

One central question is what types of programs have the capacity to bolster employment opportunities within communities of high joblessness? There is widespread sentiment that interventions designed to lure employers or otherwise stimulate employment opportunities in areas of high joblessness typically have minimal impacts, although the evidence base is not entirely conclusive.[72] While the range of community development programs that arose out of the War on Poverty have been effective in some areas, such as generating affordable housing, these initiatives have been less effective in generating employment opportunities.

The most notable recent intervention designed to entice employers to disadvantaged areas is the Enterprise Zones/Empowerment Communities programs, implemented in the Clinton era. There are questions about whether these programs were put in place with resources sufficient to give them a chance to succeed, but as implemented there is mixed evidence as to whether they created employment opportunities.[73] The alternative approach to addressing joblessness is to invest in human capital of residents via job training or workforce education programs. These programs have a long history and have been closely evaluated, with mixed results. However, one recent example of a success story bears mentioning. The Jobs-Plus program, implemented in the 1990s by the federal Department of Housing and Urban Development, was designed to saturate designated public housing complexes with training and services, such as child care, to enable residents to enter the workforce, while also providing rent-based incentives encouraging work. An experimental evaluation of the program, where public housing sites were randomized to receive the intervention, showed strong results for outcomes related to employment and financial well-being.[74]

A broad interpretation of the results from Jobs-Plus suggests that when a place, such as a housing project, is saturated with services and incentives designed to facilitate employment, there may be fairly substantial economic benefits for residents. A more narrow interpretation is also plausible, however. The narrow interpretation would suggest that when an intensive set of interventions is implemented effectively and in a strong labor market, there may be fairly substantial economic benefits for residents who take advantage of the program. The most important point made in the narrow interpretation is that we do not know whether an intervention focusing on the supply side of the labor market will be effective in a weak market, when there is less demand for workers. In addition, we do not know whether the gains made in the strong labor market of the 1990s have persisted as the economy cooled down.

Given the mixed results from this literature and the uncertainty surrounding even the strongest findings from a program like Jobs-Plus, it would be a mistake to rely primarily on this type of human capital intervention to confront the problem of joblessness in urban neighborhoods. During economic downturns, direct intervention designed to guarantee employment to willing workers may be necessary. One recent model for how this might work comes from the New Hope program in Milwaukee.[75]

New Hope emerged out of the efforts of a unique mix of community activists, policy experts, and business leaders in Milwaukee. At the heart of the program was a contract that required eligible participants, who included all women *and men* with low-income living in one of Milwaukee's low-income neighborhoods, to work at least thirty or more hours per week. In return for proof of employment, participants received earnings supplements that brought them above the poverty line, and they received subsidized child care and health insurance. If they were unable to find work in the private sector, participants were guaranteed a temporary community service job.

The program might be seen as similar to the many experimental programs that were implemented prior to the passage of the national welfare reform legislation of 1996. But in truth, New Hope differed from these programs in several subtle but important ways. Unlike traditional welfare programs, in the New Hope program men were eligible for services whether or not they were married or had children. In this sense, the program represents one of the first work-support programs to address the needs of nonwhite men, a group that has seen its employment prospects progressively worsen over the past several decades. One of the under-reported facts about race and unemployment is that racial discrepancies in employment are driven almost entirely by men. Whereas black and white working-age women work at about the same rates, black men have substantially higher levels of joblessness than white men.[76] This empirical fact means that programs for which men are eligible are likely to have a much larger impact on joblessness than programs restricted to women or restricted to caregivers. By offering guaranteed, temporary community-service employment and targeting individuals in low-income neighborhoods, the program implicitly acknowledged that opportunities in the private sector are not sufficient for some segments of the population, even during a period of economic growth. Furthermore, the program offered the type of generous work supports that provided participants with a real chance to succeed in employment. The program was built on the idea that "if you work, you should not be poor," and the income, child care, and health insurance subsidies made good on this ideal. Lastly, the program staff made a conscious, careful effort to treat participants with respect and dignity, a departure from the bureaucracies that have been developed to administer traditional welfare programs.

Applicants to New Hope were randomly assigned to either the experimental group, which received all services, or a control group, which received no services through the program. The randomization allowed for a rigorous evaluation of the impact of the program, and has provided clear evidence that this type of intensive work-support strategy has the potential to substantially improve the lives of participants, with impacts that extend across generations. While participants who were already working full-time did not experience any improvements in earnings or employment, those who were not even working part-time worked more and had higher wages after taking part in the program. Adults experienced better mental and physical health through their participation in the program, and children were more likely to be in high-quality child care centers if their families took part in New Hope. Interestingly, children in families that received New Hope services showed improvements in school performance, with impacts on reading and overall effects that were especially pronounced for boys. Perhaps most importantly for a program designed to support work, New Hope reduced poverty among families that participated.

The findings from New Hope provide strong evidence that if individuals are supported in their efforts to enter the labor force, they and their children will benefit. One must keep in mind that the program was implemented during a strong economy, and it is therefore impossible to speculate on whether the results from New Hope would be the same if the program were replicated during a period of recession or high unemployment. When it was implemented, the most important features of New Hope were the wage supplements and other benefits provided to participating individuals to make work pay. In periods of economic downturn, the most important feature of this type of program may be the guarantee of minimum-wage public-service employment for individuals who are unemployed. This component of the program thus merits more detailed attention.

The idea of guaranteed employment has a long history in the United States, but it is an idea that is fraught with controversy. The best-known example of public-service employment programs is the Depression-era Works Progress Administration. But other programs that have featured a public-service employment component have been implemented in various forms and in different locations throughout the country—and not always in times of high unemployment, as the case of New Hope makes clear. The most comprehensive and balanced analysis of the various programs that have been implemented in the United States was written in the period of welfare reform by labor economist David Ellwood and his co-author, Elisabeth Welty, and I draw heavily on their work in my assessments of the potential impacts of public-service employment initiatives.[77]

Ellwood and Welty's review considers many of the most common critiques of public-service employment proposals, including the potential for inefficiency or displacement of other public or private sector workers, the absence of long-term impacts on employment and earnings trajectories of participants, and the costs of such programs. In each case, it is a mistake to minimize the risks of a program that is poorly designed or implemented. However, the authors' conclusions suggest that these critiques might be overstated for programs that are designed well and implemented at appropriate times—in particular, when demand for labor from the private sector is weak, and thus the potential for displacement is reduced.

One conclusion reached by Ellwood and Welty is that the potential for displacement is reduced substantially if public-service jobs are created that do not replicate work already being done, either in the private or public sector. For instance, the Civilian Conservation Corps (CCC) was used to improve public lands in ways that would not have been carried out in the absence of the program, which reduced the likelihood that private sector workers would be replaced by participants in the CCC. Ellwood and Welty's review makes clear that there will always be some displacement in any public-service employment program, but evidence from several programs suggests that the amount of displacement can be relatively small under certain conditions. If employment is targeted toward individuals who are different from the low-wage workforce, if jobs are temporary, and if unique assignments are given to workers, then there is less potential for public-service jobs to replace currently existing jobs.

A second, related concern is that creating new jobs will alter the demand for labor in the private sector, raising wages and reducing the overall number of jobs available. This concern is minimized if programs pay less than similar work in the private sector, if public-service employment is temporary, and if targeted populations are limited to those who are unemployed and live in high-unemployment areas.

Beyond these basic concerns about inefficiencies that might be created in the low-wage labor market, there are other important questions regarding the value of public-service jobs to the community and to the individual worker, as well as the costs of such programs. Costs of running public-service employment programs are a major issue because of the large administrative costs, which in many cases compose about half of a program's total budget.[78] If combined with other work supports, as in New Hope, the costs are much higher—although any declines in other forms of social services or in crime that result from such a program would reduce the overall fiscal burden. In terms of the "value" of public-service jobs, there is minimal evidence that community-service jobs have positive impacts on participants' long-term economic trajectories. I would argue that the true goal of such programs is not only to improve individuals' long-term prospects in the labor market, however, but also to reduce economic insecurity and avoid concentrated joblessness during periods of economic downturn. That said, there is a legitimate concern that placing people into useless jobs might be counterproductive. Surveying the literature on this topic, Ellwood and Welty argue that newly created community-service jobs typically are not seen as "make-work," but are viewed as quite valuable for communities. This is especially true if the jobs that are created focus on visible projects that would not be completed in the absence of the public-service program. This type of job is also the least likely to interfere with or create inefficiencies in the low-wage labor market.

The arguments made by Ellwood and Welty are largely supported by a review of public-service employment programs in Organization for Economic Cooperation and Development (OECD) countries.[79] In addition to noting how common this type of program is in OECD countries other than the United States, the review suggests that the programs that have been most effective are those that combine public service employment with training and work supports and individual plans designed to facilitate the transition into the labor force. These programs are less effective if they are designed as part of a "carousel" of support, in which individuals are allowed to circulate through periods of supported unemployment, public service employment, back to supported unemployment, and so forth.

The last round of calls for public service employment came during the period of welfare reform, in the mid-1990s.[80] William Julius Wilson reviewed several proposals for guaranteed public employment and settled on a proposal for a federal program that would employ any willing worker in public service employment at wages below the minimum wage.[81] Wilson proposed an increase in the minimum wage and an expansion of the Earned Income Tax Credit to go along with the guarantee of employment, so that workers who accepted public service jobs would still have an incentive to enter the private sector, yet would not be in deep poverty while working in the public sector. Ellwood, in his former role as the assistant secretary for planning and evaluation at the U.S. Department of Health and Human Services, attempted to craft welfare reform legislation that would include a guarantee of public employment as a last resort for welfare recipients leaving the rolls.[82] This component of welfare reform ultimately was removed from the legislation, but the idea gained credibility.[83]

Through at least 2010 the Obama administration has relied on general economic stimulus to drive employment growth. There is debate about how many jobs the stimulus package of 2009 has created, but one certainty is that it has not resolved the problem of concentrated joblessness. Over the years in which this book has been written, widespread unemployment has remained the most serious threat to the stability of urban communities, and the persistence of joblessness has the potential to reverse many of the positive changes in poor urban neighborhoods that have occurred over the past fifteen years or so.

With this possibility in mind, New Hope provides a possible model for the type of federal investment that is likely to stabilize communities while providing benefits for families that extend across generations. The details on implementation and costs of such a program are beyond the scope of this book, but the detailed study of New Hope conducted by Greg Duncan and colleagues provides substantial guidance on these matters.[84] The crucial aspects of such a program are that it should be available to anyone living in high unemployment areas who is jobless and who is willing to work at least thirty hours per week, regardless of income, gender, and family structure. A public service employment component, offered for only a fixed amount of time, would ensure that participants continue to look for employment in the private sector—offering only the minimum wage, this would still be an option of last resort, a guaranteed job for those who have no other alternatives. A creative approach to the types of jobs created by the program would allow the program to put residents to work in support of the larger community, creating a potential benefit for workers as well as for the area itself.[85]

In 2008, the federal government responded to the financial crisis by guaranteeing that financial institutions would not collapse, but no corresponding guarantee was made to the nation's urban communities. By promising a job to every willing worker in the nation's most distressed communities, the government would provide relief to individual workers while providing a signal that these communities will not be allowed to disintegrate.

Investing in Children's Environments

Developmental psychologists have argued for some time that early childhood environments are crucial for setting children on a positive trajectory. But there is surging momentum behind early childhood investments driven in large part by new research on the importance of children's settings in early childhood and by the research of James Heckman, the Nobel Prize–winning economist who has made a persuasive case for the relative efficiency of investing in children early in life.[86] Heckman's analysis is powerful in its logic and in its implications. He points to research from experimental early education programs, such as the Perry preschool program, which has followed students as they moved beyond the program and into adulthood and found that children who were assigned to receive quality care as part of the program had greater educational attainment, were more likely to be employed, and were less likely to be involved in crime as adults. The cognitive, social, and emotional skills developed in such programs are essential for children as they prepare for the school environment and ultimately the work environment. Where Heckman's work differs from much of the developmental literature is in his calculations of the costs and benefits of such investments. Developing a model based on the rates of return for investments at different points in an individual's life, Heckman argues that those made early in a child's life (before the age when children are eligible for universal schooling) are particularly efficient forms of investment, in part because of the cumulative effects that emerge when children begin their lives in nurturing, enriching environments.

Larry Aber, one of the most prominent scholars of child development and social policy, has argued persuasively for programs to push forward the nation's commitment to its children by providing quality learning environments to children before they reach the age of six and are eligible for kindergarten.[87] The disturbing irony is that this is arguably the age when investments in children would be most effective, yet children of this age receive the least amount of resources from states and the federal government.[88] Aber proposes several possible initiatives, including direct public provision of high-quality early child care, childhood development vouchers that could be used to pay for high-quality care or for parents to care for their own children, and a universal infant/toddler allowance. There is great appeal in such universal programs, which in theory would be more likely to garner widespread political support.

In the short term, Aber and his colleague Ajay Chaudry argue for a targeted expansion of early childhood education to children living in the most disadvantaged neighborhoods—places where families lack the resources to seek out high-quality child care and where communities have the least amount of resources to provide quality environments for children.[89] One of the most ambitious social interventions designed to address this acute need is underway in the Harlem Children's Zone (HCZ), a program that offers a unique set of services and resources for children beginning in the womb and extending through young adulthood.[90] The HCZ has received a tremendous amount of attention in the popular press, due in part to the charisma of its founder, Geoffrey Canada, and in part to the Obama administration's proposal to replicate the project in twenty Promise Neighborhoods across the country.[91]

But the attention is also attributable to the truly unique vision of the program. The HCZ is a system of programs that are designed to saturate roughly one hundred Harlem blocks with services, learning opportunities, safe environments, and resources designed to provide children living in the zone with the opportunity to prosper. Canada has secured enormous private sector investment in order to provide a "conveyor belt" of programs for children, ranging from "Baby College," a course designed for new and expecting parents, to charter schools that will eventually run from pre-K through twelfth grade, to violence prevention programs and other social services for youth.

The most original aspect of the HCZ is not found in the details of its programs, but rather in the philosophy of the zone. The HCZ represents an investment in children throughout childhood, from the womb through college. A crucial idea underlying the Zone is that it is essential to reach children early in their lives, but equally important is the idea that it is essential to retain children in the program, to link them with services and opportunities that will carry them straight through the college years.

In this way, the philosophy underlying Canada's vision recognizes that the disadvantages faced by children in America's poorest neighborhoods are not experienced at any one critical point in a child's life, but are continually faced at each stage of childhood. While early interventions like Head Start may help set children on a trajectory of success, only a sustained commitment to these children, a continuum of resources and support, can hope to ensure that they are not overwhelmed by the challenges they face. Further, the disadvantages confronting a child are often a continuation of disadvantages faced by his/her parents, which is part of the reason why the first stage in Canada's conveyor belt attempts to reach out to parents before the child is born.

Canada has said that the true indicator of the HCZ's success, in his mind, is graduation from college. If a child who has proceeded through the Zone's conveyor belt of programs successfully makes her way through college, the Zone has succeeded. This measure of success is in line with one aspect of the HCZ's philosophy, as college graduation represents the culmination of a commitment that must extend throughout the duration of childhood and into young adulthood. There are other indicators of progress that can be measured along the way, however, such as scores on statewide achievement tests. The early results from an evaluation of students' performance on such tests suggest that the Zone—or, more specifically, the Promise Academy—is achieving notable success.[92] The evaluation was conducted by Will Dobbie and Roland Fryer, the latter a professor of economics at Harvard. Dobbie and Fryer have evaluated the effects of attendance at the Promise Academy by exploiting the fact that acceptance into the school is granted by a lottery system in years when there are more applicants than slots available.[93] Comparing lottery winners to losers, the authors find evidence for substantial impacts of acceptance into the Promise Academy on students' test scores. If the results hold up, they suggest that the impact of attending a Promise Academy for children who enter in kindergarten is enough to close the gap between white and black children on tests of achievement in both math and English.

These results provide hope for those who believe that through intensive, sustained investments in children's environments it is possible to give all children a true chance to succeed, even if they are being raised in the nation's most disadvantaged communities. But there are at least two reasons for caution in interpreting these findings. The first is that the strong positive effects arising from acceptance into the Promise Academy have not been found in evaluations of a broader range of charter schools. While some studies have found marginal improvements in test scores attributable to acceptance into charter schools, much of the evidence available suggests largely mixed and inconclusive results.[94] This mixed evidence makes one wonder whether it is possible to replicate the success of the Harlem Children's Zone schools without the resources and the leadership enjoyed by HCZ.

The second reason for caution is that the results from the Dobbie and Fryer evaluation truly reveal the power of the school setting to influence children's academic trajectories. The study focuses on attendance at the Promise Academy, but it does not allow for a test of the community-wide transformation that Canada's rhetoric describes. Canada talks about his vision for the Zone as a place where the ideals and goals of his programs are felt beyond the individual families that take part in these programs and "contaminate" the area, infecting all residents in the Zone. This idea of contamination may seem abstract, but in fact it is crucial to understanding the mission of HCZ. In distinguishing the philosophy of the HCZ's schools from other well-regarded charter schools operating in the area, for instance, Canada argues against the notion that the students in his schools should be made to feel distinct from their neighborhood peers, superior to them or different from them in terms of culture, discipline, and behavior. His goal is not to teach his children that they can move on to a better environment; his goal is to infect that environment with the ideals and the resources that are provided in the schools.

If the Harlem Children's Zone is successful, according to these standards, it will transform the one hundred blocks that it covers. It will bring about a new hope among the children of the Zone, a new appreciation for the role of education in facilitating mobility, a new perspective toward child development among parents, and perhaps a new commitment to the community. For a place-based intervention such as the HCZ, these indicators should stand alongside individual-level outcomes, like individual test scores or rates of college graduation among program participants, as critical measures of success.

The Dobbie and Fryer study tells us little about whether the Harlem Children's Zone will bring about a transformation of the zone itself, one that extends beyond the parents and children who have been lucky enough to move through the system of programs that are offered in the Zone. We don't know whether the hopes and aspirations of Canada will seep into the young men in Harlem who have watched older cohorts of young men enter adulthood without a reasonable expectation that they can obtain a job that would support a family. We don't know whether the ideals of the Zone will persuade young men and women that their future is worth the personal investment and discipline required to persevere in school, prepare themselves for the workforce, and commit themselves to supporting and raising their children. We don't know whether the lessons learned in Baby College will be shared throughout the community, so that parents throughout the Zone will be focused on providing safe and stimulating environments for their young children. We don't know whether the example set in Canada's schools will inspire leaders of other schools in the district to set similarly high goals and to make a similar commitment to every student in their schools.

These unanswered questions reflect what might be considered the true measures of success for a program like Canada's, which is designed to saturate an area with the resources that are crucial for the development of every child. How can we understand whether the HCZ, or other programs like it, are working to bring about this type of transformation?

We can look to the Jobs-Plus program, described briefly above, as an example. The impact of Jobs-Plus was evaluated through an experiment in which places—in this case housing developments—were randomly assigned to receive the intervention or to be in the control group. By randomizing places, as opposed to people, it becomes possible to estimate the impact of the intervention on the place as a whole by comparing the outcomes of places in the treatment group to the same outcomes among places in the control group.[95]

In assessing the impact of a program like the Harlem Children's Zone, one might imagine an experiment in which neighborhoods are randomized to receive a continuum of resources and services like those offered in the HCZ. In practice, this is very similar to what President Obama has proposed already in his idea of Promise Neighborhoods. However, instead of simply replicating the HCZ in twenty Promise Neighborhoods across the country, an experimental approach would first select a larger number of neighborhoods, all of which had similarly high levels of crime, poorly functioning schools, high rates of teenage childbearing, and so forth. Among these neighborhoods, a smaller number would be randomly assigned to receive the intervention, consisting of a comprehensive set of services and resources similar to those offered in the Harlem Children's Zone.[96] Designing the program in this way would be directly equivalent to what the Obama administration has proposed, but it has the advantage of allowing for a rigorous assessment of whether the program is actually effective in reducing crime, raising test scores, reducing teenage childbearing, and so forth.

Unfortunately, the political challenges associated with randomly selecting communities to receive funding through the Promise Neighborhoods initiative have won out, and there is no plan for a rigorous evaluation of the program. As a consequence, my fear is that several years down the road scholars will have no convincing evidence to determine whether the program has been effective in transforming targeted communities. This is unfortunate—already there are strong indications that if an ambitious initiative like the Harlem Children's Zone is implemented properly, with sufficient funding and dynamic leadership, it is possible to transform individual children's lives. What we don't know is whether this energy can be replicated across the country, and whether it is possible to change entire communities.

This concluding chapter is being written during a time of major change in America's urban neighborhoods. Joblessness is widespread, housing markets in many American cities have collapsed, foreclosures have spread across the nation, and many urban neighborhoods are emptying out. These changes are playing out as I write, and the consequences for urban communities and their residents are not yet clear.

But before this rapid collapse took hold, the data available on trends in the degree of concentrated poverty across the nation's urban neighborhoods suggested movement in a positive direction. While poverty became increasingly concentrated through the 1970s and 1980s, this trend reversed in the 1990s, and the number of extreme high-poverty neighborhoods declined.[97] Data on crime trends reinforced this optimistic perspective on the future of the nation's urban communities. Over the 1990s crime dropped by almost half across the country, with even steeper declines in many cities.[98] In New

York City, the poster child for the "Great American Crime Decline," there were roughly two thousand homicides each year at the start of the 1990s—fifteen years or so later, the city averages somewhere between five hundred and six hundred homicides per year, and it is now one of the safest of America's big cities. Researchers have put forth a pile of hypotheses to explain the remarkable decline in crime over this period, including changes in the age structure of U.S. cities, growth in the number of police on the streets, changes in the strategies used by police, growth in the incarcerated population, improvements in urban economies, and even changes in immigration, abortion laws, and lead paint laws.[99] There is evidence that provides some support for any and all of these theories, but the reality is that the crime decline was likely caused by a combination of several contributing factors, and it is exceedingly difficult to identify the precise effect of any single cause.[100] The one certainty is that the decline in violent crime across many American cities has made these cities more livable and less dangerous, and these changes are most pronounced in the nation's urban ghettos.

On the basis of these two trends showing major declines in crime and concentrated poverty, one might reach the reasonable conclusion that the problem of the inherited ghetto is one that is going away. But this perspective ignores what has happened to the nation over the past few years. In the closing years of the 2000s, the nation's financial system moved to the brink of collapse, and the country fell into a sustained recession from which it is only beginning to recover. Joblessness has skyrocketed, and despite an enormous influx of funding into the nation's economy through the American Recovery and Reinvestment Act, unemployment has barely fallen. Newly available data indicate that the drop in concentrated poverty that occurred over the 1990s has reversed, once again.[101]

The end of the real estate boom and the collapse of many urban housing markets have left communities across the country vulnerable to abandonment and decay. Not surprisingly, the impact of the foreclosure wave is most pronounced in heavily minority areas—areas that were targeted by predatory lenders.[102] An analysis of mortgage data from 172 cities across the nation found that high-income African Americans and Latinos were more than three times more likely to receive subprime loans than high-income whites and were close to twice as likely to receive such loans as even low-income whites.[103] In May 2010 the *New York Times* published an interactive map showing foreclosures in New York City neighborhoods from 2006 through 2008. By 2008, the red dots representing properties in foreclosure had spread throughout the city, and in several predominantly nonwhite communities, like Bushwick and Bedford-Stuyvesant in Brooklyn, Central Harlem in Manhattan, Jamaica and St. Albans in Queens, and the South Bronx, the clusters of red dots covered much of the community.[104] In these communities, entire swaths of homes have been foreclosed and abandoned, provoking neighbors who remain to wonder aloud about the fate of the block.[105]

They are right to worry. Research has found that home ownership is associated with a range of positive outcomes for families and for communities and that foreclosure rates are highly associated with subsequent crime.[106] When combined with widespread joblessness and the fiscal crises faced by many cities and states, the mortgage crisis that is clearing out some urban neighborhoods poses a major threat to urban America. The threat is not simply that urban residents are losing their homes and their jobs; it is that communities are losing their population base along with their financial base. These developments raise the frightening possibility that many of the gains made in American cities over the 1990s—the drops in crime, the declines in concentrated poverty, the increases in home ownership—may be reversed in the near future.

My point in describing these troubling developments is not to suggest that urban neighborhoods are on the verge of a crisis. Rather, my point is that recent trends in urban America, whether positive or negative, have to be seen in the context of the broader set of forces, economic and political, that have served to maintain urban inequality for the last several decades. For instance, while assessing the importance of the decline in concentrated poverty that took place during the 1990s, it is important to recognize that, despite these declines, there were still almost twice as many high-poverty neighborhoods in 2000 as there were in 1970.[107] In considering how important the drop in violent crime has been to America's cities, we must consider also the fact that hundreds of thousands of prisoners will be returning to a small number of concentrated areas in the coming years. Without major supports, these returning prisoners will have limited capacity to enter the labor force or to support their families.

In short, by focusing on trends over short periods of time we run the risk of being distracted from the enduring set of forces that have served to reinforce urban inequality over the last several decades. In a similar way, by focusing too narrowly on current political debates or recent policy proposals we run the risk of forgetting the lessons learned from policies and politics of the recent past.

This latter point is particularly relevant in the current political and economic environment. The election of Barack Obama in 2008 inspired incredible optimism at a time of uncertainty for the nation. From his work as a community organizer in Chicago to his proposal to expand the Harlem Children's Zone model, Obama has demonstrated a unique concern for urban communities, and the Obama administration has shifted attention toward the nation's cities and metropolitan areas in a manner that has not been done since the Johnson administration.[108] The establishment of the White House Office of Urban Affairs announced this shift in priorities, and the policies proposed over time have demonstrated the sincerity of the shift.[109] The most extensive administration initiatives have been designed to make cities more competitive and more vibrant, and they have reflected the ideas and calls for action from some of the nation's most prominent urban scholars.[110] The administration also has put forth the most innovative proposals for supplementary, place-based investments in four decades with its Promise Neighborhoods and Choice Neighborhoods initiatives, part of a broader set of programs falling under the umbrella of the White House Neighborhood Revitalization Initiative.[111] In their ideals, these two proposals reflect the types of programs that have the potential, in theory, to transform some of the nation's most disadvantaged neighborhoods.

At the same time, these initiatives share the same shortcomings that have limited the effectiveness of many of the most promising urban initiatives of the past several decades. Both the Promise and Choice Neighborhoods programs are extremely modest in scope. In each case, only a small number of communities across the country will be affected, and it is unrealistic to think that the funding that is proposed could possibly produce the type of transformative impacts that the Harlem Children's Zone appears to be creating. One could argue that the modest scale of an initiative like Promise Neighborhoods may be appropriate, considering the uncertainty about whether such a program can be effective. But one very clear lesson from the urban initiatives proposed as part of the War on Poverty is that temporary, underfunded investments in communities will not alter the multigenerational problem of the inherited ghetto.

The lesson from initiatives like Model Cities and the Community Action Program is clear: promising ideas and programs are not sufficient to produce sustained change in the lives of families or communities. What is needed is *durable* urban policy, meaning policy with the capacity to create permanent changes in families' lives, and policy that is designed to be less vulnerable to the changing political mood in Washington or to the fluctuations of the business cycle.

I have described a set of examples that illustrate the types of programs and policies that would reflect a durable urban policy. Perhaps more important than any of the programs I have described are the set of strategies that will be necessary to sustain a commitment to these programs, and to the communities for which they are designed. Scholars of community organization and political processes have proposed a range of strategies that would be required to develop policies with the potential to be sustained over time. These strategies are essential if we are to sever the multigenerational link between neighborhood disadvantage and racial inequality. Just as the effects of the last four decades of public policy continue to shape the lives of today's ghetto residents, a sustained investment in urban neighborhoods has the potential to improve the life chances of urban families and ameliorate racial inequality for generations to come.

Notes

Chapter 1: Introduction

1. Wattenberg and Scammon, 1973.

2. See also Freeman, 1976; Smith and Welch, 1986.

3. This expansion of the black middle class was accompanied by growth in inequality within the black population, as new opportunities available to African Americans were enjoyed primarily by a segment of the population that was able to take advantage of expanded civil rights and affirmative action policies. For instance, see Hout, 1984; Smith and Welch, 1986; Wilson, 1978, 2011. At the same time, subsequent research has argued persuasively that much of the new opportunity available to African Americans was a product of affirmative action and black political mobilization and was "fragile" because it was heavily dependent on the unstable political environment. See Collins, 1983, 1997; Freeman, 1976; Pomer, 1986.

4. Bobo, 2011; Stoll, 2005.

5. Tabulations are based on family income among non-Hispanic blacks in the March supplements to the Current Population Survey, downloaded via the Integrated Public Use Microdata Series (IPUMS): Ruggles et al., 2010.

6. Williams, 2011.

7. Waters, Ueda, and Marrow, 2007.

8. Waters and Ueda, 2007.

9. Isaacs, 2007.

10. Logan, 2007.

11. Isaacs, 2007.

12. Isaacs, 2007.

13. Dreier, Mollenkopf, and Swanstrom, 2001; Jargowsky, 1997; Lobao, Hooks, and Tickamyer, 2007; Logan and Molotch, 1987; Massey, 2007; Massey and Denton, 1993; Wilson, 1987.

14. Gans offers a similar argument for an empirical focus on multigenerational poverty: Gans, 2011.

15. About 98 percent of Americans classified themselves as either white or black in the 1970 Census.

16. New research from specific cities is beginning to look at how second-generation immigrants are faring in early adulthood, and it will be possible in the coming ten years or so to conduct a national analysis of multigenerational families of immigrants in the PSID. For a recent book on the second generation of immigrants in the New York metropolitan area, see Kasinitz et al., 2008.

17. Chandler, 1972; Dreier, Mollenkopf, and Swanstrom, 2001; Dubofsky, 1969; Goering, 2007b; Sidney, 2003; Squires, 1992.

18. Massey and Denton, 1993.

19. The December 2008 issue of *City & Community* features a symposium on the ghetto concept, which touches on this history and on contemporary usage. Other diverse and seminal interpretations of the ghetto concept can be found in Clark, 1965; Sennett, 1994; Spear, 1969; Wacquant, 2004; Wirth, 1928. Mary Pattillo (2003) puts forth an alternative defi-

nition that focuses purely on areas of predominantly black population that may extend beyond neighborhoods where poverty is concentrated.

20. Drake and Cayton, 1933; DuBois, 1899. One major exception to the use of the term "ghetto" to describe black communities is Wirth's classic book *The Ghetto*, which described Chicago's Jewish ghetto of the 1920s and compared it with Jewish ghettos in other settings: Wirth, 1928.

21. While debates continue about whether ghetto communities in the United States exhibit a specific set of features or a specific form, there is substantial convergence amongst urban scholars regarding the centrality of "process" in defining the concept of the "ghetto." By "process" I am referring to the set of actions, events, and forces—economic, political, and demographic—that lead to segments of urban populations being separated residentially by race and class.

There is further debate on which processes have been most important for the "ghettoization" of urban neighborhoods. As Mario Small has documented in his research, a central reason for this lack of clarity is that the forces at work to create ghetto communities across the United States have been extremely diverse. Whereas Small argues that this diversity should lead scholars to abandon all but the most basic, demographic uses of the term "ghetto," I would argue that this diversity simply means it is necessary to develop a definition that is flexible enough to encompass the wide range of processes that have been important in creating ghetto communities in the United States. To get a sense of debates about whether American ghettos exhibit a specific form, compare the following studies: Small, 2007; Wacquant, 2008. See also Chaddha and Wilson, 2008; Small, 2008.

22. Blokland, 2008, p. 373.

23. Hirsch, 1983; Massey and Denton, 1993; Osofsky, 1971; Spear, 1969; Wacquant, 1993.

24. Gieryn, 2000.

25. Sampson, 2003, 2012.

26. Brooks-Gunn, Duncan, Klebanov, and Sealand, 1993; Burdick-Will et al., 2010; Sampson, Sharkey, and Raudenbush, 2008.

27. Cohen and Dawson, 1993. For related work on neighborhood poverty, neighborhood institutions, and individual and collective civic engagement, see Sampson et al., 2005; Stoll, 2001.

28. Hellerstein and Neumark, 2011; Hellerstein, Neumark, and McInerney, 2008; Holzer, 1991; Ihlanfeldt and Sjoquist, 1998; Kain, 1992.

29. George Galster has provided a comprehensive list of all of the theoretical mechanisms linking neighborhood advantage or disadvantage with individual social or economic outcomes: Galster, 2011.

30. Alba and Logan, 1993; Alba, Logan, and Stults, 2000b; Crowder, South, and Chavez, 2006; Logan, 2011.

31. Alba, Logan, and Stults, 2000a; Logan et al., 1996.

32. Drake and Cayton, 1933; DuBois, 1899; Sampson and Morenoff, 1997.

33. Massey, 2007; Massey, Gross, and Shibuya, 1994; Sampson, Raudenbush, and Earls, 1997; Wilson, 1987.

34. Jargowsky, 1997; Massey and Denton, 1993; Massey, Gross, and Shibuya, 1994; Quillian, 1999.

35. Brooks-Gunn, Duncan, Klebanov, and Sealand, 1993; Ellen and Turner, 1997; Goering and Feins, 2003; Jencks and Mayer, 1990; Sampson, Morenoff, and Gannon-Rowley, 2002.

36. This point is noted in Mare, 2001, p. 484. An exception is Massey's recent book on the American stratification system: Massey, 2007.

37. There have been several important advances in theory and measurement of "neighborhoods" in sociology, although it is still only possible to analyze most core economic and demographic characteristics at the level of the census tract or, in some cases, the block group. For more extensive discussions of the issue and some novel approaches to measurement, see Coulton et al., 2001; Grannis, 1998; Hipp, 2007; Lee et al., 2008.

38. Harding et al., 2005; Jencks and Tach, 2006; Kluegel and Smith, 1981.

39. Wilson, 1987.

40. Logan, 1978; Massey and Denton, 1993; Quillian, 1999, 2003; Massey, 2007.

41. Bowles, Gintis, and Osborne Groves, 2005; Corcoran, 1995; Solon, 1992; Solon, Ashenfelter, and Card, 1999.

42. Bowles and Gintis, 2002.

43. For example, see DuBois, 1899; Hannerz, 1969; Liebow, 1967.

44. Elliott et al., 1996; Sampson, Morenoff, and Gannon-Rowley, 2002; Sampson and Wilson, 1995; Wilson, 1987, 1996.

Chapter 2: The Inheritance of the Ghetto

1. Wilson, 1987.

2. Feagin and O'Brien, 2004.

3. Massey and Denton, 1993.

4. Massey and Denton, 1993, 1988, 1989.

5. Alba, Logan, and Bellair, 1994; Flippen, 2004; Frankenberg, Lee, and Orfield, 2003; Logan, 2011; Logan, Stults, and Farley, 2004.

6. Block and Block, 1993.

7. Altman and Low, 1992; Elder, King, and Conger, 1996; Fried, 1982; Gerson, Stueve, and Fischer, 1977.

8. Massey and Denton, 1993.

9. Turner et al., 2002; Yinger, 1995.

10. Green, Strolovitch, and Wong, 1998.

11. Dreier, Mollenkopf, and Swanstrom, 2001; Massey and Denton, 1993; Yinger, 1995.

12. Cutler, Glaeser, and Vigdor, 1999; Logan, Stults, and Farley, 2004.

13. Bobo and Zubrinsky, 1996; Charles, 2000.

14. Harris, 1999, 2001; Krysan, 2002.

15. Ellen, 2000.

16. Gramlich, Laren, and Sealand, 1992; Sampson, 2012.

17. Quillian, 2003; South and Crowder, 1997.

18. Note that this estimate is slightly different from results published in Sharkey (2008) because the current analysis includes additional years of data running through the 2007 PSID survey.

19. The appendix Web site is: http://sociology.as.nyu.edu/object/patricksharkey.html.

20. The strength of the relationship between parents' and children's neighborhood environments is strongest for children who were raised in the northeast and weakest for children raised in the south. In all regions, the persistence of neighborhood inequality is stronger if children remain in the same county when they reach adulthood. But again, this relationship is weakest for children who are raised in the south.

Chapter 3: A Forty-Year Detour on the Path toward Racial Equality

1. Special thanks to Michael Friedson, who provided excellent research assistance on the case studies of all five cities.

2. For instance, historian Ira Berlin argues that the dominant role of migration in the African American experience, from the Middle Passage to the Great Migration, elevated the importance of places in the lives of African Americans—one might speculate that this type of unique connection to places could help to explain why African Americans have stayed in cities that have deteriorated over the last several decades. See: Berlin, 2010. Other research indicates that African Americans are unique in the degree to which they live among immediate and extended family members, which may also play a role in maintaining ties to places. See Spilimbergo and Ubeda, 2004.

3. Sjoquist, 2000.

4. Bayor, 1996; Browning, Marshall, and Tabb, 1990.

5. Bayor, 2000.

6. Ihlanfeldt and Sjoquist, 2000.

7. Ihlanfeldt and Sjoquist, 2000; Thompson, 2000.

8. O'Hare and Frey, 1992.

9. Data on population and segregation come from the US2010 Project, sponsored by the Russell Sage Foundation and the American Communities Project at Brown University: http://www.s4.brown.edu/us2010/index.htm.

10. Bayor, 1996.

11. National Advisory Commission on Civil Disorders, 1968.

12. Dubofsky, 1969. See also chap. 4 of Dreier, Mollenkopf, and Swanstrom, 2001.

13. Schill, 2007.

14. Turner and Ross, 2005; Turner et al., 2002.

15. Turner et al., 2002.

16. Turner and Ross, 2005. See also Lacy, 2007.

17. Apgar and Calder, 2005; Turner et al., 2002.

18. Elkin, 1987.

19. Hanson, 2003; Lowe, 2008.

20. Phillips, 2006.

21. Hanson, 2003.

22. Kemper, 2005.

23. See, for instance, Marcuse and Van Kempen, 2002.

24. All data on population and segregation come from the US2010 Project, sponsored by the Russell Sage Foundation and the American Communities Project at Brown University: http://www.s4.brown.edu/us2010/index.htm.

25. Dreier, Mollenkopf, and Swanstrom, 2001; Massey and Denton, 1993.

26. Massey and Denton, 1993.

27. Dreier, Mollenkopf, and Swanstrom, 2001; Jackson, 1987.

28. Jackson, 1987.

29. Massey and Denton, 1993.

30. Dreier, Mollenkopf, and Swanstrom, 2001.

31. Hamilton, Mills, and Puryear, 1975; Schill and Wachter, 1995.

32. Downs, 1993, 1994.

33. Quigley and Raphael, 2004.

34. Massey and Denton, 1993.

35. Downs, 1993, 1994; Sugrue, 2003; Wacquant, 1998.

36. Anderson, 1964; Fullilove, 2005; Gans, 1962; Marcuse, 1995.

37. Hirsch, 1983; Massey and Denton, 1993; Vale, 2000.

38. Massey and Denton, 1993, p. 57.

39. Meyer, 2001.

40. Data on population and segregation come from the US2010 Project, sponsored by the Russell Sage Foundation and the American Communities Project at Brown University: http://www.s4.brown.edu/us2010/index.htm.

41. Dear and Dahmann, 2008. See also Mollenkopf, 2008; Sonenshein, 1993.

42. Dear and Dahmann, 2008; Garreau, 1991.

43. Davis, 1992.

44. Kurashige, 2010.

45. Sides, 2003.

46. Charles, 2006; Saul, 2010.

47. Saul, 2010.

48. Jargowsky, 2003.

49. Figures are based on the author's tabulations based on data from the American Community Survey, obtained through Social Explorer: www.socialexplorer.com.

50. Two unique and persuasive articles calling for a more sophisticated comparative analysis of neighborhood change can be found in Mollenkopf, 2008; Small, 2007.

51. Sugrue, 1996.

52. Bluestone and Harrison, 1982; Levy, 1987.

53. Drennan, 1991.

54. Wacquant and Wilson, 1989.

55. Drake and Cayton, 1933.

56. Wacquant and Wilson, 1989.

57. Dreier, Mollenkopf, and Swanstrom, 2001.

58. Dreier, Mollenkopf, and Swanstrom, 2001.

59. Downs, 1994; Rusk, 1993.

60. Wacquant, 2008; Wacquant and Wilson, 1989; Wilson, 1987.

61. Arum, 2000; Neckerman, 2007; Noguera, 2003; Wacquant, 1998.

62. Joseph, 1992; Wacquant, 1998. These patterns were exacerbated by the decline in the influence of central cities in state governmental policy: Weir, 1996.

63. Haar, 1975; Wilson, 2010; Caraley, 1992; Von Hoffman, 2004.

64. DeParle, 1996; Dreier, 1995; Orlebeke, 2000; Schwartz, 2010; Von Hoffman, 2004.

65. Briggs, Popkin, and Goering, 2010; Cisneros and Engdahl, 2009; Gentry, 1993; Katz et al., 2003; Popkin, 2000; Vale, 1993.

66. Some excellent examples include Kotlowitz, 1992; Merry, 1981; Popkin, 2000; Rainwater, 1970; Venkatesh, 2002.

67. Venkatesh, 2002.

68. For a fascinating political and legal history of Chicago public housing projects, see also Polikoff, 2006.

69. All data on population and segregation come from the US2010 Project, sponsored by the Russell Sage Foundation and the American Communities Project at Brown University: http://www.s4.brown.edu/us2010/index.htm.

70. Sugrue, 1996.

71. Thomas, 1997.

72. Farley, Danziger, and Holzer, 2000.

73. Farley, Danziger, and Holzer, 2000.

74. Thompson, 2004.

75. Thomas, 1997.

76. Thomas, 1997.

77. Jargowsky, 2003.

78. Farley, Danziger, and Holzer, 2000.

79. Thomas Sugrue provides perhaps the most comprehensive account of the recent history and racial climate in Detroit: Sugrue, 1996.

80. Farley, Danziger, and Holzer, 2000.

81. Sugrue, 1996.

82. Farley, Danziger, and Holzer, 2000.

83. Farley, Danziger, and Holzer, 2000.

84. Garland, 2001a.

85. Pettit and Western, 2004.

86. Western, 2006.

87. Garland, 2001b; Western, 2006.

88. Western, 2006.

89. See Western, 2006. While changes in sentencing and parole are common explanations for the progression toward mass imprisonment, the causal role that these and other policy shifts have had is difficult to determine. Research on the causes of mass imprisonment has typically concluded that an array of factors likely have contributed to the dramatic rise in incarceration over time. But this research has had difficulty isolating the impact of any specific change in the criminal justice system—for instance, Reitz (2005) argues that the abolition of parole and the establishment of determinate sentencing are not positively associated with accelerated increases in imprisonment. For more extensive treatment of this issue, see Garland, 2001a; McCall, Parker, and MacDonald, 2008; Reitz, 2005; Zimring and Hawkins, 1993.

90. Wacquant, 2001.

91. Sampson, 2011.

92. Sampson, 2011; Western, 2006; Zimring, 2007.

93. Gelman, Fagan, and Kiss, 2007.

94. Anderson, 2000; Harding, 2010; Sharkey, 2010.

95. Holzer, Offner, and Sorensen, 2005; Western, 2006.

96. Western, 2006.

97. Holzer, Raphael, and Stoll, 2004, 2006.

98. Pager, 2007.

99. Holzer, 1996.

100. Pager, 2003, 2007.

101. Research by Deirdre Royster provides a more general argument about how institutions respond to cultural expressions of masculinity differently for black and white males, with black males experiencing disproportionate sanctions for common "masculinity games" in the school setting, in the period of entrance into the labor market, and in work settings. See in particular Royster, 2007.

102. Western, 2006; Wildeman, 2009.

103. Murray, 2005; Murray and Farrington, 2008; Murray, Janson, and Farrington, 2007.

104. Sampson, 2012.

105. See: http://www.justicemapping.org/.

106. Wacquant, 2001.

107. Mincy, 2006.

108. McKee, 2008.

109. Wolfinger, 2007.

110. McKee, 2008.

111. McKee, 2008.

112. McKee, 2008.

113. Anderson, 2000; Massey, 1994.

114. Keiser, 1990.

115. Bissinger, 1997.

116. Pew Charitable Trusts, 2011.

117. Goode and Schneider, 1994.

118. Ashenfelter, Collins, and Yoon, 2006; Johnson, 2011.

119. Moynihan, 1969.

120. Ladd, 1994a.

121. One might use the term "reemergence" instead of "emergence," considering the history of efforts to promote interventions based on community participation dating back to the Progressive Era. For instance, see O'Connor, 1999.

122. Quoted in Cazenave, 2007.

123. O'Connor, 1996; O'Connor, 2001.

124. O'Connor, 2001.

125. The most comprehensive descriptions and assessments of Model Cities are found in Frieden and Kaplan, 1977; Haar, 1975.

126. Haar, 1975.

127. Warren, 1969.

128. Haar, 1975.

129. Haar, 1975; Warren, 1969.

130. Edelman, 2010; Imbroscio, 2008a, 2008b; M. Katz, 2010; Von Hoffman, 2004.

131. Edelman, 2010; Halpern, 1995; O'Connor, 1999.

132. The Area Recovery Administration is another example of an ambitious community revitalization program that was watered down and then ended just years after the legislation that established it was passed in 1961. See O'Connor, 1999.

133. Edelman, 2010.

134. Haar, 1975.

135. Edelman, 2010; Lemann, 1994.

136. Grogan and Proscio, 2001; Von Hoffman, 2004.

137. Von Hoffman, 2004.

138. Von Hoffman, 2004.

139. Busso and Kline, 2008; Ladd, 1994b; Oakley and Tsao, 2006, 2007; Rubin and Wilder, 1989; Wilder and Rubin, 1996.

140. Timberlake, 2007; Von Hoffman, 2004.

141. Jargowsky, 2003.

142. Briggs and Keys, 2009; Timberlake, 2007.

143. Kneebone and Berube, 2008.

144. Rugh and Massey, 2010.

Chapter 4: Neighborhoods and the Transmission of Racial Inequality
1. Quoted in Massey, 2011.
2. Rustin, 1965.
3. Duncan, 1968.
4. Hertz, 2005; Isaacs, 2007.
5. Hertz, 2005.
6. For evidence of this belief, see Jencks and Tach, 2006.
7. Two excellent edited volumes offer a wide range of arguments and evidence on economic and social mobility: Bowles, Gintis, and Osborne Groves, 2005; Morgan, Grusky, and Fields, 2006. The Pew Charitable Trusts also has developed an entire research initiative focused on the same topic, the Economic Mobility Project: http://www.economicmobility.org.
8. Bowles and Gintis, 2002.
9. For a review of the early estimates of intergenerational correlations, see Becker and Tomes, 1986.
10. Solon, 1992.
11. Mazumder, 2005a, 2005b.
12. Beller and Hout, 2006; Bowles, Gintis, and Osborne Groves, 2005; Corak, 2006; Grawe, 2004; Solon, 2002.
13. For instance, see Harding et al., 2005.
14. Hertz, 2005. Also see Mazumder, 2011.
15. Hertz, 2006.
16. Clark, 1965; Liebow, 1967; Rainwater, 1970.
17. Pattillo, 1999; Wilson, 1987.
18. See also Loury, 1977.
19. Alba, Logan, and Bellair, 1994; Flippen, 2004; Frankenberg, Lee, and Orfield, 2003; Logan, 2003; Logan, Stults, and Farley, 2004.
20. Datcher, 1982.
21. Corcoran and Adams, 1999; Corcoran et al., 1992; Vartanian, 1999.
22. Aaronson, 1997; Vartanian and Buck, 2005.
23. Plotnick and Hoffman, 1999.
24. Rubinowitz and Rosenbaum, 2000.
25. Rubinowitz and Rosenbaum, 2000.
26. Isaacs, 2007.
27. Nakao and Treas, 1994; Stevens and Featherman, 1981.
28. Full results for all outcomes are shown in the online appendix.
29. Brooks-Gunn, Duncan, Kato, and Sealand, 1993; Crane, 1991; Garner and Raudenbush, 1991.
30. Harding, 2003.
31. Rubinowitz and Rosenbaum, 2000.
32. Black and Sufi, 2002; Cameron and Heckman, 2001. Even earlier research analyzing national samples from the 1970s showed a substantial narrowing of black/white educational attainment differences when controlling for family background: Featherman and Hauser, 1978; Mare and Winship, 1988.
33. Blau and Duncan, 1967; Featherman and Hauser, 1978; Hout, 1984.
34. Fernandez and Su, 2004.

35. Holzer, 1987, 1991; Ihlanfeldt and Sjoquist, 1998; Kain, 1992.

36. Waldinger, 1996. See also Hellerstein and Neumark, 2011; Hellerstein, Neumark, and McInerney, 2008; Royster, 2003.

37. Charles and Hurst, 2003; Conley, 1999; Keister, 2000.

38. Conley, 1999; Oliver and Shapiro, 1995.

39. Isaacs, 2007.

40. Sharkey, 2009.

41. Alba, Logan, and Stults, 2000b; Logan and Alba, 1993; Logan et al., 1996.

42. Wilson, 1987.

43. Pattillo, 1999, p. 5.

44. For a formal econometric model of racial inequality in human capital attainment, see Loury, 1977.

Chapter 5: The Cross-Generational Legacy of Urban Disadvantage

1. Elder, Johnson, and Crosnoe, 2003.

2. Hofferth et al., 1999; Mainieri, 2004.

3. Heckman, 1995; Herrnstein and Murray, 1994.

4. Heckman, 1995; Herrnstein and Murray, 1994; Neisser et al., 1996; Nisbett, 2009.

5. Guo and Mullan Harris, 2000; Shonkoff and Phillips, 2000.

6. Winship and Korenman, 1997.

7. Carey, 2007; Nelson et al., 2007.

8. The clearest and most well-written review of this research can be found in Richard Nisbett's recent book titled *Intelligence and How to Get It: Why Schools and Cultures Count*: Nisbett, 2009. The following articles describe results from specific studies that are noteworthy: Campbell and Ramey, 1994; Campbell et al., 2002; Gross, Spiker, and Haynes, 1997; Hill, Brooks-Gunn, and Waldfogel, 2003; McCarton et al., 1997; Schweinhart and Weikart, 1997; Wasik, Bond, and Hindman, 2006.

9. Sampson, Sharkey, and Raudenbush, 2008.

10. Sanbonmatsu et al., 2006.

11. Burdick-Will et al., 2010.

12. Ludwig et al., 2009.

13. Ainsworth, 2002; Brooks-Gunn, Duncan, Klebanov, and Sealand, 1993; Brooks-Gunn, Klebanov, and Duncan, 1996; Caughy and O'Campo, 2006; Chase-Lansdale and Gordon, 1996; Chase-Lansdale et al., 1997; Duncan, Boisjoly, and Harris, 2001; Duncan, Brooks-Gunn, and Klebanov, 1994; Kohen et al., 2002; Leventhal, Xue, and Brooks-Gunn, 2006; McCullough, 2006; McCullough and Joshi, 2001; Sampson, 2008a.

14. For a full description of the methods see the online appendix that accompanies this book or see Sharkey and Elwert, 2011. The appendix is located at: http://sociology.as.nyu .edu/object/patricksharkey.html.

15. Those skeptical of any observational methods designed to study neighborhood effects might pay particular attention to the sensitivity analysis developed in the original article—the results from the sensitivity analysis suggest that the estimates of multigenerational effects are robust to major violations of the assumption of unobserved confounding. See Sharkey and Elwert, 2011.

16. Kristensen and Bjerkedal, 2007.

17. Winship and Korenman, 1997.

18. Briggs, 1997.

19. Clampet-Lundquist and Massey, 2008; Kling, Liebman, and Katz, 2007.

20. Ellen and Turner, 1997; Leventhal and Brooks-Gunn, 2000.

Chapter 6: Confronting the Inherited Ghetto: An Empirical Perspective

1. Logan, 2006.

2. Sharkey, 2007. The demographics of casualties are remarkably similar to what has been shown from other disasters in urban areas, most notably the Chicago heat wave of 1995, as documented in Klinenberg, 2002.

3. Brooks, 2005.

4. Brooks, 2007; Glaeser, 2007; MacGillis, 2007.

5. Quoted in Hirsch, 2003.

6. National Advisory Commission on Civil Disorders, 1968.

7. Goering, 2005.

8. For a sampling, see Downs, 1968; Dreier and Moberg, 1995; Fiss, 2000; Goetz, 2003; Harrison, 1974; Hartman and Squires, 2009; Hughes, 1995; Imbroscio, 2008a, 2008b; Kain and Persky, 1969; Lemann, 1994; Polikoff, 2006; Rosenbaum, 1995; Steinberg, 2009.

9. For more of a normative discussion of the issue, see Fiss, 2000; Imbroscio, 2008a; Pattillo, 2009.

10. Goering and Feins, 2003; Rubinowitz and Rosenbaum, 2000.

11. Other excellent reviews of evidence from mobility programs can be found in the following: Briggs, 1997; DeLuca and Dayton, 2009; Goetz and Chapple, 2010.

12. This point is noted in Mendenhall, DeLuca, and Duncan, 2006.

13. Kubisch et al., 2010.

14. Coulton, Theodos, and Turner, 2009.

15. The Dobbie and Fryer paper does include an analysis of the effects of living within the borders of the Harlem Children's Zone, but this is the least convincing analysis within the paper and relies on the unrealistic assumption that any effects of the HCZ programs "stop" at the boundaries that have been demarcated as part of the HCZ. This evidence is discussed in depth in the concluding chapter as well. See Dobbie and Fryer, 2009.

16. Rubinowitz and Rosenbaum, 2000.

17. Kaufman and Rosenbaum, 1992; Rosenbaum, 1995; Rosenbaum and Popkin, 1991; Rubinowitz and Rosenbaum, 2000.

18. Kaufman and Rosenbaum, 1992; Mendenhall, DeLuca, and Duncan, 2006; Rubinowitz and Rosenbaum, 2000.

19. Mendenhall, DeLuca, and Duncan, 2006; Votruba and Kling, 2009.

20. Mendenhall, DeLuca, and Duncan, 2006; Votruba and Kling, 2009.

21. A third comparison group that received standard Section 8 vouchers was also included in the study. For details see Goering and Feins, 2003.

22. Sampson, 2008a.

23. Brennan and Hill, 1999.

24. Briggs, Popkin, and Goering, 2010.

25. Kling, Liebman, and Katz, 2007; Ludwig, Liebman et al., 2008.

26. Kling, Liebman, and Katz, 2007; Sampson, 2008a.

27. Jacobs, 2007; Mathews, 2007.

28. Rosin, 2008.

29. Keels et al., 2005.

30. Burdick-Will et al., 2010.

31. Sampson, Sharkey, and Raudenbush, 2008.

32. Sanbonmatsu et al., 2006.

33. Jacob, 2004.

34. Ludwig et al., 2009.

35. A similar conclusion is reached in a paper examining the metropolitan conditions in which community change initiatives were established in the early 2000s as part of Annie E. Casey's "Making Connections" initiative. Kingsley and Williams note the wide variation in the economic conditions and in the housing markets across the fourteen sites in which the initiative was conducted, and they conclude that the goals, strategies, and obstacles to success are likely to vary dramatically across the sites as well. See Kingsley and Williams, 2010.

36. A more extensive discussion of these results can be found in Burdick-Will et al., 2010.

37. Bingenheimer, Brennan, and Earls, 2005; Kupersmidt et al., 2002; Margolin, 2005.

38. Horowitz, Weine, and Jekel, 1995; Martinez and Richters, 1993; Osofsky et al., 2004; Pynoos et al., 1987.

39. Keels et al., 2005.

40. Ferguson and Dickens, 1999.

41. Freeman, 2006.

42. Pattillo, 2007.

43. See online appendix at http://sociology.as.nyu.edu/object/patricksharkey.html.

44. Sampson, Raudenbush, and Earls, 1997; Sampson, Sharkey, and Raudenbush, 2008.

45. Sampson, Sharkey, and Raudenbush, 2008.

46. Figures 6.2a through 6.2c and table 6.1 examine the 10 percent of U.S. census tracts that experienced the largest declines from one census year to the next.

47. See also Muller, 1993; Winnick, 1990.

Chapter 7: Toward a Durable Urban Policy Agenda

1. Collins, 1997.

2. Bound and Freeman, 1992; Card, 1998.

3. Marcuse and van Kempen, 2002; Sassen, 1991.

4. McLanahan and Percheski, 2008.

5. Harding, 2010; Patterson, 2004; Small, 2004; Small, Harding, and Lamont, 2010.

6. Mark Joseph makes a similar point in calling for an end to community change "initiatives." Joseph argues that investments in communities that emerge from institutions outside of the community, and that feature defined timelines marking the beginning and ending of the initiative, are unlikely to have transformative impacts. See Joseph's essay in the following: Kubisch et al., 2010.

7. Briggs, 2005.

8. Ferguson and Dickens, 1999; Rusk, 1999.

9. Strong evidence for this argument comes from Paul Jargowsky's research demonstrating the link between metropolitan economic growth and the concentration of poverty: Jargowsky, 1997.

10. Perhaps the most comprehensive outlines of a broad-based policy agenda with the potential to reduce inequality and transform urban areas can be found in the concluding chapter of Wilson, 1996.

11. B. Katz, 2010.

12. Sjoquist, 2000. For evidence on the persistence of neighborhood inequality in Chicago, see Sampson, 2012.

13. Edelman, Holzer, and Offner, 2006; Holzer and Offner, 2006.

14. Eckholm, 2006.

15. Blank, 1997; Blank and Card, 1993; Blank and Greenberg, 2010.

16. Freeman and Holzer, 1985; Holzer and Offner, 2006; Hoynes, 1999.

17. Bureau of Labor Statistics, 2010.

18. Massey, 1990.

19. Wilson, 1987. See also Pack, 1994.

20. A report written by Manuel Pastor and Margery Austin Turner provides a persuasive set of arguments about what they refer to as "place-conscious" policies that might complement metropolitan policies. See Pastor and Turner, 2010.

21. Burdick-Will et al., 2010.

22. Edwards, 2008.

23. Polikoff, 2006.

24. Fiss, 2000.

25. Galster, 2002, 2007; Galster and Zobel, 1998. See also Brock and Durlauf, 2000.

26. Galster, 2003. This scenario most closely resembles the intended outcome of the proposal put forth by Polikoff, who suggests regulations that would limit the number of families that could enter specific neighborhoods—along with strict limits on neighborhood poverty and racial composition in destination neighborhoods.

27. Sampson, 2008a.

28. Briggs, Popkin, and Goering, 2010.

29. Briggs, Popkin, and Goering, 2010.

30. Hochschild, 2000.

31. See also Sampson and Sharkey, 2008.

32. See Smith and Welch, 1989. To provide a point of contrast, a recent study argues that migrants to the north did not fare appreciably better than migrants within the south on at least some economic outcomes: Eichenlaub, Tolnay, and Alexander, 2010.

33. Kirk, 2009; Sharkey and Sampson, 2010.

34. Kaufman and Rosenbaum, 1992; Keels, 2008; Keels et al., 2005; Votruba and Kling, 2009.

35. This idea is proposed by Jens Ludwig and Steven Raphael: Ludwig and Raphael, 2010.

36. Kirk, 2009.

37. See also Engdahl, 2009. There are hints of this approach in the Obama administration's "Transforming Rental Assistance" initiative, which is outlined in the 2011 budget proposal.

38. Bennett and Reed, 1999; Crowley, 2009; Fullilove, 2005; Kotlowitz, 2002; Venkatesh and Celimli, 2004.

39. For a classic account of displacement and a more recent account of "serial displacement" in public policy, see Fullilove, 2005; Gans, 1962.

40. On p. 9 of his chapter in the edited volume *From Despair to Hope*, Henry Cisneros, who implemented HOPE VI as Secretary of Housing and Urban Development under President Clinton, acknowledges that there was "insufficient understanding of just how much

effort was involved in helping people unfamiliar with the private market find housing." Quoted in Cisneros, 2009.

41. This was the conclusion from the well-known report of a 1992 national commission: National Commission on Severely Distressed Public Housing, 1992. See also Pastor and Turner, 2010; Vale, 1993.

42. Kingsley, 2009; Smith et al., 2010.

43. See White House Neighborhood Revitalization Initiative, 2011.

44. The design of the Choice Neighborhoods program is such that it will be extremely difficult to generate convincing evidence on whether the program is effective. I discuss this issue in detail later in the chapter, in reference to the Promise Neighborhoods program.

45. Schill, 2007.

46. Several variants of this idea have been put forth in the literature. See, for instance, Massey, 2011; Schill, 2007. One central challenge with this approach is that political administrations have a great deal of discretion in enhancing or limiting the efforts of federal agencies to enforce fair housing. Goering proposes a more comprehensive set of reforms, including the idea of transferring the enforcement of fair housing out of the hands of HUD and into a new "Equal Housing Commission." See Goering, 2007a.

47. Whether declines in housing discrimination will actually lead to substantial changes in urban communities is an open question. For a discussion of this issue, see Briggs, 2005.

48. Robert Sampson has recently published an excellent book that lays out a set of ideas about policies that can promote stable and healthy communities in urban settings. His concluding chapter provides a complement to this section of the book, as many of our ideas overlap or are otherwise consistent and Sampson offers additional thoughts on how to strengthen communities. See Sampson, 2012.

49. Ellen, 2000.

50. Recent experimental evidence indicates that when whites view images of a neighborhood that includes images of black residents versus white residents, they are more likely to rate the neighborhood unfavorably on multiple dimensions such as quality of housing, safety, and so forth. See Krysan et al., 2009; Krysan, Farley, and Couper, 2008.

51. Fullilove, 2005; Wacquant, 1998.

52. Sampson, 1999.

53. Briggs, 2005; Dreier, Mollenkopf, and Swanstrom, 2001; Schwartz, 2010.

54. Katz, 1999, 2000; Rusk, 1993.

55. Downs, 1994; Orfield, 1997; Rusk, 1993, 1999.

56. Pastor, Benner, and Matsuoka, 2009; Pastor and Turner, 2010.

57. Blackwell and Bell, 2005; Briggs, 2005; Weir, 2000.

58. Pastor and Turner, 2010; Rose, 2001.

59. Pastor and Turner, 2010.

60. Kasarda and Janowitz, 1974; Sampson, 1999, 2012; Sampson, Raudenbush, and Earls, 1997; Tilly, 1973.

61. Sampson, 1995; Skogan, 1992.

62. For research on the coordination between the police and the church in Boston, see Berrien, McRoberts, and Winship, 2000; Berrien and Winship, 2002. On community policing, see Moore, 1999.

63. For evidence on the relationship between immigration and neighborhood crime, see Sampson, 2008b. Recent evidence suggests that the entrance of new immigrant groups into

neighborhoods facilitates the breakdown of black/white segregation: Logan and Zhang, 2010.

64. Ferguson and Dickens, 1999; Grogan and Proscio, 2001; Von Hoffman, 2004.

65. Mauer, 2003; Petersilia, 2000; Travis and Petersilia, 2001.

66. Wilson, 1996. See also Gans, 1995.

67. Aber and Chaudry, 2010; Shonkoff and Phillips, 2000.

68. Heckman, 2006.

69. Holzer and Offner, 2006.

70. Bureau of Labor Statistics, 2010.

71. For instance, see Sampson, 2012; Sampson and Morenoff, 2006.

72. Dickens, 1999; Hellerstein and Neumark, 2011; Kubisch et al., 2010; Lemann, 1994.

73. Where there is some impact on local employment, it is generally found to be minimal and cost inefficient. See Greenbaum and Engberg, 2000; Ladd, 1994b; Oakley and Tsao, 2006; Peters and Fisher, 2002.

74. Bloom, Riccio, Verma, and Walter, 2005; Turner, 2005; Turner and Rawlings, 2005.

75. Details about New Hope are from Duncan, Huston, and Weisner, 2009.

76. Hellerstein and Neumark, 2011.

77. Ellwood and Welty, 2000. See also Johnson, Rynell, and Young, 2010.

78. Ellwood and Welty, 2000.

79. Brodsky, 2000.

80. Herbert Gans has written extensively about the role of public-service jobs in moving toward a "full-employment" society in several essays—see, for instance, Gans, 1993.

81. Wilson, 1996.

82. Ellwood, 1996.

83. Some states—the most notable example being Wisconsin—did experiment with community-service employment as part of a broader set of welfare reforms.

84. Duncan, Huston, and Weisner, 2009.

85. An alternative, carefully crafted approach to public-service employment during the current recession and beyond can be found in Johnson, Rynell, and Young, 2010.

86. Heckman, 2006; Heckman and Masterov, 2007; Heckman, Stixrud, and Urzua, 2006.

87. Aber, 2007; Aber and Chaudry, 2010.

88. Aber and Chaudry, 2010; Isaacs et al., 2009.

89. Aber and Chaudry, 2010.

90. Tough, 2008.

91. The Harlem Children's Zone is one of many similar initiatives that have been implemented over the last several decades focusing on community-level investments for youth, safety, education, and so forth. Others include Annie E. Casey's "Making Connections Initiative," Ford Foundation's "Neighborhood and Family Initiative," MacArthur Foundation's "New Communities Program," along with many others. For a more comprehensive discussion of this type of intervention, see Kubisch et al., 2010. There is also an extensive set of international examples of similar types of comprehensive community investment programs: Aalbers and Van Beckhoven, 2010; Conway and Konvitz, 2000.

92. Dobbie and Fryer, 2009.

93. Dobbie and Fryer also use a second approach that exploits the timing of the introduction of the Promise Academies and the spatial boundaries of the Zone to identify its impact. Results from this second approach largely support the findings reported from the lottery analysis.

94. The literature on "charter school effects" is extremely difficult to interpret and has become enmeshed in political and ideological debates. A recent study by Stanford economist Caroline Hoxby shows positive effects of acceptance into charter schools in New York City, but the magnitude of the impacts found seems exaggerated and the design of the analysis makes interpretation of the findings difficult. Other studies have shown small positive effects or null effects of being accepted into a charter school. See Hoxby, Murarka, and Kang, 2009.

95. Random assignment of places would not resolve all of the challenges associated with evaluating the impact of this type of program, a point discussed in detail in the following: Hollister and Hill, 1995.

96. More detailed description of experimental designs to analyze this type of setting-level intervention can be found in the work of Howard Bloom and Steve Raudenbush (and others). See, for instance, Bloom, 2006; Raudenbush, Martinez, and Spybrook, 2007.

97. Gould Ellen and O'Regan, 2008; Jargowsky, 2003.

98. Figures on crime trends come from Zimring, 2007.

99. Graif and Sampson, 2009; Levitt, 2004; McCall, Parker, and MacDonald, 2008; Reyes, 2007; Sampson, 2008b; Zimring, 2007.

100. Zimring, 2007.

101. Kneebone and Berube, 2008.

102. Kochhar, Gonzalez-Barrera, and Dockterman, 2009; Rugh and Massey, 2010.

103. Rivera et al., 2008.

104. See http://www.nytimes.com/interactive/2009/05/15/nyregion/0515-foreclose.html.

105. Powell and Roberts, 2009.

106. Dietz and Haurin, 2003; Ellen, Lacoe, and Sharygin, 2011; Immergluck and Smith, 2006.

107. Jargowsky, 2003.

108. Silver, 2010.

109. In particular, not enough attention has been given to the American Recovery and Reinvestment Act, which was one of the largest and most progressive social policies ever to be passed in the United States and included a great deal of funding for urban programs. For a thorough analysis of where the funds went, see Aber and Chaudry, 2010.

110. B. Katz, 2010.

111. Wilson, 2010.

References

Aalbers, Manuel B., and Ellen Van Beckhoven. 2010. "The Integrated Approach in Neighbourhood Renewal: More than Just a Philosophy?" *Tijdschrift voor economische en sociale geografie* 101:449–61.

Aaronson, Daniel. 1997. "Sibling Estimates of Neighborhood Effects." Pp. 80–93 in *Neighborhood Poverty: Vol. 2, Policy Implications in Studying Neighborhoods*, edited by J. Brooks-Gunn, G. J. Duncan, and J. L. Aber. New York: Russell Sage.

Aber, J. Lawrence. 2007. "Changing the Climate on Early Childhood." *American Prospect* (December): A4–A6.

Aber, J. Lawrence, and Ajay Chaudry. 2010. "Low-Income Children, Their Families and the Great Recession." Urban Institute, Washington, DC.

Ainsworth, James W. 2002. "Why Does It Take a Village? The Mediation of Neighborhood Effects on Educational Achievement." *Social Forces* 81:117–52.

Alba, Richard D., and John R. Logan. 1993. "Minority Proximity to Whites in Suburbs: An Individual-Level Analysis of Segregation." *American Journal of Sociology* 98:1388–1427.

Alba, Richard D., John R. Logan, and Paul E. Bellair. 1994. "Living with Crime: The Implications of Racial/Ethnic Differences in Suburban Location." *Social Forces* 73:395–434.

Alba, Richard D., John R. Logan, and Brian J. Stults. 2000a. "The Changing Neighborhood Contexts of the Immigrant Metropolis." *Social Forces* 79:587–621.

———. 2000b. "How Segregated Are Middle-Class African Americans?" *Social Problems* 47:543–58.

Altman, Irwin, and Setha M. Low. 1992. *Place Attachment*. New York: Plenum Press.

Anderson, Elijah. 2000. *Code of the Street: Decency, Violence, and the Moral Life of the Inner City*. New York: W. W. Norton.

Anderson, Martin. 1964. *The Federal Bulldozer: A Critical Analysis of Urban Renewal*. Cambridge, MA: MIT Press.

Apgar, William C., and Allegra Calder. 2005. "The Dual Mortgage Market: The Persistence of Discrimination in Mortgage Lending." Pp. 101–23 in *The Geography of Opportunity: Race and Housing Choice in Metropolitan America*, edited by X. d. S. Briggs. Washington, DC: Brookings.

Arum, Richard. 2000. "Schools and Communities: Ecological and Institutional Dimensions." *Annual Review of Sociology* 26:395–418.

Ashenfelter, Orley, William J. Collins, and Albert Yoon. 2006. "Evaluating the Role of Brown v. Board of Education in School Equalization, Desegregation, and the Income of African Americans." *American Law and Economics Review* 8:213–48.

Bayor, Ronald H. 1996. *Race and the Shaping of Twentieth-Century Atlanta*. Chapel Hill: University of North Carolina Press.

———. 2000. "Atlanta: The Historical Paradox." Pp. 42–58 in *The Atlanta Paradox*, edited by D. L. Sjoquist. New York: Russell Sage.

Becker, Gary S., and Nigel Tomes. 1986. "Human Capital and the Rise and Fall of Families." *Journal of Labor Economics* 4:1–39.

Beller, Emily, and Michael Hout. 2006. "Intergenerational Social Mobility: The United States in Comparative Perspective." *The Future of Children* 16:19–36.

Bennett, Larry, and Adolph Reed Jr. 1999. "The New Face of Urban Renewal: The Near North Redevelopment Initiative and the Cabrini-Green Neighborhood." Pp. 175–211 in *Without Justice for All: The New Liberalism and Our Retreat from Racial Equality*, edited by A. Reed Jr. Boulder, CO: Westview Press.

Berlin, Ira. 2010. *The Making of African America*. New York: Viking.

Berrien, Jenny, Omar McRoberts, and Christopher Winship. 2000. "Religion and the Boston Miracle: The Effect of Black Ministry on Youth Violence." Pp. 266–48 in *Who Will Provide? The Changing Role of Religion in American Social Welfare*, edited by M. J. Bane, B. Coffin, and R. Thiemann. Boulder, CO: Westview Press.

Berrien, Jenny, and Christopher Winship. 2002. "An Umbrella of Legitimacy: Boston's Police Department–Ten Point Coalition Collaboration." Pp. 200–228 in *Securing Our Children's Future: New Approaches to Juvenile Justice and Youth Violence*, edited by G. Katzman. Washington, DC: Brookings.

Bingenheimer, Jeffrey B., Robert T. Brennan, and Felton J. Earls. 2005. "Firearm Violence Exposure and Serious Violent Behavior." *Science* 308:1323–26.

Bissinger, Buzz. 1997. *A Prayer for the City*. New York: Random House.

Black, Sandra E., and Amir Sufi. 2002. "Who Goes to College? Differential Enrollment by Race and Family Background." National Bureau of Economic Research Working Paper 9310, Cambridge, MA.

Blackwell, Angela Glover, and Judith Bell. 2005. "Equitable Development for a Stronger Nation: Lessons from the Field." Pp. 289–309 in *The Geography of Opportunity: Race and Housing Choice in Metropolitan America*, edited by X.d.S. Briggs. Washington, DC: Brookings.

Blank, Rebecca M. 1997. "Why Has Economic Growth Been Such an Ineffective Tool against Poverty in Recent Years?" Pp. 27–41 in *Poverty and Inequality: The Political Economics of Redistribution*, edited by J. Neill. Kalamazoo, MI: W.E. Upjohn Institute for Employment.

Blank, Rebecca M., and David E. Card. 1993. "Poverty, Income Distribution, and Growth: Are They Still Connected?" *Brookings Papers on Economic Activity* 2: 285–339.

Blank, Rebecca M., and Mark H. Greenberg. 2010. "Poverty and Economic Stimulus." Brookings Institution, Washington, DC.

Blau, Peter Michael, and Otis Dudley Duncan. 1967. *The American Occupational Structure*. New York: Free Press.

Block, Carolyn R., and Richard L. Block. 1993. "Overview of the Chicago Homicide Project." Pp. 97–106 in *Questions and Answers in Lethal and Non-Lethal Violence: Proceedings of the First Annual Workshop of the Homicide Research Working Group*, edited by C. R. Block and R. L. Block. Washington, DC: National Institute of Justice.

Blokland, Talja. 2008. "From the Outside Looking In: A 'European' Perspective on the Ghetto." *City & Community* 7:372–77.

Bloom, Howard S. 2006. "The Core Analytics of Randomized Experiments for Social Research." MDRC Working Papers on Research Methodology, New York.

Bloom, Howard S., James A. Riccio, Nandita Verma, and Johanna Walter. 2005. "Promoting Work in Public Housing. The Effectiveness of Jobs-Plus. Final Report." Manpower Demonstration Research Corporation, New York.

Bluestone, Barry, and Bennett Harrison. 1982. *The Deindustrialization of America*. New York: Basic Books.

Bobo, Lawrence D. 2011. "Somewhere between Jim Crow & Post-Racialism: Reflections on the Racial Divide in America Today." *Daedalus* 140:11–36.

Bobo, Lawrence, and Camille L. Zubrinsky. 1996. "Attitudes on Residential Integration: Perceived Status Differences, Mere In-Group Preferences, or Racial Prejudice." *Social Forces* 74:883–909.

Bound, John, and Richard B. Freeman. 1992. "What Went Wrong? The Erosion of Relative Earnings and Employment among Young Black Men in the 1980s." *Quarterly Journal of Economics* 107:201–32.

Bowles, Samuel, and Herbert Gintis. 2002. "The Inheritance of Inequality." *Journal of Economic Perspectives* 16:3–30.

Bowles, Samuel, Herbert Gintis, and Melissa Osborne Groves (eds.). 2005. *Unequal Chances: Family Background and Economic Success*. New York; Princeton, NJ: Russell Sage Foundation; Princeton University Press.

Brennan, John, and Edward Hill. 1999. "Where Are the Jobs? Cities, Suburbs, and the Competition for Employment." Brookings Institution, Washington, DC.

Briggs, Xavier de Souza. 1997. "Moving Up versus Moving Out: Neighborhood Effects in Housing Mobility Programs." *Housing Policy Debate* 8:195–234.

———. 2005. "Politics and Policy: Changing the Geography of Opportunity." Pp. 310–41 in *The Geography of Opportunity: Race and Housing Choice in Metropolitan America*, edited by X. d. S. Briggs. Washington, DC: Brookings.

Briggs, Xavier de Souza, and Benjamin Keys. 2009. "Has Exposure to Poor Neighbourhoods Changed in America? Race, Risk and Housing Locations in Two Decades." *Urban Studies* 46:429–58.

Briggs, Xavier de Souza, Susan J Popkin, and John Goering. 2010. *Moving to Opportunity: The Story of an American Experiment to Fight Ghetto Poverty*. New York: Oxford University Press.

Brock, William, and Steven N. Durlauf. 2000. "Interactions-Based Models." National Bureau of Economic Research Working Paper 258, Cambridge, MA.

Brodsky, Melvin M. 2000. "Public-Service Employment Programs in Selected OECD Countries." *Monthly Labor Review* 123:31–41.

Brooks, David. 2005. "The Bursting Point." *New York Times*, September 4, p. 11.

———. 2007. "Edwards, Obama and the Poor." *New York Times*, July 31, p. A19.

Brooks-Gunn, Jeanne, Greg J. Duncan, Pamela K. Klebanov, and Naomi Sealand. 1993. "Do Neighborhoods Influence Child and Adolescent Behavior?" *American Journal of Sociology* 99:353–95.

Brooks-Gunn, Jeanne, Pamela K. Klebanov, and Greg J. Duncan. 1996. "Economic Hardship and the Development of Five- and Six-Year-Olds: Neighborhood and Regional Perspectives." *Child Development* 67:3338–67.

Browning, Rufus P., Dale Rogers Marshall, and David H. Tabb. 1990. *Racial Politics in American Cities*. New York: Longman.

Burdick-Will, Julia, Jens Ludwig, Stephen Raudenbush, Robert Sampson, Lisa Sanbonmatsu, and Patrick Sharkey. 2011. "Converging Evidence for Neighborhood Effects on Children's Test Scores: An Experimental, Quasi-experimental, and Observational Comparison." Pp. 255–76 in *Whither Opportunity? Rising Inequality, Schools, and Children's Life Chances*, edited by G. J. Duncan and R. Murnane. New York: Russell Sage.

Bureau of Labor Statistics, U.S. Department of Labor. 2010. "The Employment Situation—May 2010." Retrieved June 28, 2010; http://www.bls.gov/news.release/pdf/empsit.pdf.

Busso, Matias, and Patrick Kline. 2008. "Do Local Economic Development Programs Work?

Evidence from the Federal Empowerment Zone Program." Cowles Foundation Discussion Paper 1638. Yale University, New Haven, CT.

Cameron, Stephen V., and James J. Heckman. 2001. "The Dynamics of Educational Attainment for Black, Hispanic, and White Males." *Journal of Political Economy* 109:455–99.

Campbell, Frances A., and Craig T. Ramey. 1994. "Effects of Early Intervention on Intellectual and Academic Achievement: A Follow-up Study of Children from Low-Income Families." *Child Development* 65:684–98.

Campbell, Frances A., Craig T. Ramey, Elizabeth Pungello, Joseph Sparling, and Shari Miller-Johnson. 2002. "Early Childhood Education: Young Adult Outcomes from the Abecedarian Project." *Applied Developmental Science* 6:42–57.

Caraley, Demetrios. 1992. "Washington Abandons the Cities." *Political Science Quarterly* 107:1–30.

Card, David. 1998. "Falling Union Membership and Rising Wage Inequality: What's the Connection?" National Bureau of Economic Research Working Paper 6520, Cambridge, MA.

Carey, Benedict. 2007. "Study Quantifies Orphanage Link to I.Q." *New York Times*, December 21, p. A30.

Caughy, Margaret O'Brien, and Patricia J. O'Campo. 2006. "Neighborhood Poverty, Social Capital, and the Cognitive Development of African-American Preschoolers." *American Journal of Community Psychology* 37:141–54.

Cazenave, Noel A. 2007. *Impossible Democracy: The Unlikely Success of the War on Poverty Community Action Programs.* Albany: State University of New York Press.

Chaddha, Anmol, and William J. Wilson. 2008. "Reconsidering the 'Ghetto.'" *City & Community* 7:384–88.

Chandler, James P. 1972. "Fair Housing Laws: A Critique." *Hastings Law Journal* 24:159–214.

Charles, Camille Zubrinsky. 2000. "Neighborhood Racial-Composition Preferences: Evidence from a Multiethnic Metropolis." *Social Problems* 47:379–407.

———. 2006. *Won't You Be My Neighbor: Race, Class, and Residence in Los Angeles.* New York: Russell Sage.

Charles, Kerwin Kofi, and Erik Hurst. 2003. "The Correlation of Wealth across Generations." *Journal of Political Economy* 111:1155–82.

Chase-Lansdale, P. Lindsay, and Rachel A. Gordon. 1996. "Economic Hardship and the Development of Five- and Six-Year-Olds: Neighbourhood and Regional Perspectives." *Child Development* 67:3338–67.

Chase-Lansdale, P. Lindsay, Rachel A. Gordon, Jeanne Brooks-Gunn, and Pamela K. Klebanov. 1997. "Neighborhood and Family Influences on the Intellectual and Behavioral Competence of Preschool and Early School-Age Children." Pp. 79–118 in *Neighborhood Poverty: Context and Consequences for Children*, vol. 1, edited by J. Brooks-Gunn, G. J. Duncan, and J. L. Aber. New York: Russell Sage.

Cisneros, Henry G. 2009. "A New Moment for People and Cities." Pp. 2–13 in *From Despair to Hope: Hope VI and the New Promise of Public Housing in America's Cities*, edited by H. G. Cisneros and L. Engdahl. Washington, DC: Brookings.

Cisneros, Henry G., and Lora Engdahl (eds.). 2009. *From Despair to Hope: Hope VI and the New Promise of Public Housing in America's Cities.* Washington, DC: Brookings.

Clampet-Lundquist, Susan, and Douglas S. Massey. 2008. "Neighborhood Effects on Economic Self-Sufficiency: A Reconsideration of the Moving to Opportunity Experiment." *American Journal of Sociology* 114:107–43.

Clark, Kenneth B. 1965. *Dark Ghetto: Dilemmas of Social Power*. New York: Harper Torchbooks.

Cohen, Cathy, and Michael Dawson. 1993. "Neighborhood Poverty and African-American Politics." *American Political Science Review* 87:286–302.

Collins, Sharon M. 1983. "The Making of the Black Middle Class." *Social Problems* 30: 369–82.

———. 1997. *Black Corporate Executives: The Making and Breaking of a Black Middle Class.* Philadelphia: Temple University Press.

Conley, Dalton. 1999. *Being Black, Living in the Red : Race, Wealth, and Social Policy in America.* Berkeley, CA: University of California Press.

Conway, Maureen, and Josef Konvitz. 2000. "Meeting the Challenge of Distressed Urban Areas." *Urban Studies* 37:749–74.

Corak, Miles. 2006. "Do Poor Children Become Poor Adults? Lessons from a Cross-Country Comparison of Generational Earnings Mobility." *Research on Economic Inequality* 13: 143–88.

Corcoran, Mary. 1995. "Rags to Rags: Poverty and Mobility in the United States." *Annual Review of Sociology* 21:237.

Corcoran, Mary, and Terry Adams. 1999. "Race, Sex, and the Intergenerational Transmission of Poverty." Pp. 461–517 in *The Consequences of Growing up Poor*, edited by G. J. Duncan and J. Brooks-Gunn. New York: Russell Sage.

Corcoran, Mary, Roger Gordon, Deborah Laren, and Gary Solon. 1992. "The Association between Men's Economic Status and Their Family and Community Origins." *Journal of Human Resources* 27:575–601.

Coulton, Claudia, Jill Korbin, Tsui Chan, and Marilyn Su. 2001. "Mapping Residents' Perceptions of Neighborhood Boundaries: A Methodological Note." *American Journal of Community Psychology* 29:371–83.

Coulton, Claudia, Brett Theodos, and Margery Austin Turner. 2009. "Family Mobility and Neighborhood Change: New Evidence and Implications for Community Initiatives." Urban Institute, Washington, DC.

Crane, Jonathan. 1991. "The Epidemic Theory of Ghettos and Neighborhood Effects on Dropping out and Teenage Childbearing." *American Journal of Sociology* 96:1226–59.

Crowder, Kyle, Scott J. South, and Erick Chavez. 2006. "Wealth, Race, and Inter-Neighborhood Migration." *American Sociological Review* 71:72–94.

Crowley, Sheila. 2009. "Hope VI: What Went Wrong?" Pp. 228–47 in *From Despair to Hope: Hope VI and the New Promise of Public Housing in America's Cities*, edited by H. G. Cisneros and L. Engdahl. Washington, DC: Brookings.

Cutler, David M., Edward L. Glaeser, and Jacob Vigdor. 1999. "The Rise and Decline of the American Ghetto." *Journal of Political Economy* 107:455–506.

Datcher, Linda. 1982. "Effects of Community and Family Background on Achievement." *Review of Economics and Statistics* 64:32–41.

Davis, Mike. 1992. *City of Quartz: Excavating the Future in Los Angeles*. New York: Vintage.

Dear, Michael, and Nicholas Dahmann. 2008. "Urban Politics and the Los Angeles School of Urbanism." *Urban Affairs Review* 44:266–79.

DeLuca, Stefanie, and Elizabeth Dayton. 2009. "Switching Social Contexts: The Effects of Housing Mobility and School Choice Programs on Youth Outcomes." *Annual Review of Sociology* 35:457–91.

DeParle, Jason. 1996. "Slamming the Door." *New York Times Magazine* (October 20):52–56.

Dickens, William T. 1999. "Rebuilding Urban Labor Markets: What Community Development Can Accomplish." Pp. 381–436 in *Urban Problems and Community Development*, edited by R. F. Ferguson and W. T. Dickens. Washington, DC: Brookings.

Dietz, Robert, and Donald R. Haurin. 2003. "The Social and Private Micro-Level Consequences of Homeownership." *Journal of Urban Economics* 54:401–50.

Dobbie, Will, and Roland G. Fryer Jr. 2009. "Are High-Quality Schools Enough to Close the Achievement Gap? Evidence from a Bold Social Experiment in Harlem?" National Bureau of Economic Research Working Paper 15473, Cambridge, MA.

Downs, Anthony. 1968. "Alternative Futures for the American Ghetto." *Daedalus* 97:1331–78.

———. 1993. "Reducing Regulatory Barriers to Affordable Housing Erected by Local Government." Pp. 255–81 in *Housing Markets and Residential Mobility*, edited by G. T. Kingsley and M. A. Turner. Washington, DC: Urban Institute Press.

———. 1994. *New Visions for Metropolitan America*. Washington, DC: Brookings.

Drake, St Clair, and Horace R. Cayton. 1933. *Black Metropolis: A Study of Negro Life in a Northern City*. Chicago: University of Chicago Press.

Dreier, Peter. 1995. "Putting Cities on the National Agenda." *Urban Affairs Review* 30:645–56.

Dreier, Peter, and David Moberg. 1995. "Moving from The 'hood: The Mixed Success of Integrating Suburbia." *American Prospect* (December): 75–9.

Dreier, Peter, John H. Mollenkopf, and Todd Swanstrom. 2001. *Place Matters: Metropolitics for the Twenty-First Century*. Lawrence: University of Kansas Press.

Drennan, Matthew P. 1991. "The Decline and Rise of the New York Economy." Pp. 25–42 in *Dual City: Restructuring New York*, edited by J. H. Mollenkopf and M. Castells. New York: Russell Sage.

Dubofsky, Jean E. 1969. "Fair Housing: A Legislative History and a Perspective." *Washburn Law Journal* 8:149–66.

DuBois, W. E. B. 1899. *The Philadelphia Negro*. New York: Lippincott.

Duncan, Greg J., Johanne Boisjoly, and Kathleen M. Harris. 2001. "Sibling, Peer, Neighbor, and Schoolmate Correlations as Indicators of the Importance of Context for Adolescent Development." *Demography* 38:437–47.

Duncan, Greg J., Jeanne Brooks-Gunn, and Pamela K. Klebanov. 1994. "Economic Deprivation and Early Childhood Development." *Child Development* 65:296–318.

Duncan, Greg J., Aletha C. Huston, and Thomas S. Weisner. 2009. *Higher Ground: New Hope for the Working Poor and Their Children*. New York: Russell Sage.

Duncan, Otis Dudley. 1968. "Inheritance of Poverty or Inheritance of Race?" Pp. 85–110 in *On Understanding Poverty*, edited by D. P. Moynihan. New York: Basic Books.

Eckholm, Erik. 2006. "Plight Deepens for Black Men, Studies Warn." *New York Times*, March 20, p. 18. Edelman, Peter. 2010. "The Next War on Poverty." *Democracy* 10:21–33.

Edelman, Peter, Harry J. Holzer, and Paul Offner. 2006. *Reconnecting Disadvantaged Young Men*. Washington, DC: Urban Institute Press.

Edwards, John. 2008. "Building One America." *Pathways* (Winter): 8–10.

Eichenlaub, Suzanne C., Stewart E. Tolnay, and J. Trent Alexander. 2010. "Moving Out but Not Up." *American Sociological Review* 75:101–25.

Elder, Glen H., Monica Kirkpatrick Johnson, and Robert Crosnoe. 2003. "The Emergence and Development of Life Course Theory." Pp. 3–19 in *Handbook of the Life Course*, edited by J. T. Mortimer and M. J. Shanahan. New York: Kluwer.

Elder, Glen H., Valarie King, and Rand D. Conger. 1996. "Attachment to Place and Migration Prospects: A Developmental Perspective." *Journal of Research on Adolescence* 6:397–425.

Elkin, Stephen L. 1987. "State and Market in City Politics: Or, the "Real" Dallas." Pp. 25–51 in *The Politics of Urban Development*, edited by C. N. Stone and H. T. Sanders. Lawrence: University of Kansas Press.

Ellen, Ingrid Gould. 2000. *Sharing America's Neighborhoods: The Prospects for Stable Racial Integration*. Cambridge, MA: Harvard University Press.

Ellen, Ingrid Gould, and Margery A. Turner. 1997. "Does Neighborhood Matter? Assessing Recent Evidence." *Housing Policy Debate* 8:833–64.

Ellen, Ingrid Gould, Johanna Lacoe, and Claudia Sharygin. 2011. "Do Foreclosures Cause Crime?" Furman Center for Real Estate and Urban Policy Working Paper, New York.

Elliott, Delbert, William J. Wilson, David Huizinga, Robert J. Sampson, Amanda Elliott, and Bruce Rankin. 1996. "Effects of Neighborhood Disadvantage on Adolescent Development." *Journal of Research in Crime and Delinquency* 33:389–426.

Ellwood, David T. 1996. "Welfare Reform as I Knew It: When Bad Things Happen to Good Policies." *American Prospect* (May-June): 22–9.

Ellwood, David T., and Elisabeth D. Welty. 2000. "Public Service Employment and Mandatory Work: A Policy Whose Time Has Come and Gone and Come Again?" Pp. 299–372 in *Finding Jobs: Work and Welfare Reform*, edited by D. E. Card and R. Blank. New York: Russell Sage.

Engdahl, Lora. 2009. "New Homes, New Neighborhoods, New Schools: A Progress Report on the Baltimore Housing Mobility Program." Poverty and Race Research Action Coalition, Washington, DC.

Farley, Reynolds, Sheldon Danziger, and Harry J. Holzer. 2000. *Detroit Divided*. New York: Russell Sage.

Feagin, Joe, and Eileen O'Brien. 2004. *White Men on Race: Power, Privilege, and the Shaping of Cultural Consciousness*. Boston: Beacon Press.

Featherman, David L., and Robert M. Hauser. 1978. *Opportunity and Change*. New York: Academic Press.

Ferguson, Ronald F., and William T. Dickens (eds.). 1999. *Urban Problems and Community Development*. Washington, DC: Brookings.

Fernandez, Roberto M., and Celina Su. 2004. "Space in the Study of Labor Markets." *Annual Review of Sociology* 30:545–69.

Fiss, Owen M. 2000. "What Should Be Done for Those Who Have Been Left Behind?" *Boston Review* (Summer):1–8.

Flippen, Chenoa. 2004. "Unequal Returns to Housing Investments? A Study of Real Housing Appreciation among Black, White, and Hispanic Households." *Social Forces* 82:1523–51.

Frankenberg, Erica, Chungmei Lee, and Gary Orfield. 2003. "A Multiracial Society with Segregated Schools: Are We Losing the Dream?" Civil Rights Project, Harvard University, Cambridge, MA.

Freeman, Lance. 2006. *There Goes the 'Hood: Views of Gentrification from the Ground Up*. Philidelphia: Temple University Press.

Freeman, Richard B. 1976. *Black Elite: The New Market for Highly Educated Black Americans*. New York: McGraw-Hill.

Freeman, Richard B., and Harry J. Holzer. 1985. "Young Blacks and Jobs—What We Now Know." *Public Interest* 78:18–31.

Fried, Marc. 1982. "Residential Attachment: Sources of Residential and Community Satisfaction." *Journal of Social Issues* 38:107–19.

Frieden, Bernard J., and Marshall Kaplan. 1977. *The Politics of Neglect: Urban Aid from Model Cities to Revenue Sharing*. Cambridge, MA: MIT Press.

Fullilove, Mindy. 2005. *Root Shock: How Tearing up City Neighborhoods Hurts America, and What We Can Do About It*. New York: Ballantine.

Galster, George C. 2002. "An Economic Efficiency Analysis of Deconcentrating Poverty Populations." *Journal of Housing Economics* 11:303–29.

———. 2003. "The Effects of MTO on Sending and Receiving Neighborhoods." Pp. 365–82 in *Choosing a Better Life*, edited by J. Goering and J. Feins. Washington, DC: Urban Institute Press.

———. 2007. "Neighbourhood Social Mix as a Goal of Housing Policy: A Theoretical Analysis." *European Journal of Housing Policy* 7:19–43.

———. 2012. "The Mechanisms of Neighborhood Effects: Theory, Evidence and Policy Implications." Pp. 23–56 in *Neighbourhood Effects Research: New Perspectives*, edited by M. v. Ham, D. Manley, N. Bailey, L. Simpson, and D. Maclennan. Dordrecht: Springer.

Galster, George C., and Anne Zobel. 1998. "Will Dispersed Housing Programmes Reduce Social Problems in the US?" *Housing Studies* 13:605–22.

Gans, Herbert. 1962. *The Urban Villagers*. New York: Free Press.

Gans, Herbert J. 1993. "Planning for a Labor-Intensive Economy." Pp. 244–54 in *People, Plans, and Policies: Essays on Poverty, Racism, and Other National Urban Problems*, edited by H. J. Gans. New York: Columbia University Press/Russell Sage.

———. 1995. *The War against the Poor: The Underclass and Antipoverty Policy*. New York: Basic Books.

———. 2011. "The Challenge of Multigenerational Poverty." *Challenge* 54:70–81.

Garland, David. 2001a. "Introduction: The Meaning of Mass Imprisonment." *Punishment & Society* 3:5–7.

———. 2001b. *Mass Imprisonment: Social Causes and Consequences*. London: Sage.

Garner, Catherine L., and Stephen W. Raudenbush. 1991. "Neighborhood Effects on Educational Attainment: A Multilevel Analysis." *Sociology of Education* 64:251–62.

Garreau, Joel. 1991. *Edge City: Life on the New Frontier*. New York: Anchor.

Gelman, Andrew, Jeffrey Fagan, and Alex Kiss. 2007. "An Analysis of the New York City Police Department's 'Stop-and-Frisk' Policy in the Context of Claims of Racial Bias." *Journal of the American Statistical Association* 102:813–23.

Gentry, Richard C. 1993. "Comment on Lawrence J. Vale's 'Beyond the Problem Projects Paradigm: Defining and Revitalizing "Severely Distressed" Public Housing.'" *Housing Policy Debate* 4:175–82.

Gerson, Kathleen, C. Ann Stueve, and Claude S. Fischer. 1977. "Attachment to Place." Pp. 139–61 in *Networks and Places: Social Relations in the Urban Setting*, edited by C. S. Fischer, R. M. Jackson, C. A. Stueve, K. Gerson, L. McCallister Jones, and M. Baldassare. New York: Free Press.

Gieryn, Thomas F. 2000. "A Space for Place in Sociology." *Annual Review of Sociology*, 463–96.

Glaeser, Ed. 2007. "Where Edwards Is Right." *New York Sun*, August 7. (Online: http://www.nysun.com/opinion/where-edwards-is-right/60007).

Goering, John. 2005. "Expanding Housing Choice and Integrating Neighborhoods: The MTO Experiment." Pp. 127–49 in *The Geography of Opportunity: Race and Housing Choice in Metropolitan America*, edited by X. d. S. Briggs. Washington, DC: Brookings.

———. 2007a. "The Effectiveness of Fair Housing Programs and Policy Options." Pp. 253–86 in *Fragile Rights within Cities: Government, Housing, and Fairness*, edited by J. Goering. Lanham, MD: Rowman & Littlefield.

———. 2007b. "Introduction and Overview." Pp. 1–18 in *Fragile Rights within Cities: Government, Housing, and Fairness*, edited by J. Goering. Lanham, MD: Rowman & Littlefield.

Goering, John M., and Judith D. Feins. 2003. *Choosing a Better Life? Evaluating the Moving to Opportunity Social Experiment.* Washington, DC: Urban Institute Press.

Goetz, Edward G. 2003. *Clearing the Way: Deconcentrating the Poor in Urban America.* Washington, DC: Urban Institute Press.

Goetz, Edward G., and Karen Chapple. 2010. "You Gotta Move: Advancing the Debate on the Record of Dispersal." *Housing Policy Debate* 20:209–36.

Goode, Judith, and Jo Anne Schneider. 1994. *Reshaping Ethnic and Racial Relations in Philadelphia: Immigrants in a Divided City.* Philadelphia: Temple University Press.

Gould Ellen, Ingrid, and Kathy O'Regan. 2008. "Reversal of Fortunes? Lower-Income Urban Neighbourhoods in the US in the 1990s." *Urban Studies* 45:845–69.

Graif, Corina, and Robert J. Sampson. 2009. "Spatial Heterogeneity in the Effects of Immigration and Diversity on Neighborhood Homicide Rates." *Homicide Studies* 13:242–60.

Gramlich, Edward, Deborah Laren, and Naomi Sealand. 1992. "Moving into and out of Poor Urban Areas." *Journal of Policy Analysis and Management* 11:273–87.

Grannis, Rick. 1998. "The Importance of Trivial Streets: Residential Streets and Residential Segregation." *American Journal of Sociology* 103:1530–64.

Grawe, Nathan D. 2004. "Intergenerational Mobility for Whom? The Experience of High- and Low-Earning Sons in International Perspective." Pp. 58–89 in *Generational Income Mobility in North America and Europe*, edited by M. Corak. Cambridge: Cambridge University Press.

Green, Donald P., Dara Z. Strolovitch, and Janelle S. Wong. 1998. "Defended Neighborhoods, Integration, and Racially Motivated Crime." *American Journal of Sociology* 104:372–403.

Greenbaum, Robert, and John Engberg. 2000. "An Evaluation of State Enterprise Zone Policies." *Review of Policy Research* 17:29–45.

Grogan, Paul, and Tony Proscio. 2001. *Comeback Cities: A Blueprint for Urban Neighborhood Revival.* Boulder, CO: Basic Books.

Gross, Ruth T., Donna Spiker, and Christine W. Haynes. 1997. *Helping Low Birth Weight, Premature Babies: The Infant Health and Development Program.* Palo Alto, CA: Stanford University Press.

Guo, Guang, and Kathleen Mullan Harris. 2000. "The Mechanisms Mediating the Effects of Poverty on Children's Intellectual Development." *Demography* 37:431–47.

Haar, Charles M. 1975. *Between the Idea and the Reality: A Study in the Origin, Fate and Legacy of the Model Cities Program.* Boston: Little, Brown.

Halpern, Robert. 1995. *Rebuilding the Inner City: A History of Neighborhood Initiatives to Address Poverty in the United States.* New York: Columbia University Press.

Hamilton, Bruce W., Edwin S. Mills, and David Puryear. 1975. "The Tiebout Hypothesis and Residential Income Segregation." Pp. 101–18 in *Fiscal Zoning and Land Use Controls: The Economic Issues*, edited by E. S. Mills and W. E. Oates. Lexington, MA: D.C. Heath.

Hannerz, Ulf. 1969. *Soulside: Inquiries into Ghetto Culture and Community.* New York: Columbia University Press.

Hanson, Roy. 2003. *Civic Culture and Urban Change: Governing Dallas.* Detroit: Wayne State University Press.

Harding, David J. 2003. "Counterfactual Models of Neighborhood Effects: The Effect of

Neighborhood Poverty on Dropping out and Teenage Pregnancy." *American Journal of Sociology* 109:676–719.

———. 2010. *Living the Drama: Community, Conflict, and Culture among Inner-City Boys*. Chicago: University of Chicago Press.

Harding, David J., Christopher Jencks, Leonard M. Lopoo, and Susan E. Mayer. 2005. "The Changing Effect of Family Background on the Incomes of American Adults." Pp. 100–44 in *Unequal Chances: Family Background and Economic Success*, edited by S. Bowles, H. Gintis, and M. Osborne Groves. Princeton, NJ: Princeton University Press.

Harris, David. 1999. "'Property Values Drop When Blacks Move in, Because . . . ': Racial and Socioeconomic Determinants of Neighborhood Desirability." *American Sociological Review* 64:461–79.

Harris, David R. 2001. "Why Are Whites and Blacks Averse to Black Neighbors?" *Social Science Research* 30:100–116.

Harrison, Bennett. 1974. "Ghetto Economic Development: A Survey." *Journal of Economic Literature* 12:1–37.

Hartman, Chester, and Gregory Squires (eds.). 2009. *The Integration Debate: Competing Futures for American Cities*. New York: Routledge.

Heckman, James J. 1995. "Lessons from the Bell Curve." *Journal of Political Economy* 103:1091–1120.

———. 2006. "Skill Formation and the Economics of Investing in Disadvantaged Children." *Science* 312:1900–1902.

Heckman, James J., and Dimitriy V. Masterov. 2007. "The Productivity Argument for Investing in Young Children." *Applied Economic Perspectives and Policy* 29:446–93.

Heckman, James J., Jora Stixrud, and Sergio Urzua. 2006. "The Effects of Cognitive and Noncognitive Abilities on Labor Market Outcomes and Social Behavior." *Journal of Labor Economics* 24:411–82.

Hellerstein, Judith K., and David Neumark. 2011. "Employment in Black Urban Labor Markets: Problems and Solutions." National Bureau of Economic Research Working Paper 16986, Cambridge, MA.

Hellerstein, Judith K., David Neumark, and Melissa McInerney. 2008. "Spatial Mismatch or Racial Mismatch?" *Journal of Urban Economics* 64:464–79.

Herrnstein, Richard, and Charles Murray. 1994. *The Bell Curve: Intelligence and Class Structure in American Life*. New York: Free Press.

Hertz, Tom. 2005. "Rags, Riches, and Race: The Intergenerational Economic Mobility of Black and White Families in the United States." Pp. 165–91 in *Unequal Chances: Family Background and Economic Success*, edited by S. Bowles, H. Gintis, and M. Osborne Groves. Princeton, NJ: Princeton University Press.

———. 2006. "Understanding Mobility in America." Center for American Progress, Washington, DC.

Hill, Jennifer, Jeanne Brooks-Gunn, and Jane Waldfogel. 2003. "Sustained Effects of High Participation in an Early Intervention for Low-Birth-Weight Premature Infants." *Developmental Psychology* 39:730–44.

Hipp, John R. 2007. "Block, Tract, and Levels of Aggregation: Neighborhood Structure and Crime and Disorder as a Case in Point." *American Sociological Review* 72:659–80.

Hirsch, Arnold R. 1983. *The Making of the Second Ghetto: Race and Housing in Chicago, 1840–1960*. Cambridge: Cambridge University Press.

———. 2003. "Second Thoughts on the Second Ghetto." *Journal of Urban History* 29:298.

Hochschild, Jennifer. 2000. "Creating Options." *Boston Review* (Summer): Online (http://bostonreview.net/BR25.3/hochschild.html).

Hofferth, Sandra, Pamela E. Davis-Kean, Jean Davis, and Jonathan Finkelstein. 1999. *The Child Development Supplement to the Panel Study of Income Dynamics: 1997 User Guide.* Ann Arbor, MI: Institute for Social Research.

Hollister, Robinson G., and Jennifer Hill. 1995. "Problems in the Evaluation of Community-Wide Initiatives." Pp. 127–72 in *New Approaches to Evaluating Community Initiatives: Concepts, Methods, and Contexts*, vol. 1, edited by J. I. Connell, A. C. Kubisch, L. B. Schoor, and C. H. Weiss. Washington, DC: Aspen Institute.

Holzer, Harry J. 1987. "Informal Job Search and Black Youth Unemployment." *American Economic Review* 77:446–52.

———. 1991. "The Spatial Mismatch Hypothesis: What Has the Evidence Shown?" *Urban Studies* 28:105–22.

———. 1996. *What Employers Want: Job Prospects for Less Educated Workers.* New York: Russell Sage.

Holzer, Harry J., and Paul Offner. 2006. "Trends in the Employment Outcomes of Young Black Men, 1979–2000." Pp. 11–38 in *Black Males Left Behind*, edited by R. B. Mincy. Washington, DC: Urban Institute Press.

Holzer, Harry J., Paul Offner, and Elaine Sorensen. 2005. "Declining Employment among Young Black Less-Educated Men: The Role of Incarceration and Child Support." *Journal of Policy Analysis and Management* 24:329–50.

Holzer, Harry J., Steven Raphael, and Michael Stoll. 2004. "Will Employers Hire Former Offenders? Employer Preferences, Background Checks, and Their Determinants." Pp. 205–43 in *Imprisoning America: The Social Effects of Mass Incarceration*, edited by M. Pattillo, D. Weiman, and B. Western. New York: Russell Sage.

———. 2006. "How Do Employer Perceptions of Crime and Incarceration Affect the Employment Prospects of Less-Educated Young Black Men?" Pp. 67–85 in *Black Males Left Behind*, edited by R. Mincy. Washington, DC: Urban Institute Press.

Horowitz, Karyn, Stevan Weine, and James Jekel. 1995. "PTSD Symptoms in Urban Adolescent Girls: Compounded Community Trauma." *Journal of American Academy of Child & Adolescent Psychiatry* 34:1353–61.

Hout, Michael. 1984. "Occupational Mobility of Black Men: 1962 to 1973." *American Sociological Review* 49:308–22.

Hoxby, Caroline M., Sonali Murarka, and Jenny Kang. 2009. "How New York City's Charter Schools Affect Achievement." New York City Charter Schools Evaluation Project, Cambridge, MA.

Hoynes, Hilary W. 1999. "The Employment, Earnings, and Income of Less Skilled Workers over the Business Cycle." National Bureau of Economic Research Working Paper 7188, Cambridge, MA.

Hughes, Mark Alan. 1995. "A Mobility Strategy for Improving Opportunity." *Housing Policy Debate* 6:271–97.

Ihlanfeldt, Keith R and David L Sjoquist. 1998. "The Spatial Mismatch Hypothesis: A Review of Recent Studies and Their Implications for Welfare Reform." *Housing Policy Debate* 9:849–92.

———. 2000. "The Geographic Mismatch between Jobs and Housing." Pp. 116–27 in *The Atlanta Paradox*, edited by D. L. Sjoquist. New York: Russell Sage.

Imbroscio, David L. 2008a. "Fighting Poverty with Mobility: A Normative Policy Analysis." *Review of Policy Research* 21:447–61.

———. 2008b. "United and Actuated by Some Common Impulse of Passion: Challenging the Dispersal Consensus in American Housing Policy Research." *Journal of Urban Affairs* 30:111–30.

Immergluck, Dan, and Geoff Smith. 2006. "The Impact of Single-Family Mortgage Foreclosures on Neighborhood Crime." *Housing Studies* 21:851–66.

Isaacs, Julia B. 2007. "Economic Mobility of Black and White Families." Pp. 71–80 in *Getting Ahead or Losing Ground: Economic Mobility in America*, edited by J. B. Isaacs, I. V. Sawhill, and R. Haskins. Pew Charitable Trusts Economic Mobility Project, Washington, DC.

Isaacs, Julia B., Tracy Vericker, Jennifer Macomber, and Adam Kent. 2009. "Kids' Share: An Analysis of Federal Expenditures on Children through 2008." Urban Institute and Brookings Institution, Washington, DC.

Jackson, Kenneth T. 1987. *Crabgrass Frontier: The Suburbanization of the United States*. New York: Oxford University Press.

Jacob, Brian A. 2004. "Public Housing, Housing Vouchers, and Student Achievement: Evidence from Public Housing Demolitions in Chicago." *American Economic Review* 94:233–58.

Jacobs, Joanne. 2007. "Sending Poor Kids to Middle-Class Schools Doesn't Fix a Thing; It Doesn't Produce Better Test Scores or Improve Dropout Rates." *Chicago Sun-Times*, October 7, p. B3.

Jargowsky, Paul. 1997. *Poverty and Place: Ghettos, Barrios and the American City*. New York: Russell Sage.

———. 2003. "Stunning Progress, Hidden Problems: The Dramatic Decline of Concentrated Poverty in the 1990s." Brookings Institution, Washington, DC.

Jencks, Christopher, and Susan E. Mayer. 1990. "The Social Consequences of Growing up in a Poor Neighborhood." Pp. 111–86 in *Inner-City Poverty in the United States*, edited by L. E. Lynn and M. G. H. McGeary. Washington, DC: National Academy Press.

Jencks, Christopher, and Laura Tach. 2006. "Would Equal Opportunity Mean More Mobility?" Pp. 23–58 in *Mobility and Inequality: Frontiers of Research in Sociology and Economics*, edited by S. Morgan, D. Grusky, and G. Fields. Palo Alto, CA: Stanford University Press.

Johnson, Clifford M., Amy Rynell, and Melissa Young. 2010. "Publicly Funded Jobs: An Essential Strategy for Reducing Poverty and Economic Distress throughout the Business Cycle." Urban Institute, Washington, DC.

Johnson, Rucker C. 2011. "Long-Run Impacts of School Desegregation & School Quality on Adult Attainments." National Bureau of Economic Research Working Paper 16664, Cambridge, MA.

Joseph, Lawrence B. 1992. "Coping with the New Fiscal Federalism: Changing Patterns of Federal and State Aid to Chicago." *Research in Urban Policy* 4:207–27.

Kain, John F. 1992. "The Spatial Mismatch Hypothesis: Three Decades Later." *Housing Policy Debate* 3:371–460.

Kain, John F., and Joseph J. Persky. 1969. "Alternatives to the Gilded Ghetto." *Public Interest* (January): 74–86.

Kasarda, John, and Morris Janowitz. 1974. "Community Attachment in Mass Society." *American Sociological Review* 39:328–39.

Kasinitz, Philip, John H. Mollenkopf, Mary C. Waters, and Jennifer Holdaway. 2008. *Inherit-*

ing the City: The Children of Immigrants Come of Age. Cambridge, MA: Harvard University Press and Russell Sage Foundation.

Katz, Bruce. 1999. "Beyond City Limits: A New Metropolitan Agenda." Pp. 303–31 in *Setting National Priorities: The 2000 Elections and Beyond*, edited by R. D. Reischauer and H. J. Aaron. Washington, DC: Brookings.

——— (ed.). 2000. *Reflections on Regionalism*. Washington, DC: Brookings.

———. 2010. "Obama's Metro Presidency." *City & Community* 9:23–31.

Katz, Bruce, Karen Dastorel Brown, Margery A. Turner, Mary Cunningham, and Noah Sawyer. 2003. "Rethinking Local Affordable Housing Strategies: Lessons from 70 Years of Policy and Practice." Brookings Institution and Urban Institute, Washington DC.

Katz, Michael B. 2010. "Narratives of Failure? Historical Interpretations of Federal Urban Policy." *City & Community* 9:13–22.

Kaufman, Julie E., and James E. Rosenbaum. 1992. "The Education and Employment of Low-Income Black Youth in White Suburbs." *Educational Evaluation and Policy Analysis* 14:229–240.

Keels, Micere. 2008. "Second-Generation Effects of Chicago's Gautreaux Residential Mobility Program on Children's Participation in Crime." *Journal of Research on Adolescence* 18:305–52.

Keels, Micere, Greg J. Duncan, Stefanie Deluca, Ruby Mendenhall, and James Rosenbaum. 2005. "Fifteen Years Later: Can Residental Mobility Programs Provide a Long-Term Escape from Neighborhood Segregation, Crime, and Poverty?" *Demography* 42:51–73.

Keiser, Richard A. 1990. "The Rise of a Biracial Coalition in Philadelphia." Pp. 49–74 in *Racial Politics in American Cities*, edited by R. P. Browning, D. R. Marshall, and D. H. Tabb. New York: Longman.

Keister, Lisa A. 2000. *Wealth in America: Trends in Wealth Inequality*. New York: Cambridge University Press.

Kemper, Robert V. 2005. "Dallas–Fort Worth: Toward New Models of Urbanization, Community Transformation, and Immigration." *Urban Anthropology* 34:125–49.

Kingsley, G. Thomas. 2009. "Taking Advantage of What We Have Learned." Pp. 263–97 in *From Despair to Hope: Hope VI and the New Promise of Public Housing in America's Cities*, edited by H. G. Cisneros and L. Engdahl. Washington, DC: Brookings.

Kingsley, G. Thomas, and Ashley Williams. 2010. "Metropolitan Contexts for Community Initiatives: Contrasts in a Turbulent Decade." Urban Institute, Washington, DC.

Kirk, David S. 2009. "A Natural Experiment on Residential Change and Recidivism: Lessons from Hurricane Katrina." *American Sociological Review* 74:484–505.

Klinenberg, Eric. 2002. *Heat Wave: A Social Autopsy of Disaster in Chicago*. Chicago: University of Chicago Press.

Kling, Jeffrey, Jeffrey Liebman, and Lawrence Katz. 2007. "Experimental Analysis of Neighborhood Effects." *Econometrica* 75:83–119.

Kluegel, James R., and Elliott R. Smith. 1981. "Beliefs about Stratification." *Annual Review of Sociology* 7:29–56.

Kneebone, Elizabeth, and Alan Berube. 2008. "Reversal of Fortune: A New Look at Concentrated Poverty in the 2000s." Brookings Institution Metropolitan Policy Program, Washington, DC.

Kochhar, Rakesh, Ana Gonzalez-Barrera, and Daniel Dockterman. 2009. "Through Boom and Bust: Minorities, Immigrants and Homeownership." Pew Research Center, Washington, DC.

Kohen, Dafna E., Jeanne Brooks-Gunn, Tama Leventhal, and Clyde Hertzman. 2002. "Neighbourhood Income and Physical and Social Disorder in Canada: Associations with Young Children's Competencies." *Child Development* 73:1844–60.

Kotlowitz, Alex. 1992. *There Are No Children Here: The Story of Two Boys Growing up in the Other America*. New York: Doubleday.

Kristensen, Petter, and Tor Bjerkedal. 2007. "Explaining the Relation between Birth Order and Intelligence." *Science* 316:1717.

Krysan, Maria. 2002. "Whites Who Say They'd Flee: Who Are They, and Why Would They Leave?" *Demography* 39:675–96.

Krysan, Maria, Mick P. Couper, Reynolds Farley, and Tyrone A. Forman. 2009. "Does Race Matter in Neighborhood Preferences? Results from a Video Experiment." *American Journal of Sociology* 115:527–59.

Krysan, Maria, Reynolds Farley, and Mick P. Couper. 2008. "In the Eye of the Beholder." *Du Bois Review: Social Science Research on Race* 5:5–26.

Kubisch, Anne C., Patricia Auspos, Prudence Brown, and Tom Dewar (eds.). 2010. *Voices from the Field III: Lessons and Challenges from Two Decades of Community Change Efforts*. Washington, DC: Aspen Institute.

Kupersmidt, Janis B., Ariana Shahinfar, Mary Ellen Voegler-Lee, Annette M. La Greca, Wendy K. Silverman, Eric M. Vernberg, and Michael C. Roberts. 2002. "Children's Exposure to Community Violence." Pp. 381–401 in *Helping Children Cope with Disasters and Terrorism*. Washington, DC: American Psychological Association.

Kurashige, Scott. 2010. *The Shifting Grounds of Race: Black and Japanese Americans in the Making of Multiethnic Los Angeles*. Princeton, NJ: Princeton University Press.

Lacy, Karyn. 2007. *Blue-Chip Black: Race, Class, and Status in the New Black Middle Class*. Berkeley: University of California Press.

Ladd, Helen F. 1994a. "Big City Finances." Pp. 201–69 in *Big-City Politics, Governance, and Fiscal Constraints*, edited by G. E. Peterson. Washington, DC: Urban Institute.

———. 1994b. "Spatially Targeted Economic Development Strategies: Do They Work?" *Cityscape* 1:193–218.

Lee, Barrett A., Sean F. Reardon, Glenn Firebaugh, Chad R. Farrell, Stephen A. Matthews, and David O'Sullivan. 2008. "Beyond the Census Tract: Patterns and Determinants of Racial Segregation at Multiple Geographic Scales." *American Sociological Review* 73:766–91.

Lemann, Nicholas. 1994. "The Myth of Community Development." *New York Times Magazine* (January 9).

Leventhal, Tama, and Jeanne Brooks-Gunn. 2000. "The Neighborhoods They Live In: Effects of Neighborhood Residence upon Child and Adolescent Outcomes." *Psychological Bulletin* 126:309–37.

Leventhal, Tama, Yange Xue, and Jeanne Brooks-Gunn. 2006. "Immigrant Differences in School-Age Children's Verbal Trajectories: A Look at Four Racial/Ethnic Groups." *Child Development* 77:1359–74.

Levitt, Steven 2004. "Understanding Why Crime Fell in the 1990s: Four Factors That Explain the Decline and Six That Do Not." *Journal of Economic Perspectives* 18:163–90.

Levy, Frank. 1987. *Dollars and Dreams: The Changing American Income Distribution*. New York: Norton.

Liebow, Elliott. 1967. *Tally's Corner: A Study of Negro Streetcorner Men*. Boston: Little, Brown.

Lobao, Linda M., Gregory Hooks, and Ann R. Tickamyer (eds.). 2007. *The Sociology of Spatial Inequality*. Albany: State University of New York Press.

Logan, John R. 1978. "Growth, Politics, and the Stratification of Places." *American Journal of Sociology* 84:404–16.

———. 2003. "Ethnic Diversity Grows, Neighborhood Integration Lags." Pp. 235–55 in *Redefining Urban and Suburban America: Evidence from Census 2000, Vol. 1*, edited by B. Katz and R.E. Lang. Washington, DC: Brookings.

———. 2006. "The Impact of Katrina: Race and Class in Storm-Damaged Neighborhoods." Spatial Structures in the Social Sciences, Brown University, Providence, RI.

———. 2007. "Who Are the Other African Americans? Contemporary African and Caribbean Immigrants in the United States." Pp. 49–67 in *The Other African Americans: Contemporary African and Caribbean Immigrants in the United States*, edited by Y. Shaw-Taylor and S. A. Tuch. Lanham, MD: Rowman & Littlefield.

———. 2011. "Separate and Unequal: The Neighborhood Gap for Blacks, Hispanics and Asians in Metropolitan America." US2010 Project, Brown University/Russell Sage, Providence, RI.

Logan, John R., and Harvey L. Molotch. 1987. *Urban Fortunes: The Political Economy of Place*. Berkeley: University of California Press.

Logan, John R., and Richard D. Alba. 1993. "Locational Returns to Human Capital: Minority Access to Suburban Community Resources." *Demography* 30:243–68.

Logan, John R., Richard D. Alba, Thomas McNulty, and Brian Fisher. 1996. "Making a Place in the Metropolis: Locational Attainment in Cities and Suburbs." *Demography* 33:443–53.

Logan, John R., Brian J. Stults, and Reynolds Farley. 2004. "Segregation of Minorities in the Metropolis: Two Decades of Change." *Demography* 41:1–22.

Logan, John R., and Charles Zhang. 2010. "Global Neighborhoods: New Pathways to Diversity and Separation." *American Journal of Sociology* 115:1069–1109.

Loury, Glenn C. 1977. "A Dynamic Theory of Racial Income Differences." Pp. 153–86 in *Women, Minorities, and Employment Discrimination*, edited by P. A. Wallace and A. M. Lamond. Lexington, MA: Lexington Books.

Lowe, Theodore M. 2008. "Racial Politics in Dallas in the Twentieth Century." *East Texas Historical Journal* 46:27–41.

Ludwig, Jens, Brian A. Jacob, Michael Johnson, Greg J. Duncan, and James E. Rosenbaum. 2009. "Neighborhood Effects on Low-Income Families: Evidence from a Natural Housing-Voucher Experiment in Chicago." University of Chicago Working Paper, Chicago.

Ludwig, Jens, Jeffrey Liebman, Jeffrey Kling, Greg J. Duncan, Lawrence Katz, Ronald Kessler, and Lisa Sanbonmatsu. 2008. "What Can We Learn about Neighborhood Effects from the Moving to Opportunity Experiment?" *American Journal of Sociology* 114:144–88.

Ludwig, Jens, and Steven Raphael. 2010. "The Mobility Bank: Increasing Residential Mobility to Boost Economic Mobility." Hamilton Project/Brookings Institution, Washington, DC.

MacGillis, Alec. 2007. "Obama Says He, Too, Is a Poverty Fighter." *Washington (DC) Post*, July 19, p. A4.

Mainieri, Tina. 2004. *The Panel Study of Income Dynamics Child Development Supplement: User Guide for CDS-II*. Ann Arbor, MI: Institute for Social Research.

Marcuse, Peter. 1995. "Interpreting Public Housing History." *Journal of Architectural and Planning Research* 12:240–58.

Marcuse, Peter, and Ronald van Kempen. 2002. *Of States and Cities: The Partitioning of Urban Space*. Oxford: Oxford University Press.

Mare, Robert D. 2001. "Observations on the Study of Social Mobility and Inequality." Pp. 477–88 in *Social Stratification: Class, Race and Gender in Sociological Perspective*, edited by D. B. Grusky. Boulder, CO: Westview Press.

Mare, Robert D., and Christopher Winship. 1988. "Ethnic and Racial Patterns of Educational Attainment and School Enrollment." Pp. 173–203 in *Divided Opportunities: Minorities, Poverty, and Social Policy*, edited by G. Sandefur and M. Tienda. New York: Plenum Press.

Margolin, Gayla. 2005. "Children's Exposure to Violence: Exploring Developmental Pathways to Diverse Outcomes." *Journal of Interpersonal Violence* 20:72–81.

Martinez, Pedro, and John E. Richters. 1993. "The NIMH Community Violence Project: II. Children's Distress Symptoms Associated with Violence Exposure." *Psychiatry: Interpersonal and Biological Processes* 56:22–35.

Massey, Douglas S. 1990. "American Apartheid: Segregation and the Making of the Underclass." *American Journal of Sociology* 96:329–57.

———. 1994. "Getting Away with Murder: Segregation and Violent Crime in Urban America." *University of Pennsylvania Law Review* 143:1203–32.

———. 2007. *Categorically Unequal: The American Stratification System*. New York: Russell Sage.

———. 2011. "The Past & Future of American Civil Rights." *Daedalus* 140:37–54.

Massey, Douglas S., and Nancy Denton. 1993. *American Apartheid: Segregation and the Making of the Underclass*. Cambridge, MA: Harvard University Press.

Massey, Douglas S., and Nancy A. Denton. 1988. "The Dimensions of Residential Segregation." *Social Forces* 67:281–315.

———. 1989. "Hypersegregation in U.S. Metropolitan Areas: Black and Hispanic Segregation along Five Dimensions." *Demography* 26:373–91.

Massey, Douglas S., Andrew B. Gross, and Kumiko Shibuya. 1994. "Migration, Segregation, and the Geographic Concentration of Poverty." *American Sociological Review* 59:425–45.

Mathews, Jay. 2007. "Neighborhoods' Effect on Grades Challenged." *Washington (DC) Post*, August 14, p. A4..

Mauer, Marc. 2003. "Introduction: The Collateral Consequences of Imprisonment." *Fordham Urban Law Journal* 30:1491–1500.

Mazumder, Bhashkar. 2005a. "The Apple Falls Even Closer to the Tree than We Thought." Pp. 80–99 in *Unequal Chances: Family Background and Economic Success*, edited by S. Bowles, H. Gintis, and M. Osborne Groves. New York: Russell Sage and Princeton University Press.

———. 2005b. "Fortunate Sons: New Estimates of Intergenerational Mobility in the United States Using Social Security Earnings Data." *Review of Economics & Statistics* 87:235–55.

———. 2011. "Black-White Differences in Inter-Generational Economic Mobility in the U.S." U.S. Census Bureau, Washington, DC.

McCall, Patricia L., Karen F. Parker, and John M. MacDonald. 2008. "The Dynamic Relationship between Homicide Rates and Social, Economic, and Political Factors from 1970 to 2000." *Social Science Research* 37:721–35.

McCarton, Cecilia M., Jeanne Brooks-Gunn, Ina F. Wallace, Charles R. Bauer, Forrest C. Bennett, Judy C. Bernbaum, R. Sue Broyles, Patrick H. Casey, Marie C. McCormick, David T. Scott, Jon Tyson, James Tonascia, and Curtis L. Meinert. 1997. "Results at Age

Eight Years of Early Intervention for Low-Birth-Weight Premature Infants: The Infant Health and Development Program." *Journal of American Medical Association* 227:126–32.

McCullough, Andrew. 2006. "Variation in Children's Cognitive and Behavioral Adjustment between Different Types of Place in the British National Child Development Study." *Social Science and Medicine* 62:1865–79.

McCullough, Andrew, and Heather Joshi. 2001. "Neighborhood and Family Influences on the Cognitive Ability of Children in the British National Child Development Study." *Social Science and Medicine* 53:579–91.

McKee, Guian A. 2008. *The Problem of Jobs: Liberalism, Race, and Deindustrialization in Philadelphia*. Chicago: University of Chicago Press.

McLanahan, Sara, and Christine Percheski. 2008. "Family Structure and the Reproduction of Inequalities." *Annual Review of Sociology* 34:257–76.

Mendenhall, Ruby, Stefanie DeLuca, and Greg Duncan. 2006. "Neighborhood Resources, Racial Segregation, and Economic Mobility: Results from the Gautreaux Program." *Social Science Research* 35:892–923.

Merry, Sally Engle. 1981. *Urban Danger: Life in a Neighborhood of Strangers*. Philadelphia: Temple University Press.

Meyer, Stephen Grant. 2001. *As Long as They Don't Move Next Door: Segregation and Racial Conflict in American Neighborhoods*. Lanham, MD: Rowman & Littlefield.

Mincy, Ronald B. (ed.). 2006. *Black Males Left Behind*. Washington, DC: Urban Institute Press.

Mollenkopf, John H. 2008. "School Is Out." *Urban Affairs Review* 44:239–65.

Moore, Mark H. 1999. "Security and Community Development." Pp. 293–337 in *Urban Problems and Community Development*, edited by R. F. Ferguson and W. T. Dickens. Washington, DC: Brookings.

Morgan, Stephen, David Grusky, and Gary Fields (eds.). 2006. *Mobility and Inequality: Frontiers of Research in Sociology and Economics*. Palo Alto, CA: Stanford University Press.

Moynihan, Daniel Patrick. 1969. *Maximum Feasible Misunderstanding: Community Action in the War on Poverty*. New York: Free Press.

Muller, Thomas. 1993. *Immigrants and the American City*. New York: New York University Press.

Murray, Joseph. 2005. "The Effects of Imprisonment on Families and Children of Prisoners." Pp. 442–62 in *The Effects of Imprisonment*, edited by A. Liebling and S. Maruna. Portland, OR: Willan.

Murray, Joseph, and David P. Farrington. 2008. "Parental Imprisonment: Long-Lasting Effects on Boys' Internalizing Problems through the Life Course." *Development and Psychopathology* 20:273–90.

Murray, Joseph, Carl-Gunnar Janson, and David P. Farrington. 2007. "Crime in Adult Offspring of Prisoners: A Cross-National Comparison of Two Longitudinal Samples." *Criminal Justice and Behavior* 34:133–49.

Nakao, Keiko, and Judith Treas. 1994. "Updating Occupational Prestige and Socioeconomic Scores: How the New Measures Measure Up." *Sociological Methodology* 24:1–72.

National Advisory Commission on Civil Disorders. 1968. *Report of the National Advisory Commission on Civil Disorders*. New York: Bantam Books.

National Commission on Severely Distressed Public Housing. 1992. *The Final Report of the National Commission on Severely Distressed Public Housing*. Washington, DC: U.S. Department of Housing and Urban Development.

Neckerman, Kathryn M. 2007. *Schools Betrayed: Roots of Failure in Inner-City Education*. Chicago: University of Chicago Press.

Neisser, Ulric, Gweneth Boodoo, Thomas J. Bouchard Jr., A. Wade Boykin, Nathan Brody, Stephen J. Ceci, Diane F. Halpern, John C. Loehlin, Robert Perloff, Robert J. Sternberg, and Susana Urbina. 1996. "Intelligence: Knowns and Unknowns." *American Psychologist* 51:77–101.

Nelson, Charles A., III, Charles H. Zeanah, Nathan A. Fox, Peter J. Marshall, Anna T. Smyke, and Donald Guthrie. 2007. "Cognitive Recovery in Socially Deprived Young Children: The Bucharest Early Intervention Project." *Science* 318:1937–40.

Nisbett, Richard E. 2009. *Intelligence and How to Get It: Why Schools and Cultures Count*. New York: W. W. Norton.

Noguera, Pedro. 2003. *City Schools and the American Dream: Reclaiming the Promise of Public Education*. New York: Teachers College Press.

Oakley, Deirdre, and Hui-shien Tsao. 2006. "A New Way of Revitalizing Distressed Urban Communities? Assessing the Impact of the Federal Empowerment Zone Program." *Journal of Urban Affairs* 28:443–71.

———. 2007. "Socioeconomic Gains and Spillover Effects of Geographically Targeted Initiatives to Combat Economic Distress: An Examination of Chicago's Empowerment Zone." *Cities* 24:43–59.

O'Connor, Alice. 1996. "Community Action, Urban Reform, and the Fight against Poverty." *Journal of Urban History* 22:586–625.

———. 1999. "Swimming against the Tide: A Brief History of Federal Policy in Poor Communities." Pp. 77–137 in *Urban Problems and Community Development*, edited by R. F. Ferguson and W. T. Dickens. Washington, DC: Brookings.

———. 2001. *Poverty Knowledge: Social Science, Social Policy, and the Poor in Twentieth-Century U.S. History*. Princeton, NJ: Princeton University Press.

O'Hare, William P., and William H. Frey. 1992. "Booming, Suburban, and Black." *American Demographics* 14:30–35.

Oliver, Melvin L., and Thomas M. Shapiro. 1995. *Black Wealth, White Wealth: A New Perspective on Racial Inequality*. New York: Routledge.

Orfield, Myron. 1997. *Metropolitics: A Regional Agenda for Community and Stability*. Washington, DC: Brookings.

Orlebeke, Charles J. 2000. "The Evolution of Low-Income Housing Policy, 1949 to 1999." *Housing Policy Debate* 11:489–520.

Osofsky, Gilbert. 1971. *Harlem: The Making of a Ghetto: Negro New York, 1890–1930*. New York: Harper Collins.

Osofsky, Howard J., Joy D. Osofsky, Bruce Sklarew, Stuart W. Twemlow, and Sallye M. Wilkinson. 2004. "Children's Exposure to Community Violence: Psychoanalytic Perspectives on Evaluation and Treatment." Pp. 237–56 in *Analysts in the Trenches: Streets, Schools, War Zones*, edited by B. Skalarow, S.W. Twemlow, S.M. Wilkinson. Mahwah, NJ: Analytic Press.

Pack, Janet Rothenberg. 1994. "The Impacts of Concentrated Urban Poverty on City Government Expenditures." University of Pennsylvania, Wharton School Real Estate Center, Philadelphia.

Pager, Devah. 2003. "The Mark of a Criminal Record." *American Journal of Sociology* 108:937–75.

———. 2007. *Marked: Race, Crime, and Finding Work in an Era of Mass Incarceration*. Chicago: University of Chicago Press.

Pastor, Manuel, Chris Benner, and Martha Matsuoka. 2009. *This Could Be the Start of Something Big: How Social Movements for Regional Equity Are Reshaping Metropolitan America.* Ithaca, NY: Cornell University Press.

Pastor, Manuel, and Margery Austin Turner. 2010. "Reducing Poverty and Economic Distress after ARRA: Potential Roles for Place-Conscious Strategies." Urban Institute, Washington, DC.

Patterson, Orlando. 2004. "Culture and Continuity: Causal Structures in Socio-Cultural Persistence." Pp. 71–109 in *Matters of Culture: Cultural Sociology in Practice*, edited by J. Mohr and R. Friedland. New York: Cambridge University Press.

Pattillo, Mary. 1999. *Black Picket Fences: Privilege and Peril among the Black Middle Class.* Chicago: University of Chicago Press.

———. 2003. "Extending the Boundaries and Definition of the Ghetto." *Ethnic and Racial Studies* 26:1046–57.

———. 2007. *Black on the Block: The Politics of Race and Class in the City.* Chicago: University of Chicago Press.

———. 2009. "Investing in Poor Black Neighborhoods, 'As Is.'" Pp. 31–56 in *Public Housing Transformation: Confronting the Legacy of Segregation*, edited by S. J. Popkin and L. A. Rawlings. Washington, DC: Urban Institute Press.

Peters, Alan H., and Peter S. Fisher. 2002. *State Enterprise Zone Programs: Have They Worked?* Kalamazoo, MI: WE Upjohn Institute.

Petersilia, Joan. 2000. "When Prisoners Return to the Community: Political, Economic, and Social Consequences." U.S. Department of Justice, National Institute of Justice, Washington, DC.

Pettit, Becky, and Bruce Western. 2004. "Mass Imprisonment and the Life Course: Race and Class Inequality in U.S. Incarceration." *American Sociological Review* 69:151–69.

Pew Charitable Trusts. 2011. "Philadelphia 2011: The State of the City." Pew Charitable Trusts, Philadelphia Research Initiative, Washington, DC.

Phillips, Michael. 2006. *White Metropolis: Race, Ethnicity, and Religion in Dallas, 1841–2001.* Austin: University of Texas Press.

Plotnick, Robert D., and Saul Hoffman. 1999. "The Effect of Neighborhood Characteristics on Young Adult Outcomes: Alternative Estimates." *Social Science Quarterly* 80:1–18.

Polikoff, Alexander. 2006. *Waiting for Gautreaux: A Story of Segregation, Housing, and the Black Ghetto.* Chicago: Northwestern University Press.

Pomer, Marshall I. 1986. "Labor Market Structure, Intragenerational Mobility, and Discrimination: Black Male Advancement out of Low-Paying Occupations, 1962–1973." *American Sociological Review* 51:650–59.

Popkin, Susan J. 2000. *The Hidden War: Crime and the Tragedy of Public Housing in Chicago.* New Brunswick, NJ: Rutgers University Press.

Powell, Michael, and Janet Roberts. 2009. "Minorities Affected Most as New York Foreclosures Rise." *New York Times*, May 1, p. A1.

Pynoos, Robert S., Calvin Frederick, Kathi Nader, William Arroyo, Alan Steinberg, Spencer Eth, Francisco Nunez, and Lynn Fairbanks. 1987. "Life Threat and Posttraumatic Stress in School-Age Children." *Archives of General Psychiatry* 44:1057–63.

Quigley, John M., and Steven Raphael. 2004. "Is Housing Unaffordable? Why Isn't It More Affordable?" *Journal of Economic Perspectives* 18:191–214.

Quillian, Lincoln. 1999. "Migration Patterns and the Growth of High-Poverty Neighborhoods, 1970–1990." *American Journal of Sociology* 105:1–37.

———. 2003. "How Long Are Exposures to Poor Neighborhoods? The Long-Term Dynamics of Entry and Exit into Poor Neighborhoods." *Population Research and Policy Review* 21:221–43.

Rainwater, Lee. 1970. *Behind Ghetto Walls: Black Families in a Federal Slum*. Chicago: Aldine.

Raudenbush, Stephen W., Andres Martinez, and Jessaca Spybrook. 2007. "Strategies for Improving Precision in Group-Randomized Experiments." *Educational Evaluation and Policy Analysis* 29:5–29.

Reitz, Kevin R. 2005. "Don't Blame Determinacy: U.S. Incarceration Growth Has Been Driven by Other Forces." *Texas Law Review* 84:1787–1802.

Reyes, Jessica Wolpaw. 2007. "Environmental Policy as Social Policy? The Impact of Childhood Lead Exposure on Crime." *B.E. Journal of Economic Analysis & Policy* 7:1–41.

Rivera, Amaad, Brenda Cotto-Escalera, Anishi Desai, Jeannette Huezo, and Dedrick Muhammad. 2008. "Foreclosed: State of the Dream 2008." United for a Fair Economy, Boston.

Rose, Kalima. 2001. "Beyond Gentrification: Tools for Equitable Development." *Shelterforce Online* (May/June); http://www.nhi.org/online/issues/117/Rose.html.

Rosenbaum, James E. 1995. "Changing the Geography of Opportunity by Expanding Residential Choice: Lessons from the Gautreaux Program." *Housing Policy Debate* 6:231–69.

Rosenbaum, James E., and Susan J. Popkin. 1991. "Employment and Earnings of Low-Income Blacks Who Move to Middle-Class Suburbs." Pp. 342–56 in *The Urban Underclass*, edited by C. Jencks and P. Peterson. Washington, DC: Brookings.

Rosin, Hanna. 2008. "American Murder Mystery." *Atlantic Monthly* (July/August):40–54.

Royster, Deirdre A. 2003. *Race and the Invisible Hand: How White Networks Exclude Black Men from Blue-Collar Jobs*. Berkeley: University of California Press.

———. 2007. "What Happens to Potential Discouraged? Masculinity Norms and the Contrasting Institutional and Labor Market Experiences of Less Affluent Black and White Men." *Annals of the American Academy of Political and Social Science* 609:153–80.

Rubin, Barry M., and Margaret G. Wilder. 1989. "Urban Enterprise Zones: Employment Impacts and Fiscal Incentives." *Journal of the American Planning Association* 55:418–31.

Rubinowitz, Leonard S., and James E. Rosenbaum. 2000. *Crossing the Class and Color Lines: From Public Housing to White Suburbia*. Chicago: University of Chicago Press.

Ruggles, Steven, J. Trent Alexander, Katie Genadek, Ronald Goeken, Matthew B. Schroeder, and Matthew Sobek. 2010. *Integrated Public Use Microdata Series: Version 5.0 [Machine-Readable Database]*. Minneapolis: University of Minnesota.

Rugh, Jacob S., and Douglas S. Massey. 2010. "Racial Segregation and the American Foreclosure Crisis." *American Sociological Review* 75:629–51.

Rusk, David. 1993. *Cities without Suburbs*. Washington, DC: Woodrow Wilson Center Press.

———. 1999. *Inside Game/Outside Game: Winning Strategies for Saving Urban America*. Washington, DC: Brookings.

Rustin, Bayard. 1965. "From Protest to Politics: The Future of the Civil Rights Movement." *Commentary* (February): 25–31.

Sampson, Robert J. 1995. "The Community." Pp. 193–216 in *Crime*, edited by J. Q. Wilson and J. Petersilia. San Francisco: Institute for Contemporary Studies.

———. 1999. "What 'Community' Supplies." Pp. 241–92 in *Urban Problems and Community Development*, edited by R. F. Ferguson and W. T. Dickens. Washington, DC: Brookings.

———. 2003. "The Neighborhood Context of Well Being." *Perspectives in Biology and Medicine* 46:S53–S73.

————. 2008a. "Moving to Inequality: Neighborhood Effects and Experiments Meet Social Structure." *American Journal of Sociology* 114:189–231.

————. 2008b. "Rethinking Crime and Immigration." *Contexts* 7:28–33.

————. 2011. "Toward a New Era in Assessing Societal Consequences." *Criminology & Public Policy* 10:819–28.

————. 2012. *Great American City: Chicago and the Enduring Neighborhood Effect.* Chicago: University of Chicago Press.

Sampson, Robert J., Doug McAdam, Heather MacIndoe, and Simon Weffer-Elizondo. 2005. "Civil Society Reconsidered: The Durable Nature and Community Structure of Collective Civic Action." *American Journal of Sociology* 111:673–714.

Sampson, Robert J., and Jeffrey Morenoff. 2006. "Durable Inequality: Spatial Dynamics, Social Processes and the Persistence of Poverty in Chicago Neighborhoods." Pp. 176–203 in *Poverty Traps*, edited by S. Bowles, S. Durlauf, and K. Hoff. Princeton, NJ: Princeton University Press.

Sampson, Robert J., and Jeffrey D. Morenoff. 1997. "Ecological Perspectives on the Neighborhood Context of Urban Poverty: Past and Present." Pp. 1–22 in *Neighborhood Poverty: Vol. 2, Policy Implications in Studying Neighborhoods*, edited by J. Brooks-Gunn, G. J. Duncan, and J. L. Aber. New York: Russell Sage.

Sampson, Robert J., Jeffrey D. Morenoff, and Thomas Gannon-Rowley. 2002. "Assessing Neighborhood Effects: Social Processes and New Directions in Research." *Annual Reviews Sociology* 28:443–78.

Sampson, Robert J., Stephen W. Raudenbush, and Felton Earls. 1997. "Neighborhoods and Violent Crime: A Multilevel Study of Collective Efficacy." *Science* 277:918–24.

Sampson, Robert J., and Patrick Sharkey. 2008. "Neighborhood Selection and the Social Reproduction of Concentrated Racial Inequality." *Demography* 45:1–29.

Sampson, Robert J., Patrick Sharkey, and Stephen W. Raudenbush. 2008. "Durable Effects of Concentrated Disadvantage on Verbal Ability among African-American Children." *Proceedings of the National Academy of Sciences* 105:845–52.

Sampson, Robert J., and William Julius Wilson. 1995. "Toward a Theory of Race, Crime and Urban Inequality." Pp. 37–54 in *Crime and Inequality*, edited by J. Hagan and R. D. Peterson. Palo Alto, CA: Stanford University Press.

Sanbonmatsu, Lisa, Jeffrey R. Kling, Greg J. Duncan, and Jeanne Brooks-Gunn. 2006. "Neighborhoods and Academic Achievement: Results from the Moving to Opportunity Experiment." *Journal of Human Resources* 41:649.

Sassen, Saskia. 1991. *The Global City: New York, London, Tokyo.* Princeton, NJ: Princeton University Press.

Saul, Scott. 2010. "Gridlock of Rage: The Watts and Rodney King Riots." Pp. 147–67 in *A Companion to Los Angeles*, edited by W. Deverall and G. Hise. Oxford: Wiley-Blackwell.

Schill, Michael H. 2007. "Implementing the Federal Fair Housing Act: The Adjudication of Complaints." Pp. 143–76 in *Fragile Rights within Cities: Government, Housing, and Fairness*, edited by J. Goering. Lanham, MD: Rowman & Littlefield.

Schill, Michael H., and Susan Wachter. 1995. "Housing Market Constraints and Spatial Stratification by Income and Race." *Housing Policy Debate* 6:141–67.

Schwartz, Alex F. 2010. *Housing Policy in the United States, Second Edition.* New York: Routledge.

Schweinhart, Lawrence J., and David P. Weikart. 1997. "The High/Scope Preschool Curriculum Comparison Study through Age 23." *Early Childhood Research Quarterly* 12:117–43.

Sennett, Richard. 1994. *Flesh and Stone: The Body and the City in Western Civilization*. London: Faber & Faber.

Sharkey, Patrick. 2007. "Survival and Death in New Orleans: An Empirical Look at the Human Impact of Katrina." *Journal of Black Studies* 37:482–501.

———. 2008. "The Intergenerational Transmission of Context." *American Journal of Sociology* 113:931–69.

———. 2009. "Neighborhoods and the Black/White Mobility Gap." Pew Charitable Trusts, Economic Mobility Project, Washington, DC.

———. 2010. "The Acute Effect of Local Homicides on Children's Cognitive Performance." *Proceedings of the National Academy of Sciences* 107:11,733–738.

Sharkey, Patrick, and Felix Elwert. 2011. "The Legacy of Disadvantage: Multigenerational Neighborhood Effects on Children's Cognitive Ability." *American Journal of Sociology* 116: 1934–81.

Sharkey, Patrick, and Robert J. Sampson. 2010. "Destination Effects: Residential Mobility and Trajectories of Adolescent Violence in a Stratified Metropolis." *Criminology* 48: 639–81.

Shonkoff, Jack P., and Deborah A. Phillips (eds.). 2000. *From Neurons to Neighborhoods: The Science of Early Childhood Development*. Washington, DC: National Academy Press.

Sides, Josh. 2003. *L.A. City Limits: African American Los Angeles from the Great Depression to the Present*. Berkeley: University of California Press.

Sidney, Mara. 2003. *Unfair Housing: How National Policy Shapes Community Action*. Lawrence: University of Kansas Press.

Silver, Hilary. 2010. "Obama's Urban Policy: A Symposium." *City & Community* 9:3–12.

Sjoquist, David L. (ed.). 2000. *The Atlanta Paradox*. New York: Russell Sage.

———. 2000. "The Atlanta Paradox." Pp. 1–14 in *The Atlanta Paradox*, edited by D. L. Sjoquist. New York: Russell Sage.

Skogan, Wesley G. 1992. *Disorder and Decline: Crime and the Spiral of Decay in American Neighborhoods*. Berkeley: University of California Press.

Small, Mario Luis. 2004. *Villa Victoria: The Transformation of Social Capital in a Boston Barrio*. Chicago: University of Chicago Press.

———. 2007. "Is There Such a Thing as 'the Ghetto'?" *City* 11:413–21.

———. 2008. "Four Reasons to Abandon the Idea of 'the Ghetto.'" *City & Community* 7:389–99.

Small, Mario Luis, David J. Harding, and Michele Lamont. 2010. "Reconsidering Culture and Poverty." *Annals of the American Academy of Political and Social Science* 629:6–27.

Smith, James P., and Finis R. Welch. 1986. "Closing the Gap: Forty Years of Economic Progress for Blacks." Rand Corporation, Santa Monica, CA.

———. 1989. "Black Economic Progress after Myrdal." *Journal of Economic Literature* 27: 519–64.

Smith, Robin, G. Thomas Kingsley, Mary K. Cunningham, Susan J. Popkin, Kassie Dumlao, Ingrid Gould Ellen, Mark Joseph, and Deborah McKoy. 2010. "Monitoring Success in Choice Neighborhoods: A Proposed Approach to Performance Measurement." Urban Institute, Washington, DC.

Solon, Gary. 1992. "Intergenerational Income Mobility in the United States." *American Economic Review* 82:393–408.

———. 2002. "Cross-Country Differences in Intergenerational Earnings Mobility." *Journal of Economic Perspectives* 16:59–66.

Solon, Gary, Orley Ashenfelter, and David Card. 1999. "Intergenerational Mobility in the Labor Market." Pp. 1761–1800 in *Handbook of Labor Economics, Vol. 3*, edited by O. Ashenfelter and D. Card. Amsterdam: North-Holland.

Sonenshein, Raphael J. 1993. *Politics in Black and White: Race and Power in Los Angeles*. Princeton, NJ: Princeton University Press.

South, Scott J., and Kyle D. Crowder. 1997. "Escaping Distressed Neighborhoods: Individual, Community, and Metropolitan Influences." *American Journal of Sociology* 102: 1040–84.

Spear, Allan H. 1969. *Black Chicago: The Making of a Negro Ghetto, 1890–1920*. Chicago: University of Chicago Press.

Spilimbergo, Antonio, and Luis Ubeda. 2004. "Family Attachment and the Decision to Move by Race." *Journal of Urban Economics* 55:478–97.

Squires, Gregory. 1992. *From Redlining to Reinvestment: Community Responses to Urban Disinvestment*. Philadelphia: Temple University Press.

Steinberg, Stephen. 2009. "The Myth of Concentrated Poverty." Pp. 213–28 in *The Integration Debate: Competing Futures for American Cities*, edited by C. Hartman and G. Squires. New York: Routledge.

Stevens, Gillian, and David L. Featherman. 1981. "A Revised Sociometric Index of Occupational Status." *Social Science Research* 10:364–95.

Stoll, Michael A. 2001. "Race, Neighborhood Poverty, and Participation in Voluntary Associations." *Sociological Forum* 16:529–57.

———. 2005. "African Americans and the Color Line." Pp. 380–414 in *The American People: Census 2000*, edited by R. Farley and J. Haaga. New York: Russell Sage.

Sugrue, Thomas J. 1996. *The Origins of the Urban Crisis: Race and Inequality in Post-War Detroit*. Princeton, NJ: Princeton University Press.

———. 2003. "All Politics Is Local: The Persistence of Localism in Twentieth-Century America." Pp. 301–26 in *The Democratic Experiment: New Directions in American Political History*, edited by M. Jacobs, W. Novak, and J. Zelizer. Princeton, NJ: Princeton University Press.

Thomas, June Manning. 1997. *Redevelopment and Race: Planning a Finer City in Postwar Detroit*. Baltimore: Johns Hopkins University Press.

Thompson, Heather A. 2004. *Whose Detroit? Politics, Labor, and Race in a Modern American City*. Ithaca, NY: Cornell University Press.

Thompson, Mark A. 2000. "Black-White Residential Segregation in Atlanta." Pp. 88–115 in *The Atlanta Paradox*, edited by D. L. Sjoquist. New York: Russell Sage.

Tilly, Charles. 1973. "Do Communities Act?" *Sociological Inquiry* 43:209–40.

Timberlake, Jeffrey M. 2007. "Racial and Ethnic Inequality in the Duration of Children's Exposure to Neighborhood Poverty and Affluence." *Social Problems* 54:319–42.

Tough, Paul. 2008. *Whatever It Takes: Geoffrey Canada's Quest to Change Harlem and America*. New York: Houghton Mifflin.

Travis, Jeremy, and Joan Petersilia. 2001. "Reentry Reconsidered: A New Look at an Old Question." *Crime & Delinquency* 47:291–313.

Turner, M. A. 2005. "Overcoming Concentrated Poverty and Isolation: Ten Lessons for Policy and Practice." Urban Institute, Washington, DC.

Turner, Margery A., and Lynette A. Rawlings. 2005. "Overcoming Concentrated Poverty and Isolation: Ten Lessons for Policy and Practice." Urban Institute, Washington, DC.

Turner, Margery A., and Stephen L. Ross. 2005. "How Racial Discrimination Affects the

Search for Housing." Pp. 81–100 in *The Geography of Opportunity: Race and Housing Choice in Metropolitan America*, edited by X. d. S. Briggs. Washington, DC: Brookings.

Turner, Margery A., Stephen L. Ross, George C. Galster, and John Yinger. 2002. "Discrimination in Metropolitan Housing Markets: National Results from Phase I of HDS 2000." U.S. Department of Housing and Urban Development, Washington, DC.

Vale, Lawrence J. 1993. "Beyond the Problem Projects Paradigm: Defining and Revitalizing 'Severely Distressed' Public Housing." *Housing Policy Debate* 4:147–74.

———. 2000. *From the Puritans to the Projects: Public Housing and Public Neighbors*. Cambridge, MA: Harvard University Press.

Vartanian, Thomas P. 1999. "Adolescent Neighborhood Effects on Labor Market and Economic Outcomes." *Social Service Review* 79:142–67.

Vartanian, Thomas P., and Page W. Buck. 2005. "Childhood and Adolescent Neighborhood Effects on Adult Income: Using Siblings to Examine Differences in Ordinary Least Squares and Fixed-Effect Models." *Social Service Review* 79:60–94.

Venkatesh, Sudhir. 2002. *American Project: The Rise and Fall of an American Ghetto*. Cambridge, MA: Harvard University Press.

Venkatesh, Sudhir, and Isil Celimli. 2004. "Tearing Down the Community." *ShelterForce Online* (November/December); http://www.nhi.org/online/issues/138/chicago.html.

Von Hoffman, Alexander. 2004. *House by House, Block by Block: The Rebirth of America's Urban Neighborhoods*. New York: Oxford University Press.

Votruba, Mark E., and Jeffrey Kling. 2009. "Effects of Neighborhood Characteristics on the Mortality of Black Male Youth: Evidence from Gautreaux, Chicago." *Social Science & Medicine* 68:814–23.

Wacquant, Loic. 1993. "Urban Outcasts: Stigma and Division in the Black American Ghetto and the French Urban Periphery." *International Journal of Urban and Regional Research* 17:366–83.

———. 1998. "Negative Social Capital: State Breakdown and Social Destitution in America's Urban Core." *Journal of Housing and the Built Environment* 13:25–40.

———. 2001. "Deadly Symbiosis: When Ghetto and Prison Meet and Mesh." *Punishment & Society* 3:95–133.

Wacquant, Loic. 2004. "Ghetto." Pp. 129–47 in *International Encyclopedia of the Social and Behavioral Sciences, Vol. 12*, edited by N. J. Smelser and P. B. Baltes. New York: Elsevier.

———. 2008. *Urban Outcasts: A Comparative Sociology of Advanced Marginality*. Malden, MA: Polity.

Wacquant, Loic, and William Julius Wilson. 1989. "The Cost of Racial and Class Exclusion in the Inner City." *Annals of the American Academy of Political and Social Science* 501:8–25.

Waldinger, Roger David. 1996. *Still the Promised City? African-Americans and New Immigrants in Postindustrial New York*. Cambridge, MA: Harvard University Press.

Warren, Roland L. 1969. "Model Cities First Round: Politics, Planning, and Participation." *Journal of the American Planning Association* 35:245–52.

Wasik, Barbara A., Mary Alice Bond, and Annemarie Hindman. 2006. "The Effects of a Language and Literacy Intervention on Head Start Children and Teachers." *Journal of Educational Psychology* 98:63–74.

Waters, Mary C., and Reed Ueda. 2007. "Introduction." Pp. 1–13 in *The New Americans: A Guide to Immigration since 1965*, edited by M. C. Waters, R. Ueda, and H. B. Marrow. Cambridge, MA: Harvard University Press.

Waters, Mary C., Reed Ueda, and Helen B. Marrow. 2007. *The New Americans: A Guide to Immigration since 1965.* Cambridge, MA: Harvard University Press.

Wattenberg, Ben J., and Richard M. Scammon. 1973. "Black Progress and Liberal Rhetoric." *Commentary* 55:35–44.

Weir, Margaret. 1996. "Central Cities' Loss of Power in State Politics." *Cityscape* 2:23–40.

———. 2000. "Coalition-Building for Regionalism." Pp. 127–53 in *Reflections on Regionalism*, edited by B. J. Katz. Washington, DC: Brookings.

Western, Bruce. 2006. *Punishment and Inequality in America.* New York: Russell Sage.

White House Neighborhood Revitalization Initiative. 2011. "Building Neighborhoods of Opportunity." Washington, DC: White House Office of Urban Affairs.

Wildeman, Christopher. 2009. "Parental Imprisonment, the Prison Boom, and the Concentration of Childhood Disadvantage." *Demography* 46:265–80.

Wilder, Margaret G., and Barry M. Rubin. 1996. "Rhetoric versus Reality: A Review of Studies on State Enterprise Zone Programs." *Journal of the American Planning Association* 62:473–91.

Williams, Timothy. 2011. "As Public Sector Sheds Jobs, Blacks Are Hit Hardest." *New York Times*, November 29, p. A16.

Wilson, William Julius. 1978. *The Declining Significance of Race: Blacks and Changing American Institutions.* Chicago: University of Chicago Press.

———. 1987. *The Truly Disadvantaged: The Inner City, the Underclass, and Public Policy.* Chicago: University of Chicago Press.

———. 1996. *When Work Disappears: The World of the New Urban Poor.* New York: Knopf.

———. 2010. "The Obama Administration's Proposals to Address Concentrated Urban Poverty." *City & Community* 9:41–49.

———. 2011. "The Declining Significance of Race: Revisited & Revised." *Daedalus* 140:55–69.

Winnick, Louis. 1990. *New People in Old Neighborhoods: The Role of New Immigrants in Rejuvenating New York's Communities.* New York: Russell Sage.

Winship, Christopher, and Sanders Korenman. 1997. "Does Staying in School Make You Smarter?" Pp. 215–34 in *Intelligence, Genes, and Success: Scientists Respond to the Bell Curve*, edited by B. Devlin, S. E. Fienberg, D. P. Resnick, and K. Roeder. New York: Springer-Verlag.

Wirth, Louis. 1928. *The Ghetto.* Chicago: University of Chicago Press.

Wolfinger, James. 2007. *Philadelphia Divided: Race & Politics in the City of Brotherly Love.* Chapel Hill: University of North Carolina Press.

Yinger, John. 1995. *Closed Doors, Opportunities Lost: The Continuing Costs of Housing Discrimination.* New York: Russell Sage.

Zimring, Frank. 2007. *The Great American Crime Decline.* New York: Oxford University Press.

Zimring, Frank, and Gordon Hawkins. 1993. *The Scale of Imprisonment.* Chicago: University of Chicago Press.

Index

Page numbers in italics refer to illustrations.

child development, 183–84. *See also* cognitive development, children's
childhood development vouchers, 191
childhood neighborhoods, and adult economic outcomes, 96–99
children of civil rights era. *See* economic mobility, and race; educational mobility, and race; occupational mobility, and race
children's environment, and public policy, 184; early childhood, 190–91; methodological issues in assessing programs, 194–95
Choice Neighborhood initiative, 177–78, 213n44
Cisneros, Henry: *From Despair to Hope*, 212n40
Civilian Conservation Corps (CCC), 188
civil rights, 48, 89
civil rights era, and racial equality, 1, 7, 9, 91
Clark, Kenneth, 96
Clinton, William Jefferson, 88, 185
cognitive development, children's: connection with community violence, 150–51; connection with neighborhoods, 124–31; estimated effects of moving out of high-poverty neighborhoods, *147*; and importance of parents' childhood neighborhood experience, 130–31; methodological problems of identifying cumulative impact of neighborhoods on, 128; and neighborhood disadvantage across consecutive generations, *119–20*; and neighborhoods, research assessing, 126–28
Comerica Park, Detroit, 72
Community Action Program (CAP), 83, 84–85, 86–87, 139, 198
community action programs, 84–88; review of, 139–40
community change initiatives, 211n6, 211n35
community development block grants, 87
community development programs, and employment, 185
community land trusts, 181

community organizers, 85
community policing, 182
Community Reinvestment Act, 88
community-service employment, 186
concentrated disadvantage: interaction with race, 13; at issue in 2008 election, 137; policy options, 172; scale of, 155; and transformation of urban labor markets, 68
"concentration effects," 171–72
contextual mobility, 16, 20, 26, 35–40; defined, 16, 17; versus geographic or residential mobility, 17–18; intergenerational mobility out of poorest and most affluent neighborhoods among African Americans and whites, *38*; over generations, 36–*37*; role in reproduction of social and economic status, 19
Corcoran, Mary, 97
crack cocaine, 88
crime, reduction in over 1990s, 195–96. *See also* violence
criminal justice system: mandatory minimum sentencing, 75; mass imprisonment, 74–79, 180, 206n89; parole, 75, 206n89; race and criminality in era of mass imprisonment, 77; "three strikes" laws, 75; truth-in-sentencing laws, 75. *See also* prison

Dallas, 55–58; immigration, 58; international finance and technology growth, 58; neighborhood poverty, 56, *57*; politics, 55–56; spread of concentrated poverty, 55; urban planning and policy, 56
Datcher, Linda, 97
deindustrialization. *See* urban labor markets, transformation of
Denton, Nancy, 25, 62
Department of Housing and Urban Development (HUD): efforts to incapacitate, 69; experimental audits of real estate industry, 53–54; Neighborhood Stabilization Program, 182
desegregation policies, 166
determinate sentencing, 206n89

Detroit, 63, 70–74; decline in white population, 70, 71; decrease in federal aid, 71; deindustrialization, 67, 70–71; desegregation, 74; downtown development projects, 71–72; federally backed home mortgages, 74; neighborhood poverty, 73; racial conflict, 71, 74; racial segregation, 70; 1967 riot, 71

Drake, St. Clair, 12

Dreier, Peter, 68

DuBois, W. E. B., 12, 16

Dudley Street Neighborhood Initiative, Boston, 139

Duncan, Greg, 190

Duncan, Otis Dudley, 91, 95

durable urban policy agenda, 12, 23, 90; community land trusts, 181; community policing, 182; durable investment in urban neighborhoods, 179–84; fair-share housing plans, 181; and mobility policy, 172–79, 198–99; "place-conscious" policies, 12, 169–72, 212n20; political coalitions, 181; public spaces, maintenance and monitoring of, 182; support systems for returning prisoners, 182–83; transportation, metropolitan wide, 181

earned income tax credit, 88, 170, 184, 189

ecological research, 14

economic downturns, disproportionate effects on poor, racially segregated communities, 171

economic growth, in the 1990s, 170

economic mobility: downward mobility, 4–5, 101; early studies of, 93–94; and income distribution, 2–3; processes of, 94

economic mobility, and race, 2, 4, 95, 99–101, *100*, 105, 106–7, 167; effects of neighborhood on, 105–7, 113, 114; racial gaps in family income, *106. See also* wealth accumulation, racial gaps

Economic Opportunity Act of 1964, 84; "special impact" amendment, 87

edge cities, 63

education: variation in quality, 14–15. *See also* school quality

educational mobility, and race, 101–2, 105, 107–9, *108, 109*

Edwards, John, 137, 172, 173, 174

election of 2008, and issue of concentrated poverty, 137

Ellen, Ingrid Gould: *Sharing America's Neighborhoods*, 179–80

Ellwood, David, 187–89, 189

Elwert, Felix, 128

Enterprise Communities/Empowerment Zones, 87–88, 185

environmental toxins, 126, 132

exclusionary zoning, 60–61, 62, 181

Fair Housing Act of 1968, 8, 9, 10, 25, 34, 53, 138, 178

fair-share housing plans, 181; role of federal government in, 213n46

federal government, and urban issues: disengagement from, 69, 83, 180; intervention in restructuring urban labor markets, 68; punitive social policies, 69, 180. *See also* federal housing policy: urban renewal

Federal Housing Administration (FHA), 59–60, 180–81

federal housing policy: federal mortgage programs, 59–60, 62; fluctuation in housing aid, 69, 168; and land use, 61, 181; public housing projects, 62, 69; restrictive covenants, 60; suburban home ownership, 60, 68, 180–81; urban renewal, 61–62

federal transportation policy, 67–68, 180

Fiss, Owen, 173, 174, 175

Ford Field, Detroit, 72

foreclosure crisis of late 2000s, 89, 182, 195, 196–97

Freeman, Lance, 152

Fryer, Roland, 192–93, 194, 210n15, 214n93

Galster, George, 173, 174

Gautreaux, Dorothy, 141

Gautreaux Assisted Housing program, 97–99, 133, 141–46, 151, 172, 173, 174–76

gentrification: and neighborhood change, 161–62, 164; research on, 152–53

geographic mobility, 17–18, 176
ghetto, inherited, 9–10, 23, 24–26, 26, 44–46, 166; and racial inequality, 92
ghetto, urban: in America, 12–13; definitions, 12–13; and interaction between race and concentrated poverty, 13, 25; and public policy, 69
global cities, emergence of, 166
Goering, John M., 213n46
Goldwater, Barry, 75
Great Migration, 67, 176, 204n2
guaranteed employment, 187–89
Harlem, 96; gentrifying neighborhoods, 152

Harlem Children's Zone, New York City, 139, 140, 191–95, 210n15, 214n91, 214n93; assessing impact of, 194–95; philosophy of, 192
Hart-Cellar Act of 1965, 2–3
Head Start, 84, 86
health insurance, 186
Heckman, James, 183, 190–91
Hertz, Tom, 95, 105
high-poverty neighborhoods: characteristics of in 1970 and 2000, 28–30, 29; joblessness, 29–30; prevalence of violence, 30–33; trend since 1990s, 89
highways and roads, federal investment in, 67–68, 180
Hispanic Americans: discrimination in housing market, 54; population in Dallas, 58; population of Los Angeles, 63
Hochschild, Jennifer, 175
Hoffman, Saul, 97
Holzer, Harry, 77, 170
home mortgage interest deduction, 60, 181
home mortgage lending, and racial discrimination, 34, 54–55, 61, 178; federal programs, 59–60, 62
home ownership, and positive outcomes for families and communities, 197
Home Owners Loan Corporation (HOLC), 58
HOPE VI, 177, 212n40
Housing Acts of 1949 and 1954, 61–62

Housing and Community Development Act of 1974, 87
housing discrimination, 34, 53–54, 178; Atlanta, 51; informal intimidation and violence, 61, 62; and local public initiatives, 60–61; and movement from passive to active enforcement, 178–79; racial steering, 53, 54; redlining, 53, 59, 62; rental housing, 34; restrictive covenants, 60, 61, 62; resulting in economic segregation, 60. *See also* federal housing policy: urban renewal; home mortgage lending, and racial discrimination; public housing projects
Housing Discrimination Study of 2000, 54
Hoxby, Caroline, 215n94
Hurricane Katrina, 136–37

immigrant population, 2–3; Dallas/Fort Worth area, 58; effect of entrance of new groups into segregated neighborhoods, 58, 63, 160–62, 213n63; growth of in lower segments of income distribution, 3; Los Angeles, 65; from West Indies and Africa, 3–4
inclusionary zoning, federal incentives for, 181
industrial land banks, 79
infant/toddler allowance, universal, 191
investment approach, to urban poverty, 139–40, 151–53

Jackson, Maynard, 50
Jacob, Brian, 148–49
Jargowsky, Paul, 65, 211n9
Jim Crow, 75
joblessness, concentrated, 183; among African American men, 184; confronting in disadvantaged communities, 184–90
Jobs-Plus program, 140, 185, 194
Johnson, Lyndon B., 53, 83, 84, 91, 138
Joseph, Mark, 211n6
Justice Mapping Center, 78

Katz, Bruce, 169
Kerner Commission Report, 1, 53, 91, 138

King, Martin Luther, Jr., 8, 138
Kingsley, G. Thomas, 211n35
Korenman, Sanders, 131
Ku Klux Klan, 55

Ladd, Helen, 84
land use and regulation, local control over, 61, 181
law-and-order rhetoric, 75
lending discrimination. *See* home mortgage lending, and racial discrimination
Liebow, Elliott: *Tally's Corner*, 96
local zoning ordinances, 60–61
Logan, John, 136
Los Angeles, 63–67; decentralized planning and governance, 63; edge cities, 63; immigration, 63–67; neighborhood poverty, 66; outmigration of white and affluent nonwhite populations, 64, 65; public housing projects, 64; Rodney King riots, 65; tension between African American community and police, 64
Los Angeles Police Department, 64–65
Low Income Housing Credit, 181
Ludwig, Jens, 149

MacArthur Foundation, New Communities Program, Chicago, 140
Making Connections initiative, 140, 211n35, 214n91
mandatory minimum sentencing, 75
Massey, Douglas, 16, 25, 26, 62, 171
mass imprisonment, 74–79, 180, 206n89; support systems for returning prisoners, 182–83. *See also* prison
metropolitan wide transportation, 181
Mikulski, Barbara, 175
mobility approach, to urban poverty policy, 137, 138
mobility gap. *See* racial mobility gap
mobility research, 17
Model Cities program, 83, 85–87, 86–87, 139, 198
Moving to Opportunity (MTO) social experiment, 126–27, 133, 134, 143–46, *147*, 172, 173, 174; political opposition to, 175

Moynihan Report, 1, 91
multigenerational disadvantage. *See* neighborhood disadvantage, multigenerational

"Neighborhood and Family Initiative," Ford Foundation, 214n91
neighborhood change: characteristics of African Americans' neighborhoods where concentrated disadvantage declined from 1980 to 1990, *161–62*; characteristics of the 10 percent of U.S. neighborhoods where concentrated disadvantage declined the most from 1970 and 1980, 1980–1990, and 1990 to 2000, *156–57*; in metropolitan areas, 158, *159–60*; relationship to rise in percentage of Latinos and foreign-born residents, 158, 161–62, 164
neighborhood change, impact of, 156–65; effects of decline in concentrated disadvantage on adult economic outcomes among African Americans, 162–63; estimating the effect of, 153–55. *See also* Moving to Opportunity (MTO) social experiment
neighborhood disadvantage, 26–27; and American ghetto, 12–16, 45; deconcentration of disadvantage, and economic benefits for African American children, 23; and downward mobility, 114–16; dynamic view of, 18; legacy of, 131–35; levels among African Americans and whites born in 1955–70 and 1985–2000, 26–28, *27*; link to children's performance on cognitive tests, 14; as mechanism for racial economic inequality, 116; persistence of, 6–7, 21, 40–44, 48; policy agenda for, 11; rigidity of, 18
neighborhood disadvantage, in childhood: impact on adult outcomes, 6–7, 117–18; impact on next generation of children, 22; racial gaps, 21–22
neighborhood disadvantage, multigenerational, 33–35; and aspirations and expectations for graduating from

neighborhood disadvantage (*continued*) college, 122–23; and attachment to neighborhood, 33; and children's anxiety toward the future, 121–22; and children's obesity, health, and depression, 120–21; for children who remain in same county and those who move to different county in adulthood, 42–43, 203n20; and effects on cognitive skills, 118–20, 119; predictors of, 42; and race, 39–40, 45

"neighborhood improvement associations," 61

neighborhoods: dimensions of, 17; effects of, based on observational survey data, 134; as an independent dimension of stratification, 15; racial and ethnic hierarchy, 15

Neighborhood Stabilization Program, Department of Housing and Urban Development (HUD), 182

New Communities Program, 140, 214n91

New Hope Program, Milwaukee, 186–90, 190

New Orleans, and Hurricane Katrina, 136–37; death of African Americans in proportion to presence in population, 136–37

New York City: deindustrialization, 67; planning and growth, 63; reduction in crime in 1990s, 196

Nisbett, Richard: *Intelligence and How to Get It: Why Schools and Cultures Count*, 209n8

Nixon, Richard, 85–86, 87

Obama Administration, 172, 177; Promise Neighborhoods proposal, 137, 191; and urban policy, 197–98

occupational mobility, and race, 103, 104, 109–11, 110; gap in annual hours worked, 104, 111, 114

Oliver, Melvin, 112

Organization for Economic Cooperation and Development (OECD) countries, public-service employment programs, 189

Pager, Devah, 77

Panel Study of Income Dynamics (PSID), 8, 48, 49–50, 56, 72, 82, 92, 94, 97, 118, 153, 155

parole, 75, 206n89

Pastor, Manuel, 181, 212n20

Pattillo, Mary, 22, 96, 153, 201n19

Perry preschool program, 190–91

Pettit, Becky, 74–75

Pew Charitable Trusts study, 114

Philadelphia, 63, 79–82; attempts to retain industrial firms in city, 79; downtown redevelopment, 80, 82; neighborhood poverty, 81; racial politics of, 79–80

Philadelphia Police Department, 80

place-based policies, 12, 169–72, 212n20

places: and racial inequality, 167; transmission of from parents to children, 47

Plotnick, Robert D., 97

police, linkages with other community institutions, 182

Polikoff, Alexander, 173, 212n26

prison, 74–79; association between parental incarceration and children's health and well-being, 78; long-term consequences of mass imprisonment for African American communities, 76; and racial inequality, 75, 78; returning prisoners, 76, 197; stigma of criminality, 77

Project on Human Development in Chicago Neighborhoods, 147, 148

Promise Academy charter schools, 140, 192–93, 214n93

Promise Neighborhoods, 137, 198

public housing projects, 62, 69; abandonment of by federal government, 180; demolishing of, 177; effort to replace with scattered-site, mixed-income housing, 177; income thresholds, 69–70; Robert Taylor Homes housing project, 70

public-service employment programs: costs of, 188; review of, 187–89; value of to communities, 188–89

public spaces, maintenance and monitoring of, 182

public transportation, lack of investment in, 68

race, and neighborhood deterioration, 180
racial inequality: from 1968 forward, 7–12; multigenerational perspective, 6–7, 10–12; neighborhood inequality, 18, 40–44, 48; and places, 167; and role of communities and cities, 5–6, 9
racial inequality, and public policy, 58–62; federal mortgage programs, 59–60; policies, informal strategies, and institutional mechanisms used to maintain, 48; and public housing, 59; racial "steering," 53, 54; redlining, 59; subsidization of white outmigration from central cities, 58–60, 180–81. *See also* mass imprisonment; prison
racial mobility gap: defined, 92; and family background, 95. *See also* economic mobility, and race; educational mobility, and race; occupational mobility, and race
racial segregation: and concentrated poverty, 171; persistence of, 25; in public housing projects, 62, 69; and urban renewal, 61–62. *See also* housing discrimination; residential mobility
racial steering, in housing market, 53, 54
racial zoning plans, 60
Rainwater, Lee: *Behind Ghetto Walls*, 96
Raudenbush, Stephen, 148
Reagan, Ronald, 87
real estate appreciation, different rates of in primarily black and primarily white communities, 112
recession of late 2000s, 196
redlining, 53, 59, 62
Reitz, Kevin R., 206n89
Rendell, Ed, 82
rental housing, racial discrimination in, 34
residential integration: resistance to, 8. *See also* housing discrimination
residential mobility, 18, 133–34; estimated effects of moving out of high-poverty neighborhoods on children's reading/language skills, *147*, 167; out of the ghetto, 141–51
residential mobility experiments, 11, 22–23; impact of, 172–73; limits of, 127; poten-

tial impact of large-scale expansion, 173–74
restrictive covenants, 60, 61, 62
Rizzo, Frank, 79–80
Robert Taylor Homes housing project, 70
Rodney King riots, 65
Romanian orphanages, and cognitive development, 125
Rosenbaum, James, 142
Royster, Deirdre, 206n101
rust belt cities, 67–68
Rustin, Bayard, 91

Sampson, Robert, 16, 20, 148, 174, 182, 213n48
Scammon, Richard M., 1
school desegregation, 83
school quality: decline in, 69; influence on children's academic careers, 193; influence on children's development through neighborhood, 132
sensitivity analysis, 209n15
Shapiro, Thomas, 112
sibling studies, 97
single parent families: and employment, 24; and race, 167
slavery, 75
Small, Mario, 202n21
social life, and geography, 14
social mobility, 18
Solon, Gary, 94
subprime loans, and race, 196
suburban prosperity: and exclusionary zoning, 181; and federal investment in highways and regional transportation systems, 180; and federally backed mortgages, 180–81; and home mortgage interest deduction, 181; and local financing of public education, 181

"three strikes" laws, 75
"tough on crime" rhetoric, 75
transportation. *See* highways and roads, federal investment in; metropolitan-wide transportation
truth-in-sentencing laws, 75
Turner, Margery, 181, 212n20

CPSIA information can be obtained
at www.ICGtesting.com
Printed in the USA
LVHW01s0842220118
563341LV00003B/8/P